THE EUCHARIST OF THE EARLY CHRISTIANS

Freel. 1984

Willy Rordorf and Others

THE EUCHARIST
OF THE
EARLY CHRISTIANS

Translated by Matthew J. O'Connell

PUEBLO PUBLISHING COMPANY

New York

Design: Frank Kacmarcik, D.F.A.

ISBN: 0-916134-33-4

CONTENTS

WHY THIS BOOK?

"The Eucharist of the Early Christians"—but why go back into the past? Is it nostalgia or fear that sends us there? Why lose ourselves in distant lands and let ourselves get bogged down in the sands of the desert? Why flee the present? We should be creating the future and struggling side by side with the men of our day!

But in a world in which technology is increasingly gaining the upper hand over man, we need space to refresh ourselves. Men need to draw breath and slake their thirst. They need a faith that is sure of itself. Far, then, from being a retreat into the past, this book is meant as a pilgrimage to the life-giving wellsprings; its aim is to make possible a vital grasp of the eucharist as expressed and experienced by the early Christians. It is good for us to acquire a sense of what life was like for the early Christians and to see what their hopes were. In so doing, we rediscover our true selves.

How, then, did the early Christians experience the eucharist? They experienced it, above all, as a time of happiness and a challenge to battle.

Earth broken open
by the hand of the Living One.
Passage accomplished
by the fire of the Spirit.
Food for our exoduses.
Bread for our tasks
and our struggles.
Wine of joy,
intoxicating;
wine for extravagant
daring deeds.
Path of hope.
Certitude of love.
Jesus Christ, Lord!

That is the eucharist of the early Christians.

If only our eucharists were like that today! The context has changed, but that does not matter. Our thirst for happiness is even greater, the struggle is just as pressing. In fact, now that I have come to understand a little better the eucharist of the early Christians, I feel more determined to live the adventure of the future, more united to my fellows, more sure of my faith in the risen Christ.

To study the eucharist of the early Christians is to open a fascinating page of the Church's life to the people of our day.

How did the idea for the book arise? In the latter part of 1970, the periodical *Parole et pain* devoted its No. 40 (September-October) to "The Eucharist in the Early Church." Later on No. 46 studied the eucharist in the third century, and No. 52 the eucharist in the fourth century.

Number 40 proved an unexpected success and was quickly out of print, so that we could not satisfy the many requests that reached us. I thought then of a collective study that would treat of the eucharist during the first five or six centuries and would appear as a volume in the *Théologie historique* published by Beauchesne in Paris. We actually started on such a book. It proved difficult, however, to find contributors who would handle such figures as Cyril of Alexandria. In addition, we came to realize that the work we were undertaking would be one more book for specialists and that, on the other hand, the first three centuries by themselves formed a unit of great interest to people today.

In this book, then, we publish a set of texts (often with revisions) that appeared originally in *Parole et pain*, Nos. 40 and 46. These include the essays on Clement of Rome, Ignatius of Antioch, Justin Martyr, Tertullian, Origen, and Cyprian of Carthage. For the remaining essays we secured new contributors (the *Didache*, Irenaeus of Lyons, Clement of Alexandria). Finally, we added a study of the *Didascalia*.

These essays form a united whole. Each author, of course, takes the approach congenial to him, but the whole seems coherent, even if a bit on the arid side. Could such dryness by avoided? In any case, here the book stands, with its faults; it meets a need, for books of this kind on this subject are few. It is now up to the reader to profit by it.

Raymond Johanny

ABBREVIATIONS

ACW   *Ancient Christian Writers*. Westminster, Md., 1946–

BAC   *Biblioteca de autores cristianos*. Madrid, 1945–

CCL   *Corpus Christianorum, Series Latina*. Tournhout, 1953–

CSEL   *Corpus Scriptorum ecclesiasticorum Latinorum*. Vienna, 1966–

DACL   *Dictionnaire d'archéologie chrétienne et de liturgie*. Paris, 1914-37

DSp   *Dictionnaire de spiritualité*. Paris, 1932–

DTC   *Dictionnaire de théologie catholique*. Paris, 1903-50

GSC   *Die griechischen christlichen Schriftsteller der ersten drei Jahrhunderte*. Leipzig, 1897–

PG   *Patrologia Graeca*, ed. J. P. Migne. Paris, 1857-66

PL   *Patrologia Latina*, ed. J. P. Migne. Paris, 1844-64

SC   *Sources chrétiennes*. Paris, 1942–

TU   *Texte und Untersuchungen zur Geschichte der altchristlichen Literatur*. Leipzig–Berlin, 1882–

Willy Rordorf

THE DIDACHE

Chapters 9 and 10 of the *Didache*, or "Teaching of the Lord, given to the nations through the Apostles," contain prayers to be said at community meals. Chapter 14 adds some notations on the Sunday liturgy as celebrated by the Christian community. These three chapters have been the subject of extensive discussion ever since Bryennios published the first printed edition of the *Didache* in 1883. In offering my own contribution to the discussion I have no intention of trying to take a completely novel approach, but would like simply to take our bearings amid all the countless studies. Where, then, do we stand today as far as the interpretation of these chapters is concerned? I suggest that these chapters represent a kind of transitional link between the Jewish tradition represented in the blessings pronounced at the table and the eucharistic anaphora as preserved in the later formularies for the Christian Mass. In the connecting link we can see the kinship of the two traditions, but we can also see what separates them.

DATE AND PLACE OF ORIGIN

Perhaps we should begin by taking a position on the date and place of origin of the *Didache*. Specialists are far from agreement on these two points. For some, the text is very ancient, dating perhaps even from the apostolic period; that is the view, for example, of J.-P. Audet, who has written a very detailed commentary on the text.[1] For others, the text dates from the beginning[2] or from the end of the second century (or even the third).[3]

Opinions on the place of origin are just as divided. Harnack believes the *Didache* was written in Egypt,[4] while Audet, Knopf, Adam, and others think it originated in Palestine or Syria.[5] My own opinion is that it was edited in Syria at the end of the first century or the beginning of the second. Unfortunately, the limits set upon this paper prevent me from spelling out my reasons for this opinion. In any event, the question of date and place does not directly concern us in dealing with the subject of the interpretation of chapters 9 and 10. Almost all scholars admit that the chapters antedated the final redaction and were introduced into the document by the editor.[6]

CHAPTERS 9, 10, AND 14 OF THE DIDACHE

Here is the text of these three chapters:[7]

Chapter 9
1. With regard to the prayer of thanksgiving [*eucharistia*], offer it in this fashion.
2. First, for the cup: "We thank you, our Father, for the holy vine of David your servant, which you have revealed to us through Jesus your servant. Glory be yours through all ages!"
3. Then for the bread broken: "We thank you, our Father, for the life and knowledge you have revealed to us through Jesus your servant. Glory be yours through all ages!
4. "Just as the bread broken was first scattered on the hills, then was gathered and became one, so let your Church be gathered from the ends of the earth into your kingdom, for yours is glory and power through Jesus Christ for all ages!"
5. Let no one eat or drink of your eucharist, except those baptized in the name of the Lord. For it is of this that the Lord was speaking when he said: "Do not give what is holy to dogs"(Matthew 7.6).

Chapter 10
1. When your hunger has been satisfied, give thanks thus:
2. "We thank you, holy Father, for your holy name which you have made to dwell in our hearts, and for the knowl-

2

edge and faith and immortality you have revealed to us through Jesus your servant. Glory be yours through all ages!

3. "All-powerful Master, you created all things for your name's sake, and you have given food and drink to the children of men for their enjoyment, so that they may thank you. On us, moreover, you have bestowed a spiritual food and drink that lead to eternal life, through Jesus your servant.

4. "Above all, we thank you because you are almighty. Glory be yours through all ages!

5. "Lord, remember your Church and deliver it from all evil; make it perfect in your love and gather it from the four winds, this sanctified Church, into your kingdom which you have prepared for it, for power and glory are yours through all ages!

6. "May grace come and this world pass away! Hosanna to the God of David! If anyone is holy, let him come! If anyone is not, let him repent! Maranatha. Amen."

7. Allow the prophets to give thanks as much as they wish.

Chapter 14

Come together on the dominical day of the Lord, break bread and give thanks, having first confessed your sins so that your sacrifice may be pure. Anyone who has a quarrel with his fellow should not gather with you until he has been reconciled, lest your sacrifice be profaned. For this is the sacrifice of which the Lord says: "In every place and at every time offer me a pure sacrifice, for I am a great king, says the Lord, and my name is marvelous among the nations" (Malachi 1.11-14).

THE INTERPRETATION OF
CHAPTERS 9 AND 10

The interpretation of chapters 9 and 10 depends chiefly on the answer to one question: Are these prayers meant for the eucharist, in the proper sense of this latter term, or are

3

they simply prayers spoken at table in connection with ordinary meals of the community? Not surprisingly, this question arose as soon as the *Didache* became known, since the beginning of chapter 9 explicitly speaks of a *eucharistia*. If the term is taken as referring to the Lord's Supper, new problems arise, since the words of institution occur nowhere in the prayers. Does this mean that the liturgical formulas given here are incomplete? Or do the prayers reflect a special form of the eucharist? Or do the prayers have nothing to do with the eucharist in the strict sense of this latter word? All these hypotheses have found defenders.

The problem becomes even more complicated if we take chapter 14 into consideration. How are we to interpret this chapter? Why should the same subject, the *eucharistia*, be discussed in two different sections? Are we to infer that chapter 14 is in fact dealing with a different subject than chapters 9 and 10?

It is certainly not easy to answer these question in a conclusive way. In fact, the variety of answers might suggest that there is no hope of ever reaching a satisfactory solution.[8] In order to give some idea of how difficult the interpretation of these chapters is, I shall give the more important answers in chronological order.

The first scholars, to my knowledge, who offered an interpretation that solves many problems, were P. Drews and, following his lead, M. Goguel.[9] They see chapters 9 and 10, on the one hand, and chapter 14, on the other, as referring to different subjects. Chapters 9 and 10 deal with communal meals for which a small group of the faithful gathered in a private home, perhaps during the week. Chapter 14 describes the eucharistic liturgy which was celebrated on Sunday by the bishop and his deacons, in the presence of the entire community. This interpretation seems quite attractive, especially since chapter 15 states that bishops and deacons are to be appointed who will

4

preside over divine services in the place of the apostles and prophets. For Drews and Goguel, chapter 14 voices a criticism of the practice, reflected in chapters 9 and 10, of taking the eucharist privately and thus tending to split the community up into small independent groups (see St. Ignatius of Antioch, *Smyrnaeans* 8 and *Philadelphians* 3-4). Chapter 14 would thus be a later addition that is intended to offset chapters 9–10.

Drews and Goguel were certainly right in regarding chapter 14 as of later provenance than chapters 9 and 10 (in fact the whole section from chapter 11 to chapter 14 inclusive is later, for reasons we cannot analyze here[10]). It seems, however, that their hypothesis of an opposition between chapter 14 and chapters 9–10 has no solid basis in the text. Why would the *Didache*, without clarifying the distinction, address the laity at one point (chapters 9–10) and the clergy at another (chapter 14) and use the same second person plural ("you") in both cases? Why would chapter 14 give so little detail on the Sunday liturgy unless that same liturgy had been discussed earlier? It would seem rather that chapter 14 simply adds a few details, called for by circumstances, to a subject already discussed in chapters 9–10.

Such was Lietzmann's thesis in his book *Messe und Herrenmahl.*[10a] It was so revolutionary that it deserves examination here, especially since it has exercised a strong influence on liturgical studies right down to our own day.

Lietzmann sought to distinguish two types of eucharist in the early Church: in the one, the commemoration of Christ's death and redemptive work was to the fore; in the other, this element, along with the idea of sacrifice, was absent. The *Apostolic Tradition* of St. Hippolytus contained an example of the first form of eucharist and became the prototype that influenced all later forms of the Mass in both the East and the West. The very existence, however, of the non-commemorative eucharist, which Lietzmann

5

regards as originating in Egypt, is quite problematic. All the Egyptian formularies of the Mass show the commemorative aspect: not only the Liturgy of St. Mark but also the more ancient formularies in the Der Balyzeh Papyrus and the *Euchologion* of Serapion of Thmuis (Serapion's anaphora does not have an anamnesis but it does contain the words of institution). In dealing with these Egyptian formularies Lietzmann was therefore obliged to fall back on the hypothesis of a later insertion.

The definitive proof for Lietzmann is the *Didache*: He interprets this as preserving the Jerusalem tradition of communal meals characterized by an atmosphere of joy, at a time when the other form of the eucharist—the Mass with its commemorative aspect, as taught by St. Paul—was gaining the upper hand. The *Didache* evidently does play an important part in Lietzmann's hypothesis. The question is whether chapters 9 and 10 will support the interpretation here given of them. If this keystone is removed, the whole edifice built by Lietzmann falls to the ground.

I shall attempt to show that these chapters contain, not a eucharistic liturgy in the strict sense, but prayers spoken at table before the eucharist proper. This is indeed the most common view today.[11] It enables us to let the text stand unchanged, whereas Lietzmann was obliged to postulate a disordered text in which 10,6 should follow upon 9,5.

The prayers of chapters 9 and 10 evidently contain turns of phrase that seem to be borrowed from the eucharistic liturgy: for example, "the bread broken" (9,4) and "a spiritual food and drink" (10,3). Two ways of explaining this fact have been excogitated. We may think, with E. Peterson,[12] that the Bryennios codex, which dates from 1056, changed originally eucharistic prayers into prayers for more everyday use at table. Or we may think that the present text contains prayers originally used at table during communal meals, and that these prayers were given eucharistic overtones because the eucharist followed immediately on the communal meal.

The second of these two explanations seems to me more in keeping with the facts. Peterson can indeed appeal for support to the fact that chapters 9 and 10 of the *Didache* are reworked in the seventh book of the *Apostolic Constitutions*, where they have evidently been taken as being eucharistic prayers. The *Constitutions* add to chapter 10 of the *Didache* the famous prayer for the *myron* or baptismal oil,[13] thereby bringing out even more strongly the eucharistic significance of chapters 9 and 10. But may we not think that this later use of the *Didache* prayers was inspired simply by the eucharistic overtones they had acquired through their context, and that the later use only carried these overtones a step further?[14] For myself, I prefer to trust the text as published by Bryennios, especially since it is hard to see how texts originally eucharistic could be transformed, after the fourth century, into prayers for the table, at the very time when the practice of the agape was disappearing.

The decisive argument against Peterson, however, is the close link we shall see to exist between these prayers of the *Didache* and the Jewish tradition of blessings for meals. The link cannot be explained except as a direct and deliberate relationship. It seems to me that the link is so evident that it must unconditionally be accepted as the starting point for any interpretation of these chapters. Father Audet's commentary has the great merit of bringing out the importance of this criterion by showing how influential the tradition of thanking God was in Israel and Judaism.[15]

The very name *eucharistia* was undoubtedly taken over from this Jewish tradition, although the latter did not use it as the Christian Church would to refer specifically to the supreme act of thanksgiving which is the Mass or Lord's Supper. Among Christian writers, the word "eucharist" acquires this special meaning at an early date: probably in

Ignatius of Antioch (*Ad Smyrnaeos* 7, 1), certainly in Justin Martyr (*Apologia I*, 6, 6) and Irenaeus (*Adversus haereses* IV, 18). On the other hand, the *Didache* was probably written before the letter of Ignatius, and we cannot assume that "eucharist" is used here only in its specifically Christian sense. This is a point for which there is corroborating evidence, as we shall see.

In Father Audet's view, chapters 9 and 10 describe an agape or "ordinary breaking of bread," which is followed by "the major eucharist" (Father Audet's expression) as partially described in chapter 14. This seems to me to be an accurate view of the matter and especially of the relationship of chapters 9 and 10 to chapter 14. The prayers set down in chapters 9 and 10 are blessings used at a meal; this meal was followed by the eucharist, as is clear from *Didache* 10, 6 which serves as an introduction to it.[16] Was the eucharist celebrated in another room? Father Audet thinks that it was, on the basis of archeological discoveries at Dura Europos. In any case, this point is of no concern to us here.

In his commentary, despite the great importance of the subject, Father Audet has not made a detailed examination of the parallelism between the Jewish and Christian traditions of prayers of blessing (specifically, the Christian tradition as attested in the *Didache*). On this point, we can make our own the very interesting conclusions which E. von der Goltz reached back in 1905.[17] To begin with, *Didache* 9 and 10 reports prayers used *at table* in connection with a community meal, as 10, 1 makes clear. This means we need consider at this point only the Jewish tradition of blessings at meals.

There is, of course, a good deal of uncertainty when it comes to dating the various customs found in this tradition. It is possible, nonetheless, to reconstruct the general course of an ordinary Jewish meal (festive meals differed only in that the ritual was more extensive). I shall take into account here only the elements that are essential for our purpose. Whenever there was a sufficient number of guests (sometimes three, sometimes ten), prayers of blessing were used. Before the meal, there was a blessing of the bread and of the wine, if there was any; according to the tradition that stems from Shammai, the wine was blessed first, then the bread. After the meal, there was a lengthy prayer of blessing at which foreigners, women, slaves, and children could not be present. [18]

This general framework of a Jewish ritual meal fits perfectly what is described in the *Didache*. Before the meal, Christians blessed the wine and the bread; then they ate and, at the end of the meal, blessed God once again. Non-baptized persons could not be present for this meal, or *eucharistia*, just as among the Jews those not admitted to the cultic rite had to absent themselves. Consequently, the prescription in 9, 5 does not prove that chapters 9 and 10 are describing the specifically Christian eucharist. This is corroborated by Hippolytus' *Apostolic Tradition* which prohibits catechumens from taking part in the agape (chapters 26–27). [19]

THE CONTENT OF CHAPTERS 9 AND 10

I shall not embark on a word by word analysis of chapters 9 and 10 and of the correspondences with the Jewish tradition. It could be shown, for example, that Christians took the Jewish blessings over the bread and the wine and gave them a new meaning: the wine recalls the vine of David, the hidden meaning of which has now been revealed in the passion of Christ, [20] and the bread is henceforth the bread that is broken, a sign of salvation and a pledge of life for the believers who eat of it.

I shall, however, offer some remarks on chapter 10, since it provides us with hints as to the origin of the Christian anaphora and, more specifically, of the *praefatio* (preface). [20a] But on what grounds can the *Didache* be said to exemplify such a *praefatio*? Well, verse 6 speaks (very

9

briefly indeed) of a preparation for participation in the eucharist (in the strict sense of this term). In order to proclaim the imminent coming of the Lord and to greet him as already present among his own (cf. the Coptic version), as well as to forbid access to communion to those who are unworthy, the *Didache* uses the same language as Paul (in 1 Corinthians 16.20-23).[21] The same terminology will be taken over by most of the later eucharistic liturgies.[22]

It follows from this that the prayers which in chapter 10 precede the invitation to communion (10, 6) must be part of the "anaphora," if we may apply this technical term to so primitive a state of the tradition. In any case, since the content of these prayers corresponds so extensively to the content of the later prefaces of the Mass, we are justified in applying the name "preface" to *Didache* 10. The value of this chapter for liturgical studies is increased by the fact that the prayers are evidently inspired by the Jewish tradition.

The great Jewish blessing at the end of the meal was in fact a sequence of four blessings. This sequence is found, in another form and a different order, in *Didache* 10.

The Jewish prayer began by praising God as king of the universe who gives food to every creature but especially to men, who are his children. *Didache* 10, 3, is clearly a version of the same theme. Christian and Jew alike address the all-powerful master of the world, but the Christian attributes to the life-giving food and drink a new meaning unknown to the Jews: they are now a reminder to Christians of the spiritual food and drink revealed by Jesus Christ—a transparent allusion to the eucharistic food and drink which are a pledge of eternal life for the believer.[23]

The second Jewish blessing was addressed to the God of Israel who had brought his people out of Egypt, entered into a covenant with them, given them the Law, and finally bestowed on them the promised land. In short, the prayer

10

praised God for his great deeds in behalf of the chosen people, deeds that make up the history of salvation. The same intention is to be seen in *Didache* 10, 2, although the content of the blessing is now specifically Christian, as the faithful address the Father who, through Jesus, formed for himself a new people from among the nations and entered into a new covenant with them. "Your holy name . . . you have made to dwell in our hearts": these words are probably a reference to baptism, since in this rite the name of God is pronounced over the candidate and transforms him into a living temple of the Holy Spirit. But baptism is for the Christian tradition what the crossing of the Red Sea had been for the Jewish tradition, namely, a rescue from this world and the beginning of a new life.[24] Finally, Christians bless God "for the knowledge and faith and immortality you have revealed to us through Jesus your servant." In these words we find the three aspects both of Christ's ministry and of the new history of salvation: the revelation of God's plan and the gift of immortality through the Holy Spirit who is present in the Church.[25]

The third of the Jewish blessings asked God to have mercy on Jerusalem, on David's house, and on the temple (this third petition evidently dates from after 70 A.D.). God is asked to deliver his people from their enemies and afflictions. Here again, we find a close parallel in *Didache* 10, 5; Christians ask God for the deliverance and gathering of the Church, but the intention is the same.

This prayer for the Church is so important that we must dwell on it for a moment, especially since a similar petition occurs in chapter 9, 4. Unfortunately, we do not have the space here to go into the meaning of the Egyptian and North African tradition.[26] On the other hand, we cannot pass over the problem of duplication in 9, 4, and 10, 5. The petition is almost identical in both passages: the faithful ask God to gather his Church from the ends of the earth into his kingdom. Now, we saw that the third of the Jewish blessings asked God to rebuild Jerusalem; such a petition

11

is, however, equivalent to "Gather the dispersed children of Israel." We may conclude, then, that the prayer for the Church is found in its proper place in *Didache* 10, 5, as part of the great blessing after a meal. The Liturgy of St. Mark shows that the prayer for the Church was still part of the *praefatio* at a later period and in Egypt; in this prayer we read: "Lord, be mindful of your holy Church, one, catholic, and apostolic, which is spread abroad from one end of the earth to the other." Here we find the prayer of the *Didache* preserved almost verbatim, although the eschatological perspective has completely disappeared (the disppearance is characteristic of the period).

But what of the duplication in *Didache* 9, 4? It seems that the prayer for the Church got itself attached to the symbol of the bread that is scattered and then gathered. I think that in the course of history this symbolism won out over another and earlier possibility, that of making the prayer for the Church a part of the preface. In my opinion we can see one moment or phase of this development in the *Euchologion* of Bishop Serapion of Thmuis (in Egypt), where *Didache* 9, 4, reappears, but this time in the setting of the prayers of consecration; more specifically, it appears between the consecration of the bread and the consecration of the wine. The prayer for the Church as symbolized in the gathered bread was thus retained into a period when the practice of having a community meal before the eucharist proper had long since disappeared. In this development, the symbol of the gathered bread, which had earlier been part of the blessing over the bread at the community meal, later became part of the consecration of the eucharistic bread. Later still, the prayer for the Church was removed from its place in the prayers of consecration and located after the epiclesis, where it is to be found today. The *Didache* thus shows us the first phase in the history of the prayer for the Church within the Christian anaphora.

Fourth
Individ
petitions

We have still to consider the fourth Jewish blessing and its parallel in the *Didache*. This fourth blessing is the longest of all, but it consists for the most part of individual petitions that probably originated at different periods. The pious Jew here addresses God as "kindly lover of men" (or "good and benevolent"), an expression that will occur frequently in Christian prefaces. *Didache* 10, 4 may reflect this part of the Jewish blessing, although the words in the *Didache* are very general. On the other hand, the very brevity of the petition in the *Didache* may mean that what we have here is simply a rubric for a more detailed prayer.[27] This is all the more likely inasmuch as spontaneous prayer (or at least prayer whose precise content was not prescribed in advance) still played an important role at this period, if we may judge by *Didache* 10, 7.[28]

I regard it as certain that chapter 10 of the *Didache*, like chapter 9, was influenced by the Jewish tradition. All the elements essential to the Jewish blessings are found in the prayer recorded in the *Didache*. Although the form has been Christianized and the order of the elements has been altered somewhat, we can once again see to what an extent Judaism was the cradle of Christianity.

We have also tried to show that the prayers of chapter 10 are to be located after the community meal and before eucharistic communion. This amounts to saying that what we have here is a kind of primitive *praefatio*. We justify this position by showing that the blessings and main petitions of the prefaces in the Christian anaphora are prefigured in the prayers of chapter 10. This thesis would be confirmed, I believe, if we took into account those resemblances between the prefaces and the Jewish blessings that have no parallel in the text of the *Didache*. I am thinking in particular of the short dialogue that begins with "Lift up your hearts"—"We have lifted them up to the Lord"; this is rather closely parallel to the dialogue between the father of the Jewish family (or the president of the assembly) and the fellow guests that introduces the great blessing. I am thinking, too, of the Christian custom of singing the *Sanctus*, which likewise is paralleled in the Jewish tradition. It is enough, however, for us to have shown that the *Didache* represents a kind of bridge between the Jewish tradition of blessings at table and the preface of the Christian anaphora. In the latter, the essential elements of the Jewish tradition live on, even while being profoundly transformed and enriched by the new liturgical heritage proper to the Christian faith.

CHAPTER 14 OF THE DIDACHE

Chapter 14, as we said earlier, refers to the meeting for "the breaking of bread" and "thanksgiving" that has already been described in chapters 9 and 10. It provides some further details which we shall describe briefly.

1. The meeting takes place on "the dominical day of the Lord." Despite the pleonastic way of describing the day, the reference is doubtless to an ordinary Sunday, Sunday being the new day for specifically Christian worship.[29] *Didache* 8, 1 attacks those "hypocrites" who fast on the second and fifth days of the week, instead of on the fourth and sixth.[30] May we suppose that in emphasizing the fact that the meeting is on Sunday *Didache* 14, 1 is making a similar point against those who would make Saturday the preferred day for worship? We cannot say so with certainty, but the possibility is not to be excluded, since other texts from the same period show us that such a "temptation" existed.[31] This would explain why the redactor of the *Didache* returns here to a subject already treated in chapters 9 and 10, and why he specifies that the community is to meet not simply on "the Lord's day" (which could mean the sabbath) but on "the dominical day of the Lord."

2. If the Sunday meeting described in *Didache* 14 is the same as the one of which chapters 9 and 10 speak, we must

suppose that it too included a community meal.[32] It follows that the assembly took place on Sunday evening, since the meal was evidently eaten in the evening. That is the situation reflected in the famous letter of Pliny the Younger on the Christians: they meet on Sunday evening "to eat their food which, whatever people may say of it, is ordinary and innocent."[32a] Acts 20.7, "On the first day of the week we met to break bread," is probably a confirmation that this was indeed the Christian custom.[33] *Didache* 9–10 and 14 belong, therefore, to a period when eucharist and agape had not yet been separated.[34]

3. We learn that the "breaking of bread" and the "thanksgiving" were accompanied by a confession of sins. Earlier, in *Didache* 4, 14, we read: "In the assembly you will confess your sins and you will not go to prayer with a bad conscience." This exhortation marks the end of the section on the "Way of Life" (chapters 1–4), which contains teaching that goes back to a Jewish source.[35] The exhortation is found in a number of texts that are parallel to the *Didache*,[36] and for this reason it is all the more interesting to see that only the *Didache* has the phrase "in the assembly." The addition brings the exhortation closer to what we find in *Didache* 14, 1-2, and turns it into a kind of commentary on the latter.

4, 14a. In the assembly, you will confess your sins	14, 1. Come together on the dominical day of the Lord, break bread and give thanks, having first confessed your sins so that your sacrifice may be pure.
4, 14b. and you will not go to prayer with a bad conscience.	14, 2. Anyone who has a quarrel with his fellow should not gather with you until he has been reconciled, lest your sacrifice be profaned.

15

From this we learn two things:

a) In the course of the eucharistic gathering, there was a public and communal confession of sins. We are not told at what point in the course of the liturgy the confession took place; the aorist participle ("having confessed," in 14, 1) indicates only that the confession came before communion, which would be obvious in any case.[37] Neither are we told how the confession was made. We might think of a recitation of the Our Father which contains the petition: "Forgive us our debts as we forgive our debtors," but the Our Father is mentioned in 8, 2, and in 8, 3 we are told that it is to be prayed thrice daily. This liturgical usage was evidently not reserved to the Sunday eucharist.

We might also think of a community prayer of the kind preserved in *I Clement* 60, 1-2: "Merciful and compassionate [God]. . . . forgive our sins and injustices, and failures and faults. Do not take account of every sin of your servants and handmaids, but purify us with your purifying truth. Direct our steps so that we may walk in holiness of heart and do what is good and pleasing to you."

b) But the confession of sins, even if sincere, was not always a sufficient preparation for communion. We are also told that there were cases of temporary "excommunication."[38] If a person had a "bad conscience," he was not to take part in the community prayer.[39] *Didache* 14, 2 now tells us what this "bad conscience" refers to: If there is a dispute between brother and brother, they must settle the dispute before coming to communion. The text makes it clear that this regulation affects both of the persons involved; neither should communicate before a reconciliation has been effected.

In reading this passage we think immediately of Matthew 5.23-24: "If you are bringing your offering to the altar and there remember that your brother has something against you, leave your offering there before the altar, go and be reconciled with your brother first, and then come back and

16

present your offering." This passage refers, of course, to worship in the temple at Jerusalem,[40] but *Didache* 14, 2 shows that the words of Jesus were quickly adapted to the new situation of Christian worship. In this context we might also cite Mark 11.25: "And when you stand in prayer, forgive whatever you have against anybody, so that your Father in heaven may forgive your failings also." This text is confirmation of the fact that reconciliation among brothers was considered a prior condition for the forgiveness of God. We know, in fact, that Christians exchanged the kiss of peace before communion, as a sign of mutual forgiveness.[41] *Didache* 14, 2 also reminds us of the situation described in 1 Corinthians 11.27-29: To communicate "worthily" is to communicate with respect for one's brothers and sisters.[42]

4. I myself would not attach too much importance to the use of the word "sacrifice" as a designation of the eucharist; it occurs twice in *Didache* 14, but it is evidently suggested by the citation of Malachi 1.11, 14, which immediately follows.[43] "Sacrifice" means here the sacrifice of thanksgiving of which the earliest Christian texts speak; these texts deliberately contrast this sacrifice with bloody sacrifices, whether Jewish or pagan.[44] Nor can we prove differently by appealing to *Didache* 13, 3, where the prophets are called the "high priests" of community. *Didache* 13, 3-7 is a reassertion, in Christian form, of the Old Testament law on the tithe owed to the high priests; the passage thus has no direct relation to chapter 14. Still less can any appeal be made to chapter 15 (on the election of bishops and deacons) in order to prove that "sacrifice" in chapter 14 refers to the eucharist as a sacrifice in a specific, ministerial sense; chapter 15 is certainly a later addition.[45]

CONCLUSIONS

If asked about the importance of the eucharistic texts in the *Didache* for the current renewal of the liturgy, I would emphasize two points:

1. The first Christian communities celebrated the eucharist in connection with a meal.[46] Some small communities are today returning to this practice. It is clear that this implies a change of viewpoint: the eucharist is no longer being treated as a solemn ritual, a mysterious sacrifice that is to be celebrated with great pomp in a cathedral, but is becoming once again a sharing by friends of a simple daily food, and this in a familiar setting, around a table. The traditional eucharist has the advantage of giving visible manifestation to an entire local Church. The small-group eucharist has the advantage of intimacy. Could we not have both forms of the eucharist in our Churches?[47]

And it emphasizes the ethical concomitant, so easily lost in the cathedral euch-

2. The *Didache* contains this fine prayer: "Just as the bread broken was first scattered on the hills, then was gathered and became one, so let your Church be gathered from the ends of the earth into your kingdom" (9, 4).[48] The image is a perfect one for the pilgrim Church. On the one hand, a local community, gathered around the one eucharistic bread and knowing that it is united in faith and reconciled through mutual forgiveness, realizes that it is in very truth the body of Christ. On the other hand, it is conscious that it is but a small fragment (a *klasma*; cf. 9, 3) of the entire body, and it prays fervently for the visible unity of all Christians. Is this not the authentic eschatological outlook Christians should have in the age of ecumenism?[49]

→ 3. ethical importance

NOTES

This is a revised and completed version of an article that appeared in the volume *Eucharisties d'Orient et d'Occident* (Lex orandi 46; Paris, 1970), pp. 65-82.

1. J.-P. Audet, *La Didachè: Instructions des apôtres* (Paris, 1958).

2. A. von Harnack, *Die Lehre der zwölf Apostel* (TU 2; Leipzig, 1886), and many others after him.

3. The "Anglo-Saxon School": for example, J. A. Robinson, especially in his book *Barnabas, Hermas and the Didache* (London, 1920); R. H. Connolly, in a series of articles in the *Journal of Theological*

Studies, 1931-39, in which he even sees some Montanist influence on the Didache; and others.

4. Cf. also R. Glover, "The Didache Quotations and the Synoptic Gospels," New Testament Studies, 5 (1958-59), 12-29; C. F. D. Moule, "A Note on Didache ix, 4," Journal of Theological Studies, N. S., 6 (1955), 240-43; R. A. Kraft, The Apostolic Fathers 3: The Didache and Barnabas (New York, 1965), p. 77; A. Vööbus, Liturgical Tradition in the Didache (Stockholm, 1968), p. 885.

5. R. Knopf, in Die Lehre der zwölf Apostel. Die zwei Klemensbriefe (Handbuch zum N. T. Die apostolischen Väter 1; Tübingen, 1920), pp. 1-40; A. Adam, "Erwägungen zur Herkunft der Didache," Zeitschrift für Kirchengeschichte, 68 (1957), 1-47; S. Giet, L'énigme de la Didachè (Paris, 1970), p. 264.

6. The antiquity of the prayers is clear from the fact that they are heavily influenced by the Jewish tradition. Note, too, the title pais ("child" or "servant") as applied to Jesus in all these prayers; it is a very early Christological title that soon disappeared from the Church's tradition. According to H. J. Gibbins, "The Problem of the Liturgical Section of the Didache," Journal of Theological Studies, 36 (1935), 383-86, the prayers date from as early as 30-70 A.D. and come from Jerusalem.

7. [Translated from the Greek text as given in Audet, op. cit., pp. 234, 236, 240, but with reference to Rordorf's French translation. The latter is by A. Tuilier and will appear in the Tuilier–Rordorf volume on the Didache in the Sources chrétiennes series. The French translation reflects a slightly different Greek text.—Tr.]

8. The same may be said of other problems in the interpretation of the Didache. Cf. F. E. Vokes, The Riddle of the Didache: Fact or Fiction? Heresy or Catholicism? (London, 1938); Giet, op. cit.

9. P. Drews, "Untersuchungen zur Didache," Zeitschrift für die neutestamentliche Wissenschaft, 5 (1904), 53-79; M. Goguel, L'Eucharistie des origines à Justin Martyr (Paris, 1910).

10. Cf. Audet, op. cit., pp. 104-20.

10a. Bonn, 1926; reprinted, 1955. English translation by D. H. G. Reese, Mass and Lord's Supper (Leiden, 1953-72).

11. Cf. J. Jeremias, The Eucharistic Words of Jesus, translated by N. Perrin (London, 1966), pp. 116-17, with bibliography; Giet, op.

19

cit., pp. 203 ff. Vööbus, *op. cit.*, pp. 61 ff. tries to prove the contrary but is not convincing.

12. "Über einige Probleme der Didache-überlieferung," in his *Frühkirche, Judentum und Gnosis* (Rome–Freiburg, 1959), pp. 156 ff. (reprinted from *Rivista di archeologia cristiana*, 27 [1951], 37-68). Peterson's view is accepted by J. Betz, "Die Eucharistia in der Didache," *Archiv für Liturgiewissenschaft*, 11 (1969), 10-48.

13. On this prayer cf. W. Rordorf, "Le baptême selon la Didachè," in *Mélanges liturgiques offert au R. P. dom Bernard Botte* (Louvain, 1972), pp. 507-8. Kraft, *op. cit.*, pp. 165-68, on the basis of this prayer, sees chapters 9–10 as describing a eucharist for the newly baptized.

14. For we must add that in the fourth century these same prayers of the *Didache* are also to be found in a non-eucharistic context, namely, in the *Logos soterias* (which is probably an authentic work of Athanasius; cf. E. von der Goltz, *Logos soterias pros ten parthenon: Eine echte Schrift des Athanasius* [TU, n.F. 14/2a; Leipzig, 1905]).

15. *Op. cit.*, pp. 372-98.

16. Cf. also J. A. Jungmann, *The Early Liturgy to the Time of Gregory the Great*, translated by F. A. Brunner (Notre Dame, 1959), pp. 35-36.

17. *Tischgebete und Abendmahlsgebete in der altchristlichen und in der griechischen Kirche* (TU, n. F. 14/2b; Leipzig, 1905). Others have likewise emphasized the importance of the Jewish tradition for the interpretation of *Didache* 9–10, but without drawing the necessary conclusions; cf. Lietzmann, *op. cit.*, pp. 164-65; M. Dibelius, "Die Mahl-Gebete der Didache," *Zeitschrift für die neutestamentliche Wissenschaft*, 37 (1938), 261-83; R. D. Middleton, "The Eucharistic Prayers of the Didache," *Journal of Theological Studies* 36 (1935), 259-67 (Middleton is the closest to E. von der Goltz). Recently, K. Hruby, "La 'birkatha-mazon,'" in *Mélanges . . . Bernard Botte*, pp. 205-22, has made a careful study of the Jewish prayers.

18. Cf. also what we know today of the Essenes!

19. Cf. also Pseudo-Athanasius, *Logos soterias* 13 (ed. E. von der Goltz; cf. note 14, above).

20

20. In my opinion, this refers to a "revelation" of the meaning of the prophecy in Genesis 49.11 (cf. Isaiah 11); cf. W. Rordorf, "La vigne et le vin dans la tradition juive et chrétienne," *Annales de l'Université de Neuchâtel 1969-1970* (Neuchâtel, 1971), pp. 135 ff.

20a. ["Anaphora" is a Greek word meaning "a carrying up or raising," and in Christian usage means "offering" and is a name for the eucharistic prayer of the Mass. *Praefatio* (preface) means "a speaking before (God and the people)"; in early Roman usage it designated the entire eucharistic prayer, but later came to mean only the opening section of that prayer.—Tr.]

21. Cf. G. Bornkamser, "Das Anathema in der urchristlichen Abendmahlsliturgie," in his *Das Ende des Gesetzes* (5th ed.; Munich, 1968), pp. 123-32.

22. This would be the place to study the *Hosanna* in the liturgy; in my view, moreover, the "If anyone is holy, etc." (*Didache* 10, 6) corresponds to the "Holy things to the holy!" of the Eastern liturgy.

23. Cf. Ignatius of Antioch, *Ad Ephesios* 20, 2. I need not emphasize the importance of the blessing of creator and creatures in all the later prefaces of the Mass.

24. Cf. J. Daniélou, *The Bible and the Liturgy* (Notre Dame, 1956), pp. 86-98.

25. We need only remind the reader that the later prefaces of the Mass, beginning with that found in the *Traditio apostolica* of St. Hippolytus, always commemorate the great events in the history of salvation.

26. Cf. L. Clerici, *Einsammlung der Zerstreuten: Liturgiegeschichtliche Untersuchung zur Vor- und Nachgeschichte der Fürbitte für die Kirche in Didache 9, 4 und 10, 5* (Liturgiewissenschaftliche Quellen und Forschungen 44; Münster, 1966).

27. Thus Harnack, *op. cit.*, p. 33; Peterson, *op. cit.*, pp. 171-72.

28. We have little detailed knowledge of this spontaneous or non-fixed prayer, but we can at least say that it was long held in honor; cf. Justin, *Apologia I*, 67; Hippolytus, *Traditio apostolica*, 9.

29. C. W. Dugmore, "Lord's Day and Easter," in *Neotestamentica et Patristica in honorem sexagenerii O. Cullmann* (Leiden, 1962), pp.

272-81, would see in the phrase a reference to Easter; for a critique of this view, cf. W. Rordorf, *Sunday: The History of the Day of Rest and Worship in the Earliest Centuries of the Christian Church*, translated by A. A. K. Graham (Philadelphia, 1968), pp. 205-15.

30. The "hypocrites" are probably not Jews, as is often assumed, but Christians who were tempted to imitate Jewish customs.

31. Cf. Ga 4.8-11; Col 2.16-17; Ignatius of Antioch, *Ad Magnesios* 9, 1-2; and the commentary on these texts in W. Rordorf, *Sabbat et dimanche* (Neuchâtel–Paris, 1972).

32. The expression "to break bread" seems to me to confirm this thesis, despite the objections of Jeremias, *op. cit.*, pp. 119-20.

32a. *Epistulae* X, 96, 7.

33. It is true that C. S. Mosna, *Storia della domenica dalle origini fino agli inizi del V. secolo* (Rome, 1969), pp. 44 ff., 83 ff., defends the view (earlier proposed by H. Riesenfeld, "The Sabbath and the Lord's Day in Judaism," in *The Gospel Tradition*, translated by E. M. Rowley and R. A. Kraft [Philadelphia, 1970], pp. 111-38) that Acts 20.7 refers to a gathering on Saturday evening; he therefore postulates that *Didache* 9-10 describes a Christian vigil on Saturday evening. For a critique of this position, cf. my review of Mosna's book in *Zeitschrift für Kirchengeschichte*, 82 (1971), 383-85.

34. In Justin Martyr, *Apologia I*, 67, the separation has already taken place.

35. Cf. W. Rordorf, "Un chapitre d'éthique judéo-chrétienne: Les Deux Voies," in *Judéo-christianisme* (Paris, 1972), pp. 109-28. (This volume = *Recherches de science religieuse* 60 [1972], nos. 1-2.)

36. These are: *Doctrina apostolorum* 4, 4; *Epistula Barnabae* 19, 12; *Canones apostolorum* 11 (in the shorter version); and *Constitutiones apostolorum* VII, 14, 17.

37. On the other hand, I am not convinced that the conjecture of Gebhardt and Harnack is necessary. They have proposed the reading *proexomologesamenoi* instead of the ms *prosexomologesamenoi* (and almost all the editors of the *Didache* have followed them). I prefer to keep the ms reading.

38. Cf. also *Didache* 10, 6: "If anyone is holy, let him come! If anyone is not, let him repent!" This is a further indication that chapters 9, 10, and 14 are closely connected each with the others.

39. *Proseuche* (prayer) despite the accompanying *sou* (your) in 4, 14 must be taken as referring to the community prayer, for the text speaks of "going to prayer." Giet, *op. cit.*, p. 88, refers to Acts 16.13 where *proseuche* means the place of Jewish worship.

40. Cf., e.g., P. Bonnard, *L'Evangile selon saint Matthieu* (Neuchâtel–Paris, 1963), p. 64.

41. Cf. Justin Martyr, *Apologia I*, 65, 2. On this point, cf. W. Rordorf, "'Wie auch wir vergeben haben unsern Schuldern' (Matth. VI, 12b)," *Studia Patristica*, 10 (Berlin, 1970), 236-41.

42. Pseudo-Athanasius, *Syntagma doctrinae* 2, seems to give this interpretation of *Didache* 4, 14.

43. Cf. Kraft, *op. cit.*, p. 174.

44. Cf. W. Rordorf, "Le sacrifice eucharistique," *Theologische Zeitschrift*, 25 (1969), 335-53, where I offer a critique of J. de Watteville's thesis in his *Le sacrifice dans les texts eucharistiques des premiers siècles* (Neuchâtel–Paris, 1966).

45. Cf. the pertinent remarks of Giet, *op. cit.*, pp. 240 ff.

46. The expressions "Holy Supper" and "Evening Meal (*Abendmahl*)" for the eucharist preserve the memory of this fact.

47. Cf. W. Rordorf, "Die Hausgemeinde der vorkonstaninischen Zeit," in C. W. Williams (ed.), *Kirche: Tendenzen und Ausblicke* (Gelnhausen–Berlin, 1971), pp. 190-96, 235-36.

48. The passage has been taken over into a number of recent eucharistic liturgies.

49. Cf. W. Rordorf, "Eglise de l'attente," *Communion* (formerly *Verbum caro*), no. 95 (1970), 86-96.

CLEMENT OF ROME

In the year 95 or 96, toward the end of the reign of Domitian, "the Church of God sojourning at Rome" wrote a letter to "the Church of God sojourning at Corinth."[1] A schism had just erupted at Corinth: one or two agitators (47, 6)[2] were plotting against the presbyters, some of whom, despite their worthy lives, were removed from a ministry they had been exercising in a blameless manner (44, 6). The letter provides no detailed information of the occasion for such a plot.[3]

The Roman Church, which sends the letter, knows itself to possess an authority to which the Church addressed must submit.[4] The Roman Church issues orders and expects the Church at Corinth to obey them.[5] It expects that the deputies sent to Corinth will soon return with news that peace and harmony have been re-established and order restored (65, 1).[6] And, as a matter of fact, Corinth does submit: Dionysius, bishop of Corinth in the time of Pope Soter (166–175), writes to the latter that the letter of Clement to the Church of Corinth is still read in the liturgical assembly. The respect thus given to the letter seems comparable to the respect given to the Scriptures, but we cannot conclude from this that Clement's letter was in fact put on a par with the Scriptures.[7]

It is not known whether the Corinthian presbyters who had been deposed approached the Church of Rome as a court of appeals, told of their problem, and asked Rome's intervention, or whether the Church of Rome came to know of the situation at Corinth and took the initiative in intervening in the affairs of another Church. In either case, the conclusion seems inescapable that the present letter is, in the words of P. Batiffol, "the epiphany of the Roman primacy."[8] Far from excusing itself for interfering in the affairs of another Church, the Church of Rome asks pardon rather for not having intervened sooner, as a person asks pardon for having delayed in fulfilling an obligation. The reason for the delay, we are told, is "the sudden series of misfortunes and calamities that have struck" the Church of Rome (1, 1).[9]

The letter from Rome does not tell us its author's name, but is presented as a message from one Church to another. Very ancient tradition claims, however, that the letter was the work of Pope St. Clement, fourth bishop of Rome; it is the only authentic work of his that has survived.[10]

THE EUCHARIST IN ITS CONTEXT (CHAPTERS 40–41)

What testimony about the eucharist does Clement's letter to the Corinthians supply? To begin with, the noun *eucharistia* does not occur at all, while the verb *eucharistein* occurs twice (38, 2 and 4). The meaning of the verb would be simply "to give thanks (to God)," if we choose to treat it as an example of classical Greek. However, Clement's thinking is thoroughly biblical; he constantly cites the Old Testament in the Septuagint Greek translation in which *eucharistein* translates the Hebrew verb *barak*, "to bless." In all likelihood, then, Clement's *eucharistein* refers to the blessings addressed to God on account of his various gifts and of all that he himself is.[11]

Even if Clement does not use the terms that later became technical designations for the eucharist, the reality is present in the letter as far as the sacrificial aspect of the eucharist is concerned. It is spoken of as having replaced the various sacrifices of the Old Testament and thus as being itself a sacrifice. It has been instituted by the Lord and is closely connected with the hierarchy, whose essential function it is to offer sacrifices.

25

These statements are found in chapters 40, 1-5, and 41, 1-2. To appreciate their full meaning, we must situate them in their context. A rapid sketch of this context will not be out of place here.[12]

Since its foundation by Paul the Apostle, the Church of Corinth had provided magnificent examples of the Christian virtues and had been a model for other Christian Churches (1–2). Then jealousy (*zelos*) entered the picture and has caused "worthless men to rise up against the worthy" (3, 3). The jealousy that we see to be the cause of rivalries and hatreds in the Old Testament from Cain to Saul (3–4) is also at work now, as the story of "the athletes in the days closest to us" shows (5, 1). Clement then goes on to give an extremely valuable testimony (5–6) concerning the apostolic origins of the Church of Rome, the martyrdom of Peter, the apostolate and martyrdom of Paul,[13] and the persecution which is raging "among us" (6, 1).[14]

In order to fight against jealousy, we must obey "the renowned and holy rule given us by our tradition"(7, 2).[15] This rule teaches repentance and conversion[16] in accordance with the Scriptures (7–8). It also prescribes obedience and humility (9–15), for humility begets peace, gentleness, obedience, and sincerity. The example of Christ, who came in humility and was wounded for our sins, was prefigured long before by the prophets and many others whose lives are an invitation to us to return to the peace ordained in the beginning by "the Father and Creator of the entire universe" (16–20). The harmony that rules in the heavens, the seas, and the bowels of the earth is a further lesson in harmonious unity.[17] Clement seems here to be echoing one or other Stoic philosopher; the Stoics, as is well known, taught that the world is harmoniously ordered.

Christians must therefore live in a manner worthy of God, respect the authorities, honor the presbyters,[18] and apply themselves to virtue by keeping ever before them their

26

faith in Christ[19] and cultivating sincerity and a reverential
fear of God, the sovereign judge and author of that resurrection "of which he gave the first fruits when he raised the
Lord Jesus Christ from the dead" (24, 1). Clement sees an
intimation of the resurrection in the succession of the sea-
sons, in the coming of day after night, and even in the
legend of the phoenix which arises from its own ashes
(Clement does not seem to have seriously doubted the
truth of this story).

God is faithful to his promises. He sees and hears everything; this divine power becomes a ceaseless invitation to
holiness (26–30). So does the example of the patriarchs
(31–34) and the magnificent blessings God has prepared
for those who love him. "Such is the path, beloved, by
which we shall find our savior, Jesus Christ, the high priest
of our offerings (*ton archihierea ton prosphoron hemon*), the
protector and helper of our weakness" (36, 1).[20] Such a use
of sacrificial language is important in view of what will be
said later.

Chapter 37, 1-4, alludes to the discipline of the Roman
armies, a discipline that made a strong impression on Clement; he sees it as a model for the order that should reign
in the Church. The order within the human body, in which
the members are subordinate to the head[21] leads him to
make the same point (37, 5). It is necessary that "the body
which we form in Christ Jesus be preserved in its integrity"
and that "each person be subject to his neighbor, according
to the gift assigned him" (38, 1). Order should be seen
everywhere.

The conclusion is that order is indispensable to the Church
of God: not any order but the order willed by God. Human
beings, "who live in houses made only of clay" (39, 5) and
who nonetheless arrogate to themselves a power that is not
from God, are evidently insane. Clement has no soft feel-
ings toward those who incited the revolt against the presbyters of Corinth.

27

It is at this point that Clement speaks of sacrifices and the hierarchy. Here is what he says:

40, 1. All this is evident to us.[22] We have studied the depths of the divine knowledge and must therefore do in proper order (*taxei*) all that the Master bids us do at determined moments. 2. He has bidden us celebrate the offerings (*prosphoras*) and the services (*leitourgias*) not randomly or without order but at determined times and hours. 3. He himself has determined by his supreme will where and by whom he wants them celebrated, so that everything may be done in a holy manner, according to his good pleasure, and in a way acceptable to his will. 4. Those, therefore, who present their offerings (*prosphoras*) at the appointed time are acceptable and blessed, for in obeying the prescriptions of the Master they do not go astray. 5. The high priest has been given functions proper to him (*idiai leitourgiai*); the priests have special places (*idios topos*) assigned to them; the Levites have their special services (*idiai diakoniai*); and the layman is bound by the prescriptions for the laity.

41, 1. Brothers, let each of us please God in the rank proper to him; let him have a good conscience and not violate the rule (*kanona*) established for his ministry (*leitourgias*), but act with dignity (*en semnoteti*). 2. Not everywhere, brothers, are sacrifices (*thusiai*) offered—be they perpetual (*endelechismou*) or votive (*euchon*) or for sin and negligence— but only at Jerusalem. Even at Jerusalem, they are not offered (*prospheretai*) in every place, but only on the altar (*thusiasterion*) before the sanctuary, after the offering has been carefully examined by the high priest and the ministers mentioned above. 3. Those, therefore, who act contrary to the order that is according to God's will are punished by death. 4. As you can see, brothers, the higher the knowledge of which we have been judged worthy, the greater the danger to which we are exposed.

Clement goes on to explain the origin of the hierarchy and

28

to show the close connection between the hierarchy and the exercise of cultic functions:

42, 1. Jesus Christ was sent from God, and the apostles were evangelized for our sake by the Lord Jesus Christ. 2. Christ, then, came from God, and the apostles from Christ; in both ways, the apostles were in proper order in accordance with God's will. 3. Having received their instructions and having been fully convinced by the resurrection of our Lord Jesus Christ. . . . 4. They proclaimed the good news from place to place and village to village. They tested their first fruits [i.e., converts] and appointed them to be overseers (*episkopous*) and ministers (*diakonous*) of the future believers.[23]

After some words on the rivalries that arose within the Jewish priesthood in the time of Moses and Aaron (43), Clement adds:

44, 2. [The apostles] established the rule that when they [the overseers and ministers the apostles had appointed] should die, other tested (*dedokimasmenoi*) men should succeed them in their cultic ministry (*leitourgian*). 3. We regard it as unjust, therefore, to remove from their cultic functions (*leitourgias*) those who were put in charge by the apostles or by other eminent men (*ellogimon andron*) with the approbation of the entire Church. . . . 4. It is no small sin for us to take the functions of overseership (*episkopes*) from men who have presented the offerings (*prosenegkotas ta dora*) in a blameless and holy manner.

The Gifts

We note, first of all, the parallelism Clement sets up between Old Testament cultic acts and those of the New Testament; the same terms are used to describe both. The principal act of the Mosaic cultus was the offering of sacrifices in accordance with a minutely detailed set of ritual prescriptions; it follows that the principal act of New Testament worship is likewise a sacrifice. Clement does not use the word "eucharist," but he evidently knows the reality to which we point when we use this word. There is no doubt that in his eyes the eucharist corresponds to, while also bringing to perfection, the sacrifices of the old law, and that it is a sacrifice.

The offering of sacrifices in the Old Testament and indeed everything involved in the public exercise of worship required the intervention of the Levitic priesthood. So too do the rites of the New Testament require the intervention of a priesthood which is the specific attribute of a hierarchy. The rites are the main function of overseers who have been appointed either by the apostles, who themselves received their powers from Christ, or by other eminent men[24] whom the apostles appointed as their successors. The overseers are also called presbyters, for in Clement's day the two terms had not yet everywhere acquired the different meanings with which we are familiar and which are exemplified in the letters of St. Ignatius of Antioch about a decade later.

This priesthood (hierosune: 43, 2) is a "special reality" not possessed by those who have not received it by transmission from the apostles or their successors; such nonpossessors are laymen. Under the old law the various members of the Levitic priesthood had their special functions.[25] So too, under the new law, there are differing functions for the overseer-presbyters and for the ministers. It is unthinkable for Clement that the members of the hierarchy and the faithful should have equal roles in the celebration of the liturgical sacrifice. No, it is for the overseers and presbyters alone to "present the gifts," and they must do it in a manner beyond reproach. Clement thus gives the eucharist a clearly ecclesiastical character.

The cultic service of the members of the hierarchy is not carried out according to the whim of the individual or the creativity of a more or less fruitful imagination or the more or less successful innovations of the celebrants. Everything

30

must be done in order (*taxei*), because there is a rule (*kanon*), established by Christ and handed on by the apostles, which each one must follow if he is to remain faithful to the will of Christ. Here again the parallel with the Old Testament holds.

We should remember this appeal to tradition which was issued before the end of the first century. The tradition goes back to the apostles and, via the apostles, to Christ, and is a rule which no one may legitimately violate.

In describing the liturgical and sacrifical institutions of the Church Clement uses, as we have seen, the terminology of the Greek Bible, which translated as best it could the Hebrew words for the various categories of sacrifice. He speaks of *thusiai, leitourgiai, prosphorai, euchai*, and sacrifices for sin that were offered on the altar (40–41). In 44, 4, he grieves that men who had presented the gifts (*ta dora*) in a holy manner were deposed from their overseership. In 35, 12, and 52, 3, he speaks of the sacrifice of praise (*thusia aineseos*) with explicit reference to Psalm 49 (50).19. We may be tempted to see in this last phrase a simple reference to the public prayer that had the psalms for its center. But the Septuagint uses the phrase to translate the Hebrew *todah*, which, according to 2 Chronicles 29.31; 33.16, and Leviticus 7.14; 22.29, meant an offering of victims, accompanied by a presentation of unleavened bread (cf. Leviticus 7.11; Amos 4.5).

In Clement's view, then, the various types of Old Testament sacrifice are summed up in the unique sacrificial act that is the celebration of the eucharist. This celebration was established and regulated by Christ, while the apostles added further details. In it, the overseers and presbyters act as high priests (*archihiereus*) and present the *prosphorai* and *dora* to God. [26] In point of fact, the action of the overseers and presbyters is ministerial, since it is Jesus Christ who is "the high priest of our offerings" (36, 1). Clement nowhere sets down a theory of the Christian sacrifice; he

31

uses ideas well known in the Roman Church in whose name he speaks, and in the Church of Corinth which he is addressing. His readers were familiar with the teaching on sacrifice of the author of the Letter to the Hebrews and by St. Paul in the First Letter to the Corinthians (11.23-29).

[handwritten margin note: That is not a passage on sacrifice!]

Clement continues his exhoration by asking his readers not to "rend and tear the members of Christ" (46, 7). The Corinthian schism "has led many astray, discouraged many, plunged many into doubt, and brought grief upon us all" (46, 9). Yet the state of tension is unrelaxed. Everyone, therefore, should read once again the exhortations and advice Paul once gave in his letter to the Corinthian community as he urged them to put an end to factions.[27] The present schism is more serious than the divisions Paul experienced. Any and every division must be eliminated so that men *[handwritten: people]* may live in love (47–50).

The authors of the schism are urged to acknowledge their sin and repent (51–52). Long ago, Moses interceded with God for his guilty people and offered himself in their stead (53); so too, those who have caused the schism should go into exile so that peace and harmony between Christians and their presbyters may be restored (54–56). The community must pray for these guilty individuals whom Clement urgently exhorts to submit to the presbyters and cease usurping a place that does not belong to them (57–58). If the schismatics prove stubborn they are putting themselves in serious danger (59, 1).

UNIVERSAL PRAYER OF THANKSGIVING

It is at this point that Clement launches into a prayer the lyric quality of which will be obvious to everyone. The prayer has become justly famous; in style it reminds us of the eastern eucharistic anaphoras, especially that of Serapion of Thmuis.

Chapter 59.

2. In continual prayer and supplication we will ask the Creator of all things that through his beloved child Jesus Christ he would preserve intact throughout the world the counted number of the chosen. It is through Jesus that he has called us from darkness to light, from ignorance to the full knowledge of the glory of his name,   *sophia*

3. in order that we might hope in your name which is the original source of every creature. You opened the eyes of our heart so that we might know you who alone are the Most High in the heights of heaven, the Holy One who rests among the holy ones. You cast down the arrogance of the proud; you reduce to nothingness the designs of the heathen; you exalt the humble, you cast down the proud; you enrich and impoverish; you take life and you save and give life; you alone are the benefactor of the spirits and the God of all flesh. You look into the abysses and inspect the works of men. You help *mortals* men in their perils, you save the despairing. You are the Creator and overseer *Bishop* (*episkopos*) of every spirit. You multiply the nations on the earth. You have chosen from all of them those who love you through your beloved child Jesus Christ, through whom you have instructed, sanctified, and honored us.

4. We pray you, sovereign Master, to be our helper and protector. Save those of us who are afflicted; have pity on the lowly, lift up those who have fallen; show yourself to the needy, heal the sick, bring back those of your people who have gone astray; feed the hungry, free our prisoners, raise up the strengthless. Let all the nations acknowledge that you alone are God, that Jesus Christ is your child, and that we are your people and the sheep of your pasture.

Institution & Anamnesis could be inserted here

Chapter 60.

1. For you have manifested the everlasting constitution of the world through your deeds. Lord, you created the world, you who are faithful through all generations, marvelous in power and magnificence, wise in creating and

prudent in establishing what exists, good in all that we see, and faithful, merciful, and compassionate to those who trust in you. Forgive our sins and injustices and failures and faults.

2. Do not take account of every sin of your servants and handmaids, but purify us with your purifying truth. Direct our steps so that we may walk in holiness of heart and do what is good and pleasing to you and to our princes.

3. Yes, sovereign Master, make your face shine on us so that we may enjoy happiness in peace, protected by your hand and freed from all sin by your upraised arm; and free us from those who hate us unjustly.

4. Grant harmony and peace to us and all the inhabitants of the earth, as you gave harmony and peace to our fathers when they called upon you in a holy manner with faith and truth. Make us obedient to your omnipotent and glorious name, and to our princes and rulers on earth.

Interesting, in light of 6:1, on the raging persecution

Chapter 61.

1. It is you, sovereign Master, who gave them kingly power by your magnificent, indescribable might, so that we might acknowledge the glory and honor you have given them, and might be subject to them and not oppose your will. To them, Lord, grant health, peace, harmony, and stability, that they may without stumbling exercise the authority you have given them.

2. It is you, sovereign Master, heavenly king of the ages, who give the sons of men glory, honor and power over earthly things. Lord, direct their purpose according to what is good and pleasing in your sight, so that they may exercise in peace, gentleness, and piety the power you have given them, and may find you propitious to them.

3. You alone have the power to bestow all blessings and to do even greater things with us. We praise you through Jesus Christ the high priest and protector of our souls. Through him be given to you glory and majesty, now and in generation after generation and through age upon age. Amen.

Clement has not forgotten the concerns that made him address to the Corinthians his exhortations regarding peace and unity. They continue to appear throughout this prayer from the beginning. The prayer is thus an integral part of the letter.

Clement urgently asks the sovereign Master and Creator of the universe to "preserve intact throughout the world the counted number of the chosen" (59, 2). A few lines earlier, he had said: "He who carries out the commandments and orders of God will be enrolled and included in the number of those who are saved by Jesus Christ" (58, 2). The rebels at Corinth risk placing themselves outside that number by their sin and their stubborn refusal to change; it is important, therefore, to win their conversion from God, so that they may profit to the full by the salvation Jesus Christ has brought. Is Clement invoking here the doctrine of predestination? The language he uses emphasizes only the divine foreknowledge, by which God knows in advance everything that will happen, even before man begins to use his free will.[28]

Clement emphasizes the eminent part played by the Lord Jesus in the execution of God's loving plan for men. Jesus is the child of God, his beloved child,[29] and it is through him that the Father has called us from the darkness to light,[30] from ignorance to the full knowledge of his name,[31] so that we may hope in that name.[32] It is through Jesus, his beloved child, that the Father has "instructed, sanctified, and honored us" (59, 3). Redemption is explained as bringing us the true knowledge of God our Father, a holiness that consists first and foremost in liberation from sin, and honor. The "honor" undoubtedly is the honor of being a child of God, and living the life of God while still on earth, as we look forward to living that same life in heaven where we will see God as he is. Instead of "honored" we might perhaps say "glorified," although "glorified" would be *doxazein* rather than *timan*.

IN PRAISE OF GOD THE CREATOR

The movement and pattern of the prayer are to be noted. First, God's power and prerogatives are recalled. Petitions are then made to him in behalf of the afflicted, the lowly, the fallen, the needy, the sick, the straying, the hungry, the faint-hearted. The impression given is of a kind of litany or at least of a series of intentions such as we find in the Good Friday liturgy. The prayer thus resembles the prayer of the faithful or general intercessions which the reform initiated by Vatican II has now made part of the Mass and the Office. It will be worth our while to look more closely at Clement's prayer.

The first part, in which there is a shift from the third person to the second, begins with praise of the greatness and omnipotence of God (59, 3). From him comes everything that exists and to him men owe all the blessings they have. His will is to cast down the proud and exalt the lowly; he is the benefactor of spirits and the helper of men in their dangers; he sees everything and nothing escapes him.[33] All nations owe their existence to him, and out of these many and varied peoples he has chosen those who are to love him through Jesus Christ and by means of the grace which Christ has merited.

The prayer which follows (59, 4) asks the Master[34] for help in favor of the afflicted and the lowly. God is asked to bring back those of his people who have gone astray, to heal the weak,[35] to free the prisoner, to feed the hungry. May all peoples acknowledge God as the only true God and Jesus Christ as his child;[36] may they acknowledge that we are his people. In this first part, praise of God is in the foreground; prayer of petition follows as a consequence, and whatever blessings that prayer may win will contribute in turn to the glory of God. The structure and style are evidently those of the biblical "blessing."

The second part again begins with praise of God (60, 1). It offers homage to God as Creator of the world and as the God who remains faithful through all generations. He is infinitely wise and good, merciful and compassionate. The prayer then moves on to petition (end of 60, 1; 60, 2) that asks God to forgive our sins.[37] Clement is a good psychol- *theologian?* ogist and does not see evil only in the Church of Corinth; he himself and the Church of Rome, in whose name he speaks, have committed sins that require God's pardon; everyone needs to trust in God's mercy. Since God is indeed merciful, let him deign not to keep an exact count of the sins of his servants and handmaids. Let him purify his people by means of his truth[38] and direct our steps so that we may walk in holiness of heart and do only what is pleasing to him and to our princes.

The mention of the princes (*archontes*) is unexpected. It points to a fact that the *Letter to Diognetus* will emphasize later on, namely, that Christians intend to obey the laws of the country in which they live, and not in any way to disturb the functioning of civic institutions; they mean to be first-rate citizens.[39]

Clement now asks God to make his face shine on us,[40] to give us peace, protect us with his hand, and free us with his mighty arm; these formulas recall the wonders God worked in behalf of his people at their exodus from Egypt (60, 3-4). Clement begs God for harmony and peace "for us" and for all the inhabitants of the earth, the kind of harmony and peace God once gave to "our fathers"[41] when they were faithful to him.

The third part of the prayer (end of 60, 4 and 61) asks God that we be obedient not only to his name (our evident duty) but also "to our princes and rulers on earth." In Clement's mind, there isn't the slightest doubt about the origin of their power: it is from God. The power of princes and rulers is given them by a wise and good God for the sake of the peoples over whom these rulers have authority. In their leaders, even their temporal leaders, subjects must see a participation in God's authority; that is what legitimates the religious submission they give such rulers. Evidently, temporal rulers should likewise have the wisdom and good sense to know that their power is limited by divine law and that they have no right to command anything contrary to that law.

It may seem strange that Clement should urge upon his readers submission to the orders of princes, at the very time when his Roman Church has just endured tribulations and interference from the imperial authorities and when it was being forced to think back to the persecution it had endured in Nero's time. Christian writers have not shown any excessive affection for Rome, the Babylon of the Apocalypse (16.19; chapters 17–18); they sometimes thought of the Empire as the devil's tool, even though the peace the Empire established helped in the spread of the gospel. Yet Clement's thought is in a direct line with that of St. Paul who says that all authority is from God and to resist it is to resist God (Romans 13.1-7), and with that of St. Peter who says that we must be subject to established authority for the sake of God (1 Peter 2.13).

In the days of St. Peter and St. Paul the emperor was Nero, a man whose cruelty knew no bounds, as Tacitus and the Christian writers tell us. Yet Christians never failed to pray for the civil authorities. We all remember what St. Paul says in his First Letter to Timothy: "My advice is that, first of all, there should be prayers offered for everyone— petitions, intercessions and thanksgiving—and especially for kings and others in authority, so that we may be able to live religious and reverent lives in peace and quiet" (2.1-2). Later, the Apologists reminded their readers that while Christians refused to offer sacrifices to the divine emperor, since their religion forbade them to give a human being the honor due to God alone, they nonetheless prayed constantly to God for the health of the emperor, the prosperity of the empire, its victory over its enemies, and peace in the world.[42]

Clement reminds his own readers that kingly power, which is supreme power in the temporal order, comes from God as a gift from his power and generosity. Subjects must bear in mind "the glory and honor you have given them" in giving their temporal rulers a share in the divine power over men. For these leaders Clement asks "health, peace, harmony, and stability" (61, 1), all of these being necessary if rulers are to exercise their authority with wisdom and moderation, and not turn into tyrants. After a brief repetition in which he addresses God as "heavenly king of the ages" and attributes to him "glory, honor, and power over earthly things," Clement utters a special prayer for these men in authority: "Direct their purpose according to what is good and pleasing in your sight, so that they may exercise in peace, gentleness, and piety the power you have given them, and may find you propitious to them" (61, 2).

The ending of the entire prayer (61, 3) is a restatement of God's power and goodness: he is able to bestow all the favors asked of him, and even greater blessings than these. Clement addresses his own praise and that of the Church (exhomologein, "to praise,"[43] is a liturgical term designating the praise and blessing offered to God) "through Jesus Christ, the high priest and protector of our souls." The praise finds expression in a somewhat fully developed doxology; there are a number of these doxologies scattered throughout the letter.[44] From them we may easily infer that Clement was a Jew and almost incapable of writing the divine name without immediately adding a formula of praise and blessing; at the same time, we infer that he was a Hellenistic Jew, because he used the Septuagint Greek version of the Old Testament.

39

What is the character of this prayer which comes almost at the end of Clement's letter to the Corinthians? It is surely not a eucharistic prayer in the sense we normally give the term, for it does not contain the account of institution or the words of consecration. At the same time, however, by its lyricism and its stylistic likeness to prayers for the broad intentions of the Church it reminds us of those prayers which, according to St. Justin, the president of the assembly of brothers used to give thanks *epi polu*: "according to his ability," or "abundantly."[45] In other words, Clement's prayer gives every indication of being an example of the eucharistic prayer[46] as organized at Rome, a eucharistic prayer that may have provided inspiration for the Church of Corinth at its liturgical gatherings. The account of institution and the anamnesis would fit in quite naturally immediately after chapter 59.

In any event, everything in the letter of Clement to the Corinthians—the sections on sacrifices and on the origin of the hierarchy, as well as the final prayer which we have been discussing—focuses our attention on the mystery of the eucharist, as the sacrifice prefigured in the Old Testament sacrifices, and on its celebration.

NOTES

Greek text, critical editions: O. Gebhardt, A. Harnack, and T. Zahn, *Patrum apostolicorum opera* 1 (2nd ed.; Leipzig, 1876). J. B. Lightfoot, *The Apostolic Fathers*, Part 1: *Clement of Rome*, 2 vols. (2nd ed.; London, 1890), with extensive commentary. F. X. Funk, *Patres apostolici* 1 (Tübingen, 1901), with Latin translation; re-edited by K. Bihlmeyer, in *Die apostolischen Väter* (Tübingen, 1924). J. Fischer, *Die apostolischen Väter* (Munich, 1956), with German translation. G. Morin, O.S.B., published an early Latin version of the First Letter, *S. Clementis Romani Epistola ad Corinthios quae vocatur prima, in his Anecdota Maredsolana* 2 (Maredsous, 1894). This Latin text, with the Greek, is reprinted in T. Schaefer, *S. Clementis Romani Epistola ad Corinthios quae vocatur prima graece et latine* (Florilegium Patristicum 44; Bonn, 1941).

Greek text, current editions: Greek text of Funk, with French translation, in H. Hemmer, *Les Pères Apostoliques* (Paris, 1926). The Greek text of Fischer, with a French translation, in A. Jaubert, *Clément de Rome, Epître aux Corinthiens* (SC 167; Paris, 1971). Greek text of Funk-Bihlmeyer, with ancient Latin version and a Spanish translation in D. Ruiz Bueno, *Padres Apostólicos* (BAC 65; Madrid, 1950).

English translation with commentary: J. A. Kleist, *The Epistles of St. Clement of Rome and St. Ignatius of Antioch* (ACW 1; Westminster, Md. 1946). R. M. Grant and H. H. Graham, *First and Second Clement* (in R. M. Grant, ed., *The Apostolic Fathers: A New Translation and Commentary* 2 [New York, 1965]).

1. "Sojourning" translates the Greek word *paroikousa*. *Paroikein* means "to sojourn, to live as an alien," as opposed to *katoikein*, "to have a permanent residence, to live as a citizen with full rights." The true residence of the Christian is heaven; the time of his earthly life is only a preparation for his permanent residence with Christ. Similarly, the Church will obtain its permanent dwelling only when the heavenly Jerusalem of which the Apocalypse speaks (chap. 21-22) has come to pass. The same idea is felicitously expressed in Preface I for a Mass of the Dead in the Roman Missal: *dissoluta terrestris huius incolatus domo aeterna in caelis habitatio comparatur* (literally: "when the house in which they sojourn on earth has been destroyed, an eternal dwelling place awaits them in heaven"). Cf. 2 Co 5.1 for a similar idea. The *paroikousa* formula also occurs in the address of the *Martyrdom of Polycarp*.

The meaning "to live as an alien" lies behind the use of *paroikia* (Latin: *paroecia*), "parish," to designate a group of Christians in a city or territory, with a religious leader at their head and with a place in which to gather for the worship of God. But the term *parochus* which the Code of Canon Law uses for "parish priest" has a different origin: the *parochus* is a "provider," one whose function is to distribute (Greek: *parechein*) spiritual goods to his flock.

2. Earlier, in 1, 1, there is mention of "a few reckless and arrogant individuals."

3. Making use of a hypothesis formulated to account for the content of the *Didache*, A. Harnack explained the schism at Corinth as the result of a conflict between "the residential hierarchy" and "the charismatic hierarchy." W. Bauer suggested rather a move-

41

ment of a gnostic type which sought to depose the presbyters of Corinth; Rome intervened to support the "orthodox" party. But the letter says nothing of any doctrinal conflict, and gives no reason for assuming the existence of the double hierarchy so dear to Harnack.

4. Cf. L. Duchesne, *The Churches Separated from Rome*, translated by A. H. Mathew (New York, 1907), p. 84.

5. Cf. 59, 1; 63, 3-4; 65, 1.

6. These are almost the final lines of the letter.

7. Cf. the passage from Dionysius' letter which is given in Eusebius, *The History of the Church*, IV, 23, 11, translated by G. A. Williamson (Harmondsworth, England, 1965), p. 185.

8. *Primitive Catholicism*, translated by H. L. Brianceau (New York, 1911), p. 123. We should remember that John, the last of the Twelve, was still alive in Ephesus at the time of the incidents which led to the letter from Rome. We might think it more normal for the Church of Corinth to have consulted the apostle of love, especially since relations between Corinth and Ephesus were easier and better organized than those between Corinth and Rome.

9. The quoted words are a good description of the persecution carried on by Domitian against the Roman Church. Christians and Jews seem still to have been identified by the Romans, since the treasury sought to require all who "live according to Jewish law" to pay to the temple of Jupiter Capitolinus the tax they had sent for the temple at Jerusalem before the events of 70 A.D. Cf. Suetonius, *Life of Domitian*, 12.

10. The *Second Letter of Clement* is an anonymous homily of the second century; the *Clementine Homilies* and the *Clementine Recognitions* are still later as are the two *Letters to Virgins*.

11. On the meaning of the Hebrew *berakah* and the Greek *eucharistia* in the Septuagint, cf. J.-P. Audet, *La Didachè: Instructions des apôtres* (Paris, 1958), pp. 372-98.

12. Generally speaking, even educated people are unacquainted with the letter of Clement; formerly, they would be familiar at most only with the prayer of intercession, toward the end of the letter. We must bear in mind that Clement's thought is not developed according to a logical plan and with Cartesian rigor.

42

13. Paul "became a herald [of the faith] in the East and the West.
. . . After teaching the entire world about justice he reached the
limits of the West, fulfilled his martyrdom. . . . and was taken up
to the holy place" (5, 6-7). For a Roman like Clement "the limits
of the West" could be either Great Britain or the Pillars of Hercules (i.e., the Straits of Gibraltar). St. Paul did intend to go to
Spain (Rm 15.24, 28); it was while on that journey that he hoped
to stop at Rome. The testimony of Clement, who knew the traditions of the Roman Church, is an argument that Paul did make a
journey to Spain, probably a short one, after he was freed in 63 or
64.

14. "To these men of holy life was added a great multitude of
chosen people (*polu plēthos eklektōn*) . . . who left a magnificent
example among us" (6, 1). The Greek phrase given is the exact
equivalent of the *ingens multitudo* which Tacitus uses (*Annales*,
XV, 44) when speaking of the Christians put to death under
Nero. Clement knows that among these martyrs there were some
women whom he calls "Danaids and Dircae" (6, 2); he is referring
to Christian women who were condemned to play roles in the
staging of mythological stories (a favorite entertainment of the
Romans), at the end of which they were put to death. But
perhaps another reading is to be preferred at this point in the text:
gunaikes, neanides, paidiskai ("women, young girls, female children"); cf. A. Dain, "Notes sur le texte grec de l'épître de saint
Clément de Rome," *Recherches de science religieuse*, 39 (1951), pp.
353-61 (=*Mélanges Lebreton* I).

15. Note this appeal to tradition; another occurs in chap. 40-44.

16. *Metanoia*, a term that suggests a complete change of mentality
or outlook.

17. In chap. 18, Ps 50 (51), the *Miserere*, is quoted almost in its
entirety. In 20, 8, Clement speaks of "worlds beyond the ocean"
which are "ruled by the same order of the Master." Is he here
echoing those ancients who claimed that a continent lay beyond
the Atlantic? Or is he referring rather to Atlantis, an immense
island beyond the Pillars of Hercules, which according to Plato
sank into the sea because of its vice? We do not know.

18. In 21, 6, the juxtaposition of *prohēgoumenoi* ("rulers") and
presbuteroi obliges us to translate the second word not as "aged"
(in contrast to the *neoi*, "young," who are mentioned next) but as
"presbyters"; the addressees are being urged to respect the

members of the hierarchy. Compare 1 P 5.1-5.

19. Here (22, 1-5) Clement uses Ps 33 (34).12-18.

20. The text continues: "Through him we fix our eyes on the_ heights of heaven; through him we see in a mirror the pure (amo-non) and supreme (hupertaten) face of God" (36, 2). The end of chap. 38 uses language very close to that of the opening verses of the Letter to the Hebrews.

21. Compare 1 Co 12.12-26.

22. The writer is referring to the reflections that have preceded.

23. Into his citation of Is 60.17, at the end of 42, 7, Clement introduces mention of the *diakonoi*, thus altering the text of the prophet. According to the Hebrew text Isaiah says: "I will give you peace as your overseers and justice as your leaders." The Septuagint has: "I will establish your governors in peace and your leaders in justice." It is possible that the translation Clement gives was current in his circle.

24. Such men as Timothy and Titus are meant. The *ellogimoi andres* of 44, 3, are doubtless to be identified with the *dedokimas-menoi* ("tested") of 44, 2.

25. Cf. 40, 5. There is question of sacrifices offered under the old law, but a parallel is made with the sacrifices of the new law. The term "layman" found there means someone who has no sacred ministry to exercise. The ministry of the Levites is called a *diakonia*. It is possible that the Hellenistic Jews used the word *laikos* and "naturalized" it as part of the old religious language, and that it passed from there into early Christian religious language. Cf. A. Blaise, *Dictionnaire latin-français des auteurs chrétiens* (Strasbourg, 1954), at the word *laicus*.

26. For further reflections on these texts of Clement, the reader can profitably consult J. de Watteville, *Le sacrifice dans les textes eucharistiques des premiers siècles* (Neuchâtel–Paris, 1966). See also M. Goguel, *L'Eucharistie des origines à Justin Martyr* (Paris, 1910).

The sacrificial terminology of Clement should be compared with that of the Letter to the Hebrews 5.1. In Heb 13.15 *thusia aineseos* means praise addressed to God; in 13.16 *thusiai* means every good work done for God.

The compiler of the *Constitutiones apostolorum* endeavors in Book

II (25, 27, 34, 35, 53) to apply to the New Testament the terms used in the Old Testament. Thus, the *thusiai* of the Old Testament covers the *euchai*, *deeseis*, and *eucharistiai* of the New. The Old Testament spoke of *aparchai*, *dekatai*, and *dora*; the New Testament speaks of the "fruits" (*karpous*) and "works of our hands" (*erga ton cheiron*) which are presented to the overseer when he acts as high priest. In passing through his hands all these become the *prosphorai* and *dora* of the new law. Cf. the text in F. X. Funk, *Didascalia et Constitutiones apostolorum* (2 vols.; Paderborn, 1905).

"In *I Clement* the vocabulary of priesthood has Christ as its point of real reference and the old covenant as its point of typological reference, in an effort to account for the mission of the Church's leaders" (M. Jourjon, "Remarques sur le vocabulaire sacerdotal dans la I^a Clementis," in *Epektasis: Mélanges patristiques offerts au Cardinal Daniélou* [Paris, 1972], p. 110). A few lines later, the same writer says: "The priesthood of the old covenant reaches its fulfillment in Christ, the true high priest. . . . The priesthood of Jesus Christ is fulfilled in the Church. The Church can enter into communion with God only through its high priest. The evangelical service of God's people is carried on in the holy lives of men who are consecrated to God as the priests of the old covenant had been, and who, like them have the duty of providing spiritual guidance to the flock of Christ."

27. Clement refers only to what we now know as the First Letter to the Corinthians.

28. Cf. Ps 138 (139). The Secret prayer which in the old Roman Missal was the thirty-fifth of the orations *ad diversa* and was used in the ferial Masses of Lent contains analogous expressions.

29. Not *huios* ("son") but *pais* ("child") (59, 2. 3. 4) as in Is 42.1 (the first Servant Song) which is cited in Mt 12.18. Of itself *pais* is ambiguous because it is also used of Israel, the servant of God (Lk 1.54); David, the servant of God (Lk 1.69), every child (Mt 2.16; etc.); a servant (Mt 8.6); and Herod's entourage (Mt 14.2). The Acts of the Apostles use it of Jesus, probably by way of allusion to the Servant Songs of Isaiah (cf. Ac 3.13, 26; 4.27, 30). The context shows in what sense Jesus is the Child of God, who communicates his own glory to him.

30. The same idea occurs in 1 P 2.9. On redemption through "enlightenment," that is, through a passage from darkness to light, see, e.g., St. Augustine, *Tractatus in Joannem* 11, 6-16 (PL 34, 1391-96).

31. Cf. Ep 5.8-14.

32. Cf. 1 P 1.5. In Scripture "name" means the person with all his attributes. The same is true in other Semitic languages.

33. God is called the "Creator and overseer (*episkopos*) of every spirit" (59, 3).

34. The text has *despotēs* (in the vocative case), as in 61, 1 and 2. A *despotēs* is a sovereign but not tyrannical master; he is a master who possesses power and is able to use it to show his goodness and kindness.

35. Clement writes *oligopsuchountes* (literally, "the fainthearted"). The same term (*oligopsuchous*) occurs in 1 Th 5.14.

36. Note the parallelism between these expressions and those of Jn 17. Cf. A. Jaubert, *Clément de Rome, Epître aux Corinthiens* (SC 167; Paris, 1971), pp. 53-54.

37. Observe the various terms used to express violations of God's law: *anomia*, that which is not conformed to codified law; *adikia*, that which is not conformed to justice, that is, to the order established by God and outside of which no one can be just; *paraptoma*, a fall or false step; *plēmmelia*, error, negligence.

38. The Hebraism should be noted: literally, "purify us according to the purification of your truth." It is the truth that purifies souls; cf. Jesus' words to the Jews: "The truth will make you free" (Jn 8.32), and St. Paul who speaks of Christ purifying his Church in water by the word, which is the word of the living and true God (Ep 5.26).

39. *Ad Diognetum*, V, 5, 10. This composition was doubtless written in the second half of the second century, and seems to be of Alexandrian origin. 1 P 4.15 urges Christians to avoid all sins that fall under the purview of the law; cf. also 1 P 2.13-17. See H. Marrou, *A Diognète* (SC 53; Paris, 1951), or D. Ruiz Bueno, *Discurso a Diogneto* in his *Padres apostólicos* (BAC 165; Madrid, 1950).

40. Clement is here citing Ps 66 (67).2.

41. "Our fathers" are the patriarchs and prophets, and even the entire people of Israel. The history of the age of the Judges especially shows how the peace and material prosperity of the chosen people depended on their fidelity in observing the conditions of the covenant that they had concluded with God at Mt. Sinai.

42. Cf., e.g., St. Justin, *Apologia I*, 17, 3, and Tertullian, *Apologeticum*, 36-40. Tertullian is answering the objection that Christians are disloyal citizens because they are unwilling to perform an idolatrous act which their religion forbids, by offering sacrifices to the divine emperor. True enough, he says, they do refuse such acts, but the prayers of Christians for the emperor and the empire are no less sincere and genuine; these are enough to show how authentic their civic concern is. Cf. also St. Polycarp, *Epistula ad Philippenses*, 12, 3.

43. *Exhomologein* is the "confess" of a number of the psalms.

44. Cf. 20, 12; 32, 4; 38, 4; 43, 6; 45, 7; 50, 7; 58, 2; 64; 65, 2. In 20, 12, Jesus is the one for whom glory and majesty are desired. In 32, 4; 38, 4; 43, 6; and 45, 7, the doxology has God (the Father) as its addressee. In 61, 3 as in 64 and 65, 2, the doxology is addressed to God through Jesus Christ our "high priest and protector" (*archihiereus kai prostates*).

45. *Apologia I*, 65, 3. Compare, for example, the anaphora of Serapion of Thmuis, which dates from 339–360. The text is in K. Kirch (ed.), *Enchiridion fontium historiae ecclesiasticae antiquae*, nos. 476-80 (2nd ed.; Freiburg, 1914) and in A. Hänggi and I. Pahl (eds.), *Prex eucharistica: Textus e variis liturgiis antiquioribus selecti* (Spicilegium Friburgense 12; Fribourg, 1968), p. 70.

46. The compiler of the *Constitutiones apostolorum* was perhaps inspired by Clement's prayer in various passages of the liturgy he describes in Book VIII; but we can only compare the formulas, without establishing a sure dependence of the *Constitutiones* on the letter of Clement.

A.D. 110-111

IGNATIUS OF ANTIOCH

The testimony of Ignatius of Antioch is extremely important for the life of the Church, even in our day. He gave his witness at a turning point of history, a time when intense activity was being devoted to organizing communities, fostering the liturgical life, and developing Christian thought. It was a time when the first Christians, those who had known Christ, were disappearing from the scene.

It was also a difficult time. Tensions had arisen under the influence of doctrines which, in some circles, were even undermining the authentic faith.[1] These difficulties and threats, however, did not stop the forward thrust of the Church but, on the contrary, enabled communities to strengthen their sense of identity and to break through various constraining limits in order to bring the gospel to the nations of the known world. This is the context in which we must see Ignatius of Antioch.

IGNATIUS AS MAN AND BISHOP

Ignatius, born a pagan, was bishop of the community at Antioch at the beginning of the second century. Antioch was a city in which East and West met, and it exercised influence over the Churches of Asia Minor and Macedonia. About the year 110 a short-lived but violent persecution broke out against the Church of Antioch, and Ignatius was one of its first victims. In the reign of Emperor Trajan (85–117) this bishop of Antioch, according to tradition, was arrested, tried, and condemned to the beasts; then, "chained to ten leopards" (*Rom.* 5, 1), he was sent to Rome in a convoy of prisoners. It was probably at Rome that he underwent his martyrdom.

Along the route from Syria to Rome the Christian communities assembled to offer comfort and courage to their brothers in chains. Ignatius stopped at Philadelphia (7, 1), then at Smyrna where he was welcomed by Bishop Polycarp and greeted by delegations from the Christian communities of Ephesus, Magnesia (near the mouth of the Meander River), and Tralles (*Eph*. 1, 2; *Rom*. 9, 3). From Smyrna he wrote a letter of thanks to the communities of the three cities just named, as well as a letter to the Church of Rome. In this most beautiful of all his letters he asks the faithful of that Church not to take any steps that would deprive him of the joy of martyrdom. Ignatius was taken next to Troas, where he wrote to the Christians of Philadelphia and Smyrna and to Bishop Polycarp. These seven letters have survived.[2]

The letters, written on the journey to exile and martyrdom, are "earnest pleas for unity of faith and of sacrifice."[3] They were to be read over and over again in the Churches of the first centuries, for there are "none more vehement or more poignant."[4] Ignatius' letters are full of short and highly compact phrases; the style is rough, for he had to write swiftly as circumstances might allow. But their value as witness is immense, for they are an outpouring of enthusiasm and passionate love; they bring us the words of a mystic, in the fullest sense of the word, whose desire is to reach his goal as quickly as possible: to meet Christ, to be united to him in his sacrifice, to possess him forever:

"I beg you . . . let me be the food of beasts, that through them I may find God. . . . Then I will truly be a disciple of Jesus Christ, when the world does not see even my body. . . . It is good for me to die so that I may be united to Jesus Christ. . . . It is he whom I seek, the one who died for us. It is he whom I seek, the one who rose for us. . . . Allow me to be an imitator of the suffering of my God. . . . My earthly desire has been crucified, and there is no fire left in me for loving matter; there is rather a living water in me that murmurs and says within me: 'Come to the Father'" (*Rom*. 4–7).[5]

49

Most importantly, the letters of Ignatius provide us with very valuable information about life in the Christian communities at the beginning of the second century. This life was built closely around the bishop; its chief points of reference were baptism and the eucharist; it flowered in faith and love and in works of mercy, even while it resisted the gnostic threat and the various doctrinal errors that were abroad in the Church of Asia.[6] Ignatius exhorts these young Christian communities to remain closely united to Christ and the Church, to maintain the bonds of faith and love, under the leadership of the bishop and around the one altar whereon the one bread, which is the flesh of our Lord Jesus Christ, is broken in the eucharist, the sacrament of unity par excellence.

ANALYSIS OF TEXTS

What place does the eucharist hold in the thinking of Ignatius? We shall begin our answer by analyzing the texts in which the term *eucharistia* is used. It occurs four times: once in the letter to the Ephesians (13, 1), once in the letter to the Philadelphians (4), and twice in the letter to the Smyrnaeans (7, 1; 8, 1). But what does the word mean? Is the meaning the same in all four texts? This is what we must determine. We shall begin with the passage from the letter to the Ephesians, which presents some difficulty.

THE LETTER TO THE EPHESIANS

Ignatius urges the faithful to assemble more frequently: "Make every effort to assemble more frequently *eis eucharistian theou kai eis doxan*. For when you assemble frequently the powers of Satan are overcome, and his work of destruction is itself destroyed by your concordant faith" (*Eph.* 13, 1).

How are we to understand the Greek phrase? The translators and commentators do not seem quite sure. A. Lelong translates: "to offer God your eucharist and your praise,"

50

but he is careful to note: *"Eucharistian* seems to have both the general meaning of 'thanksgiving' and the narrower meaning of 'eucharist'; the eucharist, after all, is the supreme act of thanksgiving and the principal rite celebrated by the Christian assemblies."[7]

T. Camelot likewise seems unsure. He translates *eis eucharistian theou kai eis doxan* as "to offer God thanksgiving and praise," but he says in a note: *"Eucharistia* here means a prayer of thanksgiving to the glory of God, but it also means the eucharist, the memorial and repetition of the Last Supper where Jesus gave thanks over the bread and the cup (Luke 22.19-20 and parallels). This is the first example of the technical use of *eucharistia;* it occurs again in *Phil.* 4 and *Smyrn.* 7, 1, and 8, 1."[8] Here, then, Camelot connects thanksgiving and eucharist to the point of giving *eucharistia* its technical meaning. Elsewhere, however, he says that the meaning of the term is not always quite the same. In *Eph.* 13, 1, *eucharistia* should be translated as "thanksgiving," whereas "in other passages the meaning is more precise and the word has become a technical term (*Smyrn.* 7, 1; 8, 1), referring to the liturgical commemoration of the Lord's Supper."[9]

J. de Watteville, following the lead of A. Hamman,[10] prefers to translate *eucharistia* as "eucharist" and not as "thanksgiving."[11]

What conclusion shall we draw? It can be said that if the word *eucharistia* is not fully clear in *Eph.* 13, 1, in the other texts we shall be analyzing (*Smyrn.* 7, 1; 8, 1; *Phil.* 4) it does have a technical meaning and refers to the liturgical commemoration of the Supper during which the offerings are changed into the body and blood of the Lord and received as food at communion. We need not be surprised that the meaning of *eucharistia* should vary at a time when the later technical meaning was just being established. We should also realize, however, that variation does not mean opposition; after all, the supreme act of thanksgiving is the memorial of the Lord's Supper, that is, the eucharist in the technical sense.[12]

In *Eph.* 13, 1, Ignatius associates *eucharistia* and praise, just as in *Smyrn.* 7, 1, he associates *eucharistia* and prayer. Moreover, he urges the Ephesians to assemble more frequently because "when you assemble frequently the powers of Satan are overcome, and his work of destruction is itself destroyed by your concordant faith." According to *Eph.* 13, 1, then, the powers of Satan are overcome when the community gathers. But does not *Eph.* 20, 2 tell us that when "all of you together" assemble "in one faith" and "undivided harmony" it is in order to "break one bread which is a remedy bestowing immortality, an antidote preventing death and giving life in Jesus Christ forever"? In the latter text the eucharist is a remedy and an antidote; it purifies. The two texts together yield an important conclusion: it seems at the very least that the more frequent gatherings which Ignatius urges upon the Ephesians must have included the celebration of the eucharist in an atmosphere of faith, prayer, and thanksgiving. That, certainly, is the atmosphere we find in the next three texts we shall examine.

THE LETTER TO THE PHILADELPHIANS

Ignatius urges the Philadelphians to see unity in the eucharist:

"Be careful then to participate in only the one eucharist, for there is only one flesh of our Lord Jesus Christ and one cup to unite us in his blood, one altar just as there is one bishop with the presbytery and deacons, my fellow servants, so that whatever you do you do according to God" (*Phil.* 4).

This text is very important. It shows that the eucharist, as the sacrament of Christ's body and blood, is a sacrament of unity. It also brings out Ignatius' passionate longing for the

unity of all in Christ. This unity in faith and love is effected
by the eucharist. The reasoning is solid. *+ this is true - but*
sacrament, in its eater meaning, it is not -

Ignatius is putting the community on guard against those
who are pushing to schism; they follow a line of thinking
that is alien to Christianity and are out of harmony with the
passion of Christ. Being out of harmony with the passion
of Christ, they are at odds with God and the bishop and do
harm to the Church. Ignatius urges his correspondents
that if they want to preserve unity and to live in Jesus
Christ, they should participate in only the one eucharist.
The reason for so acting is simple: "There is only one flesh
(*sarx*) of our Lord Jesus Christ and one cup to unite us in
his blood, one altar just as there is one bishop with the
presbytery and deacons." The unity of the eucharist is
grounded in the unity of the flesh of Christ. Because there
is but one flesh of Christ, there can be but one eucharist,
and that is the one eucharist in which the Philadelphians
can participate. This eucharist is the flesh of Christ.

Sarx ("flesh") is the biblical word St. John uses in his Pro-
logue when he wishes to tell us that the Word became
"flesh" (John 1.14), and again in chapter 6 when he says
that the "flesh" of Christ is truly food (6.55-56). His flesh is
the source of eternal life: "The bread that I shall give is my
flesh (*sarx*), for the life of the world" (6.51). *Sarx* is used to
bring out the reality, the authenticity of Christ's human
nature in its concrete reality, and that same authenticity
must be attributed both to the Word's becoming flesh in
the incarnation and to Christ's giving up his flesh to eat in
the eucharist. At every point there is the same flesh, the
one *sarx*, of Christ.[13] The reality of Christ's human flesh in
his incarnation and the reality of his eucharistic flesh are
the objects of one and the same faith.

like the vague sense or I can

Ignatius will make the same point in his letter to the Smyrnaeans. For the moment, we may say that as Ignatius sees
it, the eucharist gives us the authentic, historical flesh of

⌐ ?

53

Christ. That is why there can be no doubt about the meaning of *eucharistia* in this passage from the letter to the Philadelphians. "Here, it is the technical term for the sacrament of Christ's body and blood, and for the sacrifice which Christians offer."[14]

how did *sacrifice get in here?*

This meaning is pinpointed and confirmed by the words *cup* and *altar*. There is only "one cup to unite us in his blood." How can this cup be anything but the cup from which Christians drink the blood of Christ at the moment of communion, thus rendering their union even closer because now they have all drunk from the one cup containing the blood of the one Christ? But even more is being said: Communion in the blood of Christ is *eis henosin tou haimatos autou*. The prepositional phrase expresses the movement or finality of something in the process of being fully realized: specifically, communion in the blood of Christ looks to a union that is constantly being effected and that is as perfect as the act leading to it.[15]

Various writers have sought to bring out this fullness of meaning in Ignatius' words.[16] Lelong, for example, explains the words "to unite us in his blood" as meaning: "'So that the union of all the faithful may result from their common participation in the one cup that contains the blood of Jesus Christ.' In the earliest Fathers, the eucharist is the principal symbol of and indeed the principal factor in the unity of the Church."[17] P. Batiffol sees in the words of Ignatius a reference to St. Paul (1 Corinthians 10.16): "We should have but a single eucharist because there is a single cup showing that his blood is one; Ignatius is alluding to the First Letter to the Corinthians: 'The cup . . . is it not a participation in the blood of Christ?'"[18]

According to O. Perler, we do not bring out the full meaning if we translate: "There is but a single cup to unite us in his blood." Ignatius has in mind the accounts of institution in Paul and Luke: "This cup is the new covenant in my blood" (1 Corinthians 11.25) "which will be poured out for you" (Luke 22.20). He wants to convey to us "the unifying outpouring of blood on the cross which becomes mysteriously present on the altar so as to unite us by the blood of the Lamb slain and in him: a single cup for union by his blood and in him, a single altar."[19]

Eis henōsin tou haimatos autou is here found in an eminently sacrificial context, for it is related to the passion of Christ (3, 3) and has in view the union of all with the one sacrifice of Christ; this union is accomplished through communion with his flesh and blood at the celebration of the eucharist, which is the sacrament of the covenant.

There is *a single altar* just as there is a single bishop with the presbytery and deacons. The altar is called the place of sacrifice or *thusiasterion*. It is one,[20] just as Christ (cf. Hebrews 13.10) and the eucharist and the Church are each one. For Ignatius the *thusiasterion* is the altar as symbol of the Church's unity. It is from the altar, the place of sacrifice, that the believer receives the bread of life.[21] *— note this one*

As symbol of the Church's unity and as place of sacrifice, the altar is the holiest of all places; there, gathered around the bishop and his presbytery, the community celebrates the eucharist in unity. This union is written in the hearts of the faithful, for it is proportioned to their union with Christ and therefore to their faith and love; it is deepened through the sharing of the same bread and the same cup.[22]

As for the bishop, it can be said that in Ignatius' view the entire cultic life of the Church has him for its center and focus. He holds the place of God (*Magn.* 6, 1; *Tral.* 3, 1); he is the visible image of the invisible Christ (*Eph.* 1, 3). "Apart from him it is not permitted to baptize or hold an agape; whereas everything that he approves is also pleasing to God. Consequently, everything done with him is safe and valid" (*Smyrn.* 8, 2).[23] Everything done with him will be in accordance with God.

Only the ordained may baptize.

Ignatius's thinking evidently rests at every point on a keen sense of unity: one flesh of Christ, one cup of his blood, one altar, one bishop. These various expressions explain and justify the existence of the one eucharist, while at the same time they tell us the meaning of the eucharist. The eucharist is a communion in the body and blood of Christ, in his flesh that he took in the incarnation and in which he suffered his passion. The eucharist is the sacrament of covenant, and it is a sacrifice. Since it unites all in Christ and among themselves, it cannot be celebrated except under the leadership of the bishop, and his presbytery.

THE LETTER TO THE SMYRNAEANS

In his letter to the Smyrnaeans, Ignatius takes up the cudgels against the heretics we know as the docetists.

"They abstain from the eucharist and from prayer, because they do not confess that the eucharist is the flesh of our Lord Jesus Christ, the flesh that suffered for our sins, and that the Father in his goodness raised this flesh up again. Those who thus reject the gift of God die amid their disputes. They will profit by practicing charity, so that they too may rise" (*Smyrn.* 7, 1).

This text is very beautiful and very important. After criticizing those who refuse to admit that Christ took flesh and who end by rejecting him entirely (5, 2), Ignatius here attacks others who deny that the flesh of Christ was real in his passion and resurrection and who are thus led to deny the reality of that same flesh in the eucharist. Evidently, these various groups were dealing with the same problem and applying the same kind of reasoning.

In the view of the docetists, Christ is by nature divine and therefore could not sully himself by contact with flesh; any bodily life he might have could only be an outward appearance, an illusion. Since he was not born of a woman and did not have a real body, he could not die on the cross or rise from the dead. Having thus done away with the scandal of a God taking flesh, that is, with the scandal of the incarnation, the docetists logically proceeded to empty the eucharist of its meaning: Christ did not take flesh, and therefore his flesh could not be present in the eucharist.

Such is the reasoning Ignatius reconstructs, and it holds together. The eucharist is the real flesh of Christ; eucharistic flesh and historical flesh are one and the same.[24] The reality of Christ's flesh in the incarnation and the reality of his flesh in the eucharist are inseparable (one and the same flesh in both mysteries), so that errors in Christology inevitably affect our understanding of the eucharist. J. Lebreton makes this point very clearly with regard to both St. John and St. Ignatius: "For John, as for Ignatius, the doctrine of the Christ and the doctrine of the eucharist are linked to the point of being inseparable. . . . In Ignatius' thinking, belief in the reality of Christ's life-giving flesh has immediate consequences for eucharistic theology."[25]

Ignatius' thinking is eminently Christological; he sees all aspects of the Christian life as forming an interlocking whole, so that if one denies any aspect of the mystery of Christ, one will ultimately be led to a denial of the reality of Christ himself in his fullness. This is surely the thinking that lies behind Ignatius' statement in *Smyrn.* 7, 1: those who abstained from the eucharist and prayer reject the *gift of God* and die amid their disputes.

What is meant by this "gift of God"? P. Batiffol takes it to mean "the incarnation, the flesh of Christ that suffered and was raised up, the reality of Christ's humanity."[26] For F. X. Funk, it refers to the eucharist,[27] while J. B. Lightfoot interprets it to refer to the redemption which embraces the incarnation and passion of Christ.[28] We believe, however, that if the text is taken in its entirety and in its context, the "gift of God" must be understood as a comprehensive whole, but with the accent on the eucharist. To abstain from the eucharist because one does not admit it to be the real flesh of Christ is, by way of consequence, to reject God's gift and condemn oneself to death. The "gift of God" thus refers to the eucharist insofar as the latter is bound up with the incarnation and is an actualization of the redemptive mystery (Christ's death and resurrection). These various aspects of the mystery are so closely connected in Ignatius' thinking as to constitute a single mystery of Christ. Therefore those who reject God's gift, that is, who do not acknowledge the real flesh of Christ in the eucharist because they deny the reality of the incarnation and the redemption, will die amid their disputes.

Ignatius goes on to say that these people will profit by practicing charity (literally, "by loving": *agapan*), for then they too will rise from the dead. In other words, they will profit by living in accordance with the sacrament of love; *agapan*[29] must here be understood in its pregnant sense of receiving the eucharist and then living out its social implications.[30] The eucharist and love are inseparable. This is why Ignatius points out that not only do the docetists abstain from the eucharist, but "they have no concern for charity, either toward the widow or the orphan, the oppressed . . . or the thirsty" (*Smyrn.* 6, 2).

Ignatius' thought is clear and solid. The eucharist, which is the sacrament of Christ's body and blood and is in continuity with the incarnation, contains the real flesh of Christ that suffered on the cross in a sacrifice of expiation for our sins. It contains his flesh that was not only sacrificed but was raised up again as well, for the death and the resurrection of Christ cannot be separated. Through love the Church must live out this entire paschal mystery. The second text that we shall examine from the letter to the Smyrnaeans speaks in even more detail of this ecclesial aspect of the eucharist.

58

ECCLESIAL DIMENSION OF THE EUCHARIST

A little further on in his letter to the Smyrnaeans, Ignatius writes:

"Let no one do anything relating to the Church, except in dependence on the bishop. Let only that eucharist be regarded as legitimate that is celebrated under the presidency of the bishop or someone the bishop appoints. Wherever the bishop is, there let the community be, just as wherever Christ Jesus is, there is the catholic Church. Only in dependence on the bishop is it permitted for anyone to baptize or celebrate the agape; whatever he approves is also pleasing to God" (*Smyrn.* 8, 1-2).

Ignatius is here recalling the teaching he has given to the Ephesians. There can be no authentic eucharist that is not celebrated under the presidency of the bishop. Because he represents Christ, he creates unity, and the community must be organized around him. Without him it is impossible to baptize or to celebrate the agape, that is, the eucharist[31] (*agapen* is parallel to *baptizein*, showing that the agape in this case is the eucharist). Baptism and the eucharist are the two basic cultic actions that generate the life and unity of the Church, the *katholike ekklesia*.

One flesh of Christ, one eucharist, one Church: there we have Ignatius' foundational thoughts. All peoples are called to come together in the universal Church, which is the body of Christ, "the one body of his Church" (*Smyrn.* 1, 2). It is likewise in the Church that the eucharist is celebrated; it is in the assembly (*epi to auto*) that the eucharist is experienced and gives life.[32] The eucharist makes it manifest that the Church is the body of Christ, and at the same time the eucharist forms or "makes" the body of Christ by making us members of that body. Ignatius plunges deeply into this mystery of unity. He writes to the Magnesians:

"Make every effort to do all things with a unanimity that has God for its source, and under the presidency of the bishop who holds the place of God. . . . Just as the Lord did nothing, by himself or by the agency of his apostles, except in dependence on the Father with whom he was one, so you should do nothing except in dependence on the bishop and the presbyters. . . . Do everything in common: one prayer, one supplication, one outlook, one hope in love and irreproachable joy: such is Jesus Christ, to whom nothing is preferable. Let all of you hasten to gather, as in a single temple of God and as around a single altar, around the one Jesus Christ who came forth from the one Father, remained one with him, and went back to him" (6, 1; 7, 1-2).

In this rich description of the liturgical worship of the Christian community, Ignatius brings out the profound unity of God's people among themselves and with Christ, as they gather around the one altar, namely, Christ. The eucharistic assembly generates unity: unity with the bishop, unity with the entire Church, and unity with Christ who is inseparably one with the Father. This union of Christ with the Father is, in fact, the source and cause of the union of all others with Christ and with each other. The unity was won in principle by the shedding of Christ's blood; it becomes a present reality and grows ever more authentic by means of the Eucharist, for all who participate in it.

The eucharist, being the memorial of the passion and resurrection of Christ, binds the members together and unites them to Christ so that they may share in his freedom from corruption, for "the head cannot be engendered apart from the members" (*Tral.* 11, 2). There we have the reason why we can share in but a single eucharist: because there is only one flesh of Christ and one cup of his blood. By giving to each person the selfsame flesh of Christ, the eucharist unites them all and builds Christ's body, the Church.

60

Our analysis of the four texts in which the word *eucharistia* appears has brought out some fundamental orientations of Ignatius' thought on the eucharist: the eucharist is in continuity with the incarnation and is a participation in the passion and resurrection of Christ. When celebrated in faith and love, under the presidency of the bishop, it is a source of unity. In the remainder of this essay we shall turn to certain further aspects of the eucharist that will enable us to grasp more fully its dynamic power.

REMEDY BESTOWING IMMORTALITY

For Ignatius of Antioch, the eucharist is a remedy that bestows immortality. The economy, that is, the divine plan of salvation, involves, says Ignatius,

"faith in him [Jesus] and love for him in his suffering and resurrection. . . . especially if the Lord reveals to me that each of you individually and all of you together, by the grace that comes from his name, gather in one faith and in Jesus Christ who was of David's line according to the flesh (Romans 1.3), Son of man and Son of God, in order to obey the bishop and the presbytery, breaking one bread which is a remedy bestowing immortality (*pharmakon athanasias*), an antidote preventing death (*antidotos tou me apothanein*) and giving life in Jesus Christ forever (*alla zen en Iesou Christo dia pantos*)" (*Eph.* 20, 1-2).

In this passage the eucharistic bread is called a "remedy bestowing immortality" and an "antidote preventing death." *Pharmakon athanasias* was a technical term in the medical profession, the name for an ointment invented by the goddess Isis and capable of curing all kinds of illnesses.[33] Ignatius applies the term to the eucharist, and the Greek Fathers would frequently repeat it later on. What Ignatius is trying to bring out is the great power of the eucharist, which does become a wellspring of immortality. The eucharist exerts a healing action, the action of Christ, our "only physician" (*Eph.* 7, 2) who came to heal

61

our wounds and give us life. The eucharist is an antidote capable of counteracting the deadly poison (*Tral.* 6, 2) of sin and uniting us forever to Christ.

The two expressions—remedy bestowing immortality, and antidote preventing death—are positive and negative ways of expressing the saving power of the eucharist to free us from sin, purify us, and establish us firmly in the life of the risen Christ, by uniting us all in the one Lord who is "our common hope" (*Eph.* 21, 2).

But the eucharist purifies, nourishes, and creates the unity of the Church only if it is received and lived in faith and love and "undivided harmony." It is precisely because the heretics do not belong to the community of faith, because they do not confess the true flesh of Christ, and because they reject the gift of God, that they abstain from the eucharist and die amid their disputes (*Smyrn.* 7, 1). Ignatius is bold in stating the requirements of the eucharist and the need for faith and love. He even goes so far as to identify faith with the flesh of Christ and love with the blood of Christ: "Arm yourselves, then, with gentle patience, and recreate yourselves in faith, which is the flesh of the Lord, and in love, which is the blood of Jesus Christ" (*Tral.* 8, 1). The same thought recurs in the letter to the Romans:

"My earthly desire has been crucified, and there is no fire left in me for loving matter; there is rather a living water in me that murmurs and says within me: 'Come to the Father.' I take pleasure no longer in corruptible food or the delights of this life. My desire is for the bread of God, which is the flesh of Jesus Christ, and for drink I desire his blood, which is incorruptible love" (7, 2-3).

Is all this simply symbolism, or a mystic's way of speaking? How are we to take these statements?

The Johannine inspiration of these texts is evident. In the sixth chapter of his Gospel, St. John expresses the idea of eternal life by means of symbols drawn from the eucharistic liturgy: bread of God, bread of life, flesh of Christ, blood of Christ. Ignatius in turn endeavors to express the incorruptible love which is eternal life, by means of similar language. He does so in a eucharistic perspective or with a eucharistic outlook. In the final analysis, however, it is not very important to determine "whether or not such passages have a strictly eucharistic meaning. Their aim is simply to remind us, in images drawn from the eucharistic liturgy, that the primary object of a Christian's faith and love is the reality of Christ's body and blood, and that in this faith the Christian will find life."[34]

Faith and love have as their object the flesh and blood of Christ who was born of David's line. This flesh and blood become the Christian's food in the eucharist, our source of immortality. They also feed him in the sense that they must be perceived and lived in and by faith and love. The two aspects are inseparable: faith and love are necessary for receiving the eucharist, but they are also the fruit of the eucharist. Faith and love are thus always concerned with the reality of Christ's flesh. The one Christ is our living bread that has come down from heaven; he it is who gives life; he it is who enables the martyr to become a "bread of Christ" (Rom. 4, 2), thanks to the bread (the eucharist) which Christians break together and offer as a memorial.

For Ignatius, faith and love are a participation in the "incorruptible love" of which the eucharistic celebration is the pledge. Here we have the full dynamism of the eucharist coming into view. When lived in faith and love, the eucharist leads the Christian to an ever more perfect union with Christ and, through Christ, with the Father, with the help of a strict regime of asceticism and renunciation ("my earthly desire has been crucified") and under the impulse of the Spirit ("living water").

What Ignatius says, then, in the letters to the Romans (7, 2-3) and the Trallians (8, 1) in no way detracts from the utter realism of Christ's flesh and of our faith in the flesh of Christ (his historical flesh, his eucharistic flesh). Far from contradicting the realism voiced in the letters to the Smyrnaeans (8, 1) and the Philadelphians (4), these other passages actually confirm it. Faith and love can be called the flesh and blood of Christ only because they presuppose the reality of that flesh and blood, and are founded upon it.

FROM EUCHARIST TO MARTYRDOM

In Ignatius' thinking, the reality of Christ's flesh makes martyrdom a necessity. This martyrdom should be approached and experienced as a eucharist, a participation in the death and resurrection of Christ.

When the Bishop of Antioch thinks of martyrdom in cultic terms, that is, as an act of worship, he thinks of it as a eucharist. It is a sacrifice offered to God; it is the supreme act of complete and definitive union with Christ and therefore becomes the perfect way of imitating him. This is why Ignatius cries out as he does in the letter to the Romans and begs his readers to "let me be the food of beasts, that through them I may find God. I am God's wheat, and the teeth of beasts shall grind me so that I will be a pure bread of Christ" (*Rom.* 4, 1).[35]

We can sense the energy, the strong feeling that pervades these lines. But how are we to take them? As the exaggerations of a mystic with a strong imagination? By no means. They are the logical conclusion of a process that begins with the eucharist. There can be no doubt that in Ignatius' mind his desire for martyrdom is the logical result of a movement toward God, a thirst for God, that urges him on to perfect imitation of and identification with Christ. Martyrdom is simply the imitation of Christ in his passion and sacrifice. Ignatius offers himself "to be poured out as a libation to God, for the altar stands ready" (*Rom.* 2, 2). As "God's wheat," he will become "a pure bread of Christ" (*Rom.* 4, 1) and "a sacrifice to God" (*Rom.* 4, 2). When he thus truly becomes a disciple of Christ and "an imitator of the passion of my God" (*Rom.* 6, 3), he will become "a freedman of Jesus Christ" and will be reborn, in him, into freedom (*Rom.* 4, 3).

The entire thinking of Ignatius in this matter is a dynamic prolongation of the eucharist. Like the eucharist, and on the basis of it, martyrdom derives its value from the passion of Christ and leads to the resurrection. Through identification with Christ and through the complete gift of self that martyrdom entails, Ignatius will fulfill in himself the radical meaning of the eucharistic sacrifice; as far as possible, he will make real in himself the eucharistic mystery that is celebrated in the sacrifice of the altar.

Need we go so far as to say that "it is the martyr himself who is to become the eucharist"?[36] Hardly. In fact, these words of Father Bouyer seem to clash with the quite valid explanation he gives of it. He says that in Ignatius' view

"the eucharist, in nourishing us with the risen Christ, associates us with his passion and, very particularly, with the *agape* which is its soul; and reciprocally, martyrdom, as realizing in our lives the perfection of *agape*, gives its whole realism to the union with the *Christus passus* brought about by the eucharist and finally reveals in us the presence of the risen Christ. In the eucharist, he has given us the seed of what he is, he has set in motion in us the process that brought him to his risen life. In martyrdom, this process unfolds and this seed bears its fruit: in suffering with Christ, not only do we rise with Him, but we become in some way the Risen One."[37]

All this seems quite reasonable and true. By any accounting, the link between eucharist and martyrdom is a matter of Christian experience and quite capable of stirring our admiration, even today. For Ignatius of Antioch, the eucharist is essentially a living and life-giving reality, a source of energy and power. In fact, it is the reality of Christ himself in the plenitude of that redemptive mystery which requires constantly to be made present and active in us and to be experienced so that it may produce its fruit of love and holiness. That is the message conveyed to us in the letters of Ignatius of Antioch.

NOTES

1. This was the period when the gnostic threat weighed heavily on the churches of Asia.

2. For the Greek text we have used the edition, with introduction, French translation, and notes, of T. Camelot, O.P.: *Ignace d'Antioche: Letters* (SC 10; 3rd ed.; Paris, 1958). English translations with commentary: J. A. Kleist, S.J., *The Epistles of St. Clement of Rome and St. Ignatius of Antioch* (ACW 1; Westminster, Md., 1946); R. M. Grant, *Ignatius of Antioch* (in R. M. Grant, ed., *The Apostolic Fathers: A New Translation and Commentary* 4 [New York, 1966]).

The seven letters will be cited as follows: *Eph.* (Ephesians), *Magn.* (Magnesians), *Tral.* (Trallians), *Rom.* (Romans), *Phil.* (Philadelphians), *Smyrn.* (Smyrnaeans), and *Pol.* (Polycarp).

3. J. Quasten, *Patrology* 1. *The Beginnings of Patristic Literature* (Westminster, Md. 1950), p. 64.

4. J. Lebreton, "The Apostolic Fathers and Their Times," in J. Lebreton and J. Zeiller, *The History of the Primitive Church*, translated by E. C. Messenger (New York, 1949), 1:429. Here is the passage from which the quoted words are taken: "These flaming words of the great martyr were read over and over again in the early Christian church in the times of the martyrs; there is none more vehement or more poignant, but what gives them superhuman beauty is the faith which inspires them; the man who speaks thus has directed all the activities of his life towards union with Christ."

5. On the mysticism of Ignatius the martyr cf. J. Liébaert, *Les*

enseignements moraux des Pères apostoliques (Recherches et synthèses, Section morale 4; Gembloux, 1970), pp. 34-35; Th. Preiss, *La vie en Christ: La mystique de l'imitation du Christ et l'unité chez saint Ignace d'Antioche* (Neuchâtel, 1952), pp. 7-45.

6. Ignatius speaks of "beasts with human faces" (*Smyrn.* 4, 1). There were the Judaizers but also the docetists; Ignatius had to deal with people who denied the reality of Christ's humanity in the incarnation, passion, and resurrection (*Tral.* 9; *Smyrn.* 2-3).

7. *Les Pères apostoliques* 3. *Ignace d'Antioche* (2nd ed.; Paris, 1927), pp. 18-19.

8. *Op. cit.*, p. 82, text and n. 1.

9. *Op. cit.*, Introduction, p. 52.

10. *La prière* 2 (Paris, 1963), p. 96. Hamman translates *Eph.* 13, 1 as follows: "See to it that you come together more frequently to offer God your eucharist and praises." A little further on, Hamman says: "*Eucharistia* means both thanksgiving and Eucharist in the narrow sense; the word thus combines prayer and liturgy, neither of these being thought of apart from the other" (p. 97).

11. *La sacrifice dans les textes eucharistiques des premiers siècles* (Neuchâtel–Paris, 1966): "In my view we must take into account (1) *Smyrn.* 7, 1: 'They abstain from the Eucharist and prayer'; (2) the parallel statement in *Magn.* 7 where, again summing up the Christian life, Ignatius immediately mentions 'a single prayer.... Hasten to gather as in a single temple of God, around one altar, around the one Jesus Christ'; (3) the fact that in the paragraph we are discussing [*Eph.* 13] St. Ignatius regards the 'eucharist' as capable of expelling demons, and that in *Eph.* 20, 2 the eucharist is presented to us a *pharmakon* full of power; and (4) the ancient usage that we find in St. Justin, for example. In the light of all these points, I prefer, with Hamman, to translate *eucharistia* here as 'eucharist' and not as 'thanksgiving.' All these texts assert a close relationship between prayer and eucharist and refer, as *Eph.* 13, 1 does, to Christian worship" (pp. 50-51).

According to M. Goguel, *L'eucharistie, des origines à Justin Martyr* (Paris, 1910), Ignatius is urging the Ephesians "to gather more frequently for the Eucharist and in order to thank God" (p. 248).

12. When Ignatius urges the Ephesians to gather more often for the eucharist, he suggests to us the question of how frequently

the eucharist was in fact celebrated. The information given us in the letters (cf. *Pol.* 4, 2) does not allow us to give a precise answer. According to Hamman, "in advising Christians to assemble more often, Ignatius seems to have in mind other meetings besides the ones on Sunday" (*op. cit.* 2:97).

13. For St. John, the eucharist, which is Christ's flesh and blood, is the sacrament of the redemptive incarnation. Cf. D. Mollat, "The Sixth Chapter of John," in J. Delorme *et al.*, *The Eucharist in the New Testament*, translated by E. M. Stewart (Baltimore, 1964), pp. 143-56, especially pp. 151-53. [This book is a translation of *Lumière et vie*, no. 31 (1957).]

14. Camelot, *op. cit.*, p. 142, n. 4.

15. *Henōsis*, "union," refers to the action of uniting; *henotēs*, "unity," is the result achieved.

16. Cf. my study, "L'eucharistie, sacrement de l'unité selon saint Ignace d'Antioche," *Parole et pain*, no. 18 (1967), pp. 40 f.

17. *Op. cit.*, p. 72.

18. *L'eucharistie: La présence réelle et la transsubstantiation* (5th ed.; Paris, 1913), p. 43.

19. "Eucharistie et unité de l'Eglise d'après saint Ignace d'Antioche," in *XXXV Congreso Eucarístico Internacional* (1952), p. 246.

20. In Christian antiquity, there was a single altar (the place of sacrifice) in each church, as a sign that the sacrifice was likewise one. Cf. *Maison-Dieu*, no. 29 (1952), on the subject of "The Mystery of the Altar."

21. "Anyone not within the sanctuary (*entos tou thusiasteriou* [literally: not within the altar]) is deprived of the bread of God" (*Eph.* 5, 2). This sentence is weighty with significance. According to the Watteville, the phrase "bread of God" (cf. also *Rom.* 7, 3) is sacrificial and must be understood in the light of Leviticus: "The phrase 'bread of God' must have been understood by readers of this letter as equivalent to 'sacrifice,' while at the same time it reminded them of John 6:33 and the body of Christ which is the supreme bread God gives us, the bread of life" (*op. cit.*, p. 52). Cf. also *Magn.* 7, 2; *Tral.* 7, 2.

22. With regard to *Phil.* 4, J. Colson observes that the altar is also the Church as united to Christ around his ministers, and the table where the eucharistic bread is broken. Cf. his *Ministre de Jésus-Christ ou le sacerdoce de l'évangile: Etude sur la condition sacerdotale des ministres chrétiens dans l'Eglise primitive* (Théologie historique 4; Paris, 1966), p. 337.

For Ignatius the altar and the church are the *place of sacrifice*. "It seems that the conception of the eucharist as the sacrifice of the Church suggested this designation" (Quasten, *op. cit.*, p. 66).

23. On the conception of ministry in Ignatius cf. M. Thurian, "L'organisation du ministère dans l'Eglise primitive selon saint Ignace d'Antioche," *Verbum caro*, no. 81 (1967), 26-38; A. Vilela, "Le presbyterium selon saint Ignace d'Antioche," *Bulletin de littérature ecclésiastique*, 3 (1973), 161-86.

24. The text of Ignatius is perfectly clear. Goguel even says of it: "The realist understanding of the Eucharist is expressed here in a manner that leaves no doubt. The flesh with which the Eucharist is identified is the flesh that suffered and was raised up. It is the very material substance of the person of Christ" (*op. cit.*, p. 250).

25. *Histoire du dogme de la Trinité* 2 (Paris, 1928), p. 288, n. 1.

26. Batiffol, *op. cit.*, p. 46.

27. *Opera patrum apostolicorum* 1 (Tübingen, 1878), p. 240.

28. *The Apostolic Fathers*, Part II: *St. Ignatius* 2 (London, 1889), p. 307.

29. For the various senses of the word agapē cf. J. Colson, *Agapè chez saint Ignace d'Antioche* (Paris, 1961).

30. O. Perler thinks that *agapān*, "to love," is "a metaphysical way of saying 'to practice charity by taking part in the Eucharistic agape which is the pledge of resurrection'"(*op. cit.*, p. 254).

31. The authors generally agree on this interpretation; cf. Batiffol, *op. cit.*, p. 41; Perler, *op. cit.*, p. 245; Lelong, *op. cit.*, p. 90; Colson, *Ministre de Jésus-Christ*, p. 338; Colson, *Agapè*, p. 72.

32. *Epi to auto* is a phrase Ignatius uses often; cf. *Magn.* 7, 1; *Phil.* 6, 2; 10, 1; *Eph.* 5, 3. It occurs in a eucharistic context in St. Paul (1 Co 11.20): "For St. Ignatius the Eucharist is both the

supreme manifestation of the Church's unity and a powerful means to effect this unity" (Goguel, *op. cit.*, p. 249).

33. Cf. Camelot, *op. cit.*, p. 90, n. 2, where he briefly summarizes a study by Th. Schermann on the "remedy bestowing immortality."

34. Camelot, *op. cit.*, pp. 54-55. Camelot points out that "symbolism does not exclude realism, but rather presupposes it and is grounded in it" (p. 55). For de Watteville, too, Ignatius' "approach, far from undermining the realism of his conception of the Eucharist . . . powerfully confirms it" (*op. cit.*, pp. 56-57). Cf. Batiffol, *op. cit.*, p. 48.

The observations of J. Liébaert are very much to the point: "The flesh of Christ—with all the fullness of meaning the word 'flesh' has in Ignatius' thinking: genuine flesh, really crucified and really risen—this flesh to which the baptized Christ is united in the Eucharist, is the very substance of the Christian faith, for the blood of the Lord that was shed on the cross and is now communicated in the sacrament, is the sign of the divine agape and the source of all charity" (*op. cit.*, p. 59).

35. The entire Letter to the Romans is exceptionally beautiful.

36. L. Bouyer, *The Spirituality of the New Testament and the Fathers*, translated by M. P. Ryan (New York, 1960), p. 202.

37. *Ibid.* Cf. also G. Bardy and A. Hamman, *La vie spirituelle d'après les Pères des trois premiers siècles* 1 (Paris, 1968), pp. 86-90. On the significance of martyrdom and its place in the early Church cf. M. Viller, *La spiritualité des premiers siècles chrétiens* (Paris, 1930), pp. 13-24.

The connection between the eucharist and martyrdom was often emphasized in the early centuries. For St. Cyprian (to take but one example) cf. M. Pellegrino, "Eucharistia e martirio in San Cipriano," in *Convivium Dominicum* (Catania, Sicily, 1959), pp. 133-50.

JUSTIN   AD 150

The importance of Justin's testimony is well known. At Rome, around the year 150, this layman taught a "philosophy" which was, in fact, a form of Christian wisdom. He taught it in his own name and not by any mandate from the Church, but a few years later his teaching was confirmed by martyrdom. He is one of those witnesses who can be believed because his death set a seal upon his life.

One of Justin's writings contains two descriptions of the eucharist, addressed to people who did not share the Christian faith, and especially to the emperors. Another work explains and justifies the eucharist, but this time to a Jewish readership. These two much-quoted statements will be the focus of our attention here. First, then, we turn to the *First Apology*, chapters 65–67.[1]

THE TESTIMONY OF THE FIRST APOLOGY

Chapter 65.

1. After we have thus cleansed the person who believes and has joined our ranks, we lead him in to where those we call "brothers" are assembled to offer prayers in common for ourselves, for him who has just been enlightened, and for all men everywhere. It is our desire, now that we have come to know the truth, to be found worthy of doing good deeds and obeying the commandments, and thus to obtain eternal salvation.

2. When we finish praying, we greet one another with a kiss.

3. Then bread and a cup containing water and wine mixed with water are brought to him who presides over the bre-

71

thren; he takes them and offers prayers, glorifying the Father of all things through the name of the Son and the Holy Spirit; and he utters a lengthy thanksgiving because the Father has judged us worthy of these gifts. When the prayer of thanksgiving is ended, all the pople present give their assent with an "Amen!"

4. ("Amen" in Hebrew means "So be it.")

5. When the president has given thanks and the people have all signified their assent, those whom we call "deacons" distribute the bread and the wine and water, over which the thanksgiving has been spoken, to each of those present; they also carry them to those who are absent.

Chapter 66.

1. This food we call "eucharist," and no one may share it unless he believes that our teaching is true, and has been cleansed in the bath of forgiveness for sin and rebirth, and lives as Christ taught.

2. For we do not receive these things as though they were ordinary food and drink. Just as Jesus Christ our Savior was made flesh through the word of God and took on flesh and blood for our savlation, so too (we have been taught) through the word of prayer that comes from him the food over which the thanksgiving has been spoken becomes the flesh and blood of the incarnate Jesus, in order to nourish and transform our flesh and blood.

3. For, in the memoirs which the apostles composed and which we call "gospels," they have told us that they were commissioned thus: Jesus took bread and, having given thanks, said: "Do this in memory of me; this is my body"; and in a like manner he took the cup and, having given thanks, said: "This is my blood," and he gave these to them alone.

4. Wicked demons have taught men to imitate all this in the mysteries of Mithras. For, as you know or can find out, there too bread and a cup of water are presented when someone is being initiated in the sacred rites, and meanwhile certain words are spoken.

72

Chapter 67.

1. Since that time, we constantly recall these events among ourselves; if we have anything, we help all who are in need, and we are constantly united with one another.

2. And for all that we eat we thank the Maker of all through his Son Jesus Christ and the Holy Spirit.

3. And on the day named after the sun, all who live in city or countryside assemble, and the memoirs of the apostles or the writings of the prophets are read for as long as time allows.

4. When the lector has finished, the president addresses us, admonishing us and exhorting us to imitate the splendid things we have heard.

5. Then we all stand and pray, and, as we said earlier, when we have finished praying, bread, wine, and water are brought up. The president offers prayers of thanksgiving, according to his ability, and the people give their assent with an "Amen!" Next, the gifts over which the thanksgiving has been spoken are distributed, and each one shares in them, while they are also sent via the deacons to the absent brethren.

6. The wealthy who are willing make contributions, each as he pleases, and the collection is deposited with the president who aids orphans and widows, those who are in want because of sickness or some other reason, those in prison, and visiting strangers; in short, he takes care of all in need.

7. The reason why we all assemble on Sunday is that it is the first day: the day on which God transformed darkness and matter and created the world, and the day on which Jesus Christ our Savior rose from the dead.

We must immediately point out that despite appearances Justin is not giving two descriptions of the eucharist. Rather, he first describes the process of Christian initiation, comprising baptism (ch. 61) and the eucharist (ch. 65–66). Against that background he explains Christian life as itself an anamnesis or remembering: the Christian remembers those in need; he remembers to pray to the Triune God; and he remembers to celebrate the day of the Lord.[2] At this

73

point Justin explains what the day of the Lord is: It is the day on which the Christian remembers creation and resurrection, and celebrates the eucharist anew. It is this that causes Justin to speak of the eucharist once again. Strictly speaking, there is no duplication, for the eucharist plays a double role in Christian life: It is part of the initiation of the person into the Christian life, and it is the focal point of the weekly celebration of the Lord's day.

In Justin's view, then, the Christian is a man who remembers the light given him in baptism and the nourishment given him in the eucharist; he does so by a life of fraternal love, prayer to the Trinity, and the celebration of Sunday. It is in the context of this understanding of Christian life that we shall study the baptismal eucharist of chapters 65 and 66; the Sunday eucharist of chapter 67 will be brought in simply to confirm our analysis.

Chapters 65 and 66, we should note, do not represent an arbitrary division of undifferentiated material. Chapter 65 gives a description, chapter 66, an explanation.

DESCRIPTION OF THE CELEBRATION

Let us recall certain points of this description:
1) The assembly: In 65, 1 Justin says that "we lead him in to where those we call 'brothers' are assembled." 67, 3 will say that "on the day named after the sun, all who live in city or countryside assemble."

2) The distinction between president and people: This distinction is clear from the entire text of 65, and is pinpointed in 65, 3, where the president performs the eucharistic action while the people ratify what he does. On the other hand, there is no specifically Christian word used to describe the role of the celebrant: "he who presides" (*proestos*: 65, 3; cf. 67, 4) is a phrase any pagan would have understood; nothing in the text allows us to speak of the celebrant as a "priest" (*hiereus*).

In his book on sacrifice in the eucharistic texts of the first centuries, de Watteville thinks there is a basis for calling the president a "priest."[3] His reasoning is all the more appealing in that it comes from a theologian in the Reformation tradition, but nonetheless we cannot accept it.

3) The deacons: This is the only technical name Justin gives for any minister. It is our opinion that the distribution of the eucharist, especially to those absent from the celebration, made this ministry known to outsiders and that pagans would or could be familiar with the word "deacon" as title of a eucharistic minister. (Consider, for example, the fact that the deacon brought the eucharist to prisoners in the jails.)

It is to be observed that in 67, 3 Justin mentions the collection immediately after speaking of the deacons bringing communion to the absent. The collection is not our modern offertory collection but a collection understood as a fruit of communion: God's gift to us turns us into givers to others. The deacon seems to be regarded as a minister of God's love that rouses fraternal love in us.

4) The similarity between the description of the eucharistic prayer here and in *Didache* 9–10: in both cases the prayer is a prayer of praise for blessings received. Note that in this description Justin does not give the words of institution; neither does *Didache* 9–10.

EXPLANATION OF THE CELEBRATION

The explanation touches on the discipline, doctrine, origin, and originality of the eucharist.

1) *Discipline*. The food, we are told, is called "eucharist." We may substitute an equivalent word and read "This food we call 'blessing'"; then we may compare the statement with 61, 12, where we are told that the baptismal washing is called "enlightenment." The name "eucharist" has

75

stuck; the name "enlightenment" has not been kept for baptism. Like the name, the conditions for receiving the eucharist—faith, baptism, a life according to Christ—have not changed since Justin's time!

2) *Doctrine.* Two points are to be noted. The first is the parallel between incarnation and eucharist. Justin says (though not very clearly) that the same divine spiritual power, namely, the Logos, is at work in both the incarnation and the eucharist. The Word of God gave flesh and blood to Christ; the Word of God eucharistizes the bread and wine. The second point is the realistic language Justin uses: This food is the flesh and blood of the incarnate Jesus. With regard to this we shall simply point out the perspective opened up when Justin says that we receive the flesh and blood of Jesus "in order to nourish and *transform (kata metabolēn)* our flesh and blood." The eucharist is here being linked to the resurrection; it brings with it the seed of the resurrection.[4]

3) *Origin.* Justin sees the eucharist as originating in the commission given the apostles in the Lord's words of institution. For the bread, Justin reproduces almost verbatim Luke 22. 19, but he inverts the order of the parts; that is, he puts first the words which he interprets, as we do, as being a command to repeat what Jesus did at the Supper.

For the cup, Justin's words are closer to those of Matthew or Mark than to those of Luke or Paul, since the words refer directly to the blood rather than to the cup of the covenant. The words "He gave these to them alone" (66, 3) certainly mean that he gave the eucharistic bread and wine to Christians only. Justin is not saying that the Lord reserved the eucharist to his apostles and, after them, to the president of the assembly, but rather that he gives the eucharist to the Christian assembly and not to the world.

Finally, in our opinion, the statement "through the word of prayer that comes from him the food over which the thanksgiving has been spoken becomes the flesh and blood" certainly refers to the words of institution. What Justin is saying, however, is rather that the eucharistic prayer has its origin in Christ (it is based on his action) than that the words of institution are part of the eucharistic prayer of his day.

4) *Originality*. When Justin mentions the similarity between the eucharist and the rites of Mithras he raises a problem which he does not resolve here, but does handle at length throughout the *First Apology*. His answer is that the religious systems which imitate Christianity are being used by the demons; they have imitated externals but have not grasped what is specific to the Christian faith. Consequently, they have mimicked the bath of baptism, but they have not been able to bestow enlightenment; they have celebrated a sacrificial meal, but never thought of the eucharistic blessing-prayer.

To supplement the valuable information given in the *First Apology* we have another document: the *Dialogue with Trypho*.[5]

THE TESTIMONY OF THE DIALOGUE WITH TRYPHO

Chapter 41

1. The offering of fine flour that was prescribed for those cleansed of leprosy was a prefiguration of the bread of the eucharist which our Lord Jesus Christ commanded us to offer in memory of the passion he underwent for the sake of those whose souls are cleansed of all evil. He so commanded us in order that we might at the same time thank God for creating the world and all it contains for man's sake, for freeing us from the evil in which we were born, and for destroying utterly the principalities and powers through him who became passible in accordance with God's will.

2. Concerning the sacrifices you used to offer, God says

through Malachi, one of the twelve [prophets]: "My will is not in you, says the Lord, nor will I accept your sacrifices from your hands. For from the rising of the sun to its setting my name is glorified by the nations, and in every place incense and pure sacrifice are offered to my name; for my name is great among the nations, says the Lord, but you have defiled it."
3. In this passage God already speaks of the sacrifices which we, the nations, offer him in every place, namely, the bread of the eucharist and the cup of the eucharist. He adds that we glorify his name, while you defile it.

Chapter 70
4. In this prophecy, too (Isaiah 33.16), God clearly speaks of the bread which our Christ has bidden us offer as a memorial of his incarnation, for the sake of those who believe in him and for whom he suffered, and of the cup which he has bidden us offer with thanksgiving as a memorial of his blood.

Chapter 117
1. All the sacrifices offered through his [Jesus'] name, as Jesus Christ ordered, that is, the sacrifices which Christians offer in every place in the world in their eucharist over bread and cup—these God tells us in advance are pleasing to him. . . .
2. . . . I, too, say that the prayers and thanksgivings offered by worthy men are the only sacrifices that are perfect and pleasing to God.
3. These are the only sacrifices that Christians have learned to offer, in the memorial (consisting) of the dry and liquid food by which they remember the passion God's Son underwent for their sake. . . .
5. There is not a single race of men . . . among whom prayers and thanksgivings are not offered to the Father, Creator of the universe, in the name of the crucified Jesus.

The *Dialogue* thus contains several passages which at least allude to the eucharist: 41, 1-3; 70, 4; 117, 1-3 and 5. Chapter 41, 1-3 is evidently the most important of the passages, and we can relate the others to it.

The context for 41, 1-3 is a discussion of prefigurations of Christ in the Old Testament: the Passover lamb and the two goats (40) and the offering of fine flour (41). In the latter Justin sees a prefiguration of the eucharist, and he refers to Malachi by way of explaining the bread used in the thanksgiving.

THE REFERENCE TO MALACHI[6]

We may compare the reference made here with the reference to the same passage in the *Didache*. The *Didache* is in no sense anti-Jewish. It sees in the text of Malachi only an order from the Lord that a pure sacrifice should be offered in every place, and it understands the Christian Sunday as being a faithful response to this command. Justin, on the other hand, understands the text of Malachi as a repudiation of Jewish sacrifices in favor of the sacrifice offered by the nations.

At the same time, we should not allow ourselves to be misled by this comparison. The *Didache* does not quote v. 10 ("My will is not in you . . . your hands"), which, from Justin's viewpoint, is essential. Nor does the *Didache* quote the words, "but you have defiled it," which Justin quotes in order to exalt the sacrifice of the nations. In addition, Justin gives the words of Malachi as a statement ("in every place incense and a pure sacrifice are offered"): God asserts the emptiness of Jewish sacrifices, and the authenticity of the sacrifice of the nations. The *Didache* reads the same words as a command from the Lord: In every place and at every time let men offer me a pure sacrifice.

CHARACTER OF THE EUCHARIST

The bread of the eucharistic thanksgiving is present in the Old Testament in the form of a type. Justin focuses on a rather small detail in the long ritual for the cleansing of lepers. In the Book of Leviticus (14.10) we read: "On the eighth day, he [the leper who has been healed] is to take two lambs without blemish, an unblemished ewe one year old, three tenths of wheaten flour mixed with oil for the libation, and one log of oil."

Amid all this array of sacrificial material Justin is careful to single out only the fine flour. He selects that which is least bulky and, at the same time, bears the closest resemblance to bread. He has no desire to make the Christian sacrifice any more material than it has to be.

Chapter 117 brings out the same concern very clearly. If we read the passage with a view to seeing exactly what the eucharist is, we find Justin locating the sacrifice (*thusia*) in the prayers (*euchai*) and thanksgivings (*eucharistiai*) of worthy men. He tells us that tradition bids the Christian offer no sacrifice but that of prayer and thanksgiving in the memorial of the passion (117, 3). After having presented the sacrifice as the sacrifice of God's priestly people (116, 3), he now emphasizes its universality (117, 5). It is proper to the eucharist, then, to be the sacrifice of the entire people (and not just of a priestly caste) and a sacrifice that can be offered anywhere in the world (and not linked with the rites of a particular people).

The offering of fine flour is a "type" (*tupos*). The word refers to a reality that calls another reality to mind by pre-figuring it. Typology presupposes the Old Testament; it also presupposes that the institutions of Israel are thought of as being prophetic. (This is important for such institutions as have been eliminated only because they have been fulfilled and transcended.) Paul seems to use the word *tupos* in the sense familiar to us, for he speaks of Adam as the "type" (*tupos*) of the One who was to come (Romans 5.14). What we have in Justin (and Paul) is the argument from prophecy, in one of its forms: The Christian institution fulfills the practices of the Jews.[7]

The bread over which the thanksgiving is spoken is a *memorial* (anamnesis). This idea of "memorial" is a Jewish idea and has often been analyzed. To celebrate a memorial of God's action in dealing with his people is to renew this active presence, to make it present and effective here and now. It is to be noted that the *Dialogue* assigns the idea of anamnesis an importance, in relation to the eucharist, that we do not find in the *First Apology*.

In discussing the matter with pagans, it was enough to show that the eucharist had its origin in a command of Jesus: "Do this." Nonetheless, the idea of memorial or anamnesis does come into the *First Apology* (67, 1), but it is applied to Christian life in its entirety, which is regarded as an anamnesis of baptism and the eucharist.

The memorial in the eucharist is the memorial of Christ's suffering. This idea was not put forward in the *First Apology* but it is strongly emphasized in the *Dialogue*. We may take the phrases referring to it in 41, 1 and divide them into two parts in order better to appreciate the riches they contain.

1. ". . . the bread of the eucharist which our Lord Jesus Christ commanded us to offer in memory of the passion he underwent. . . . " The eucharist is here presented to the Jewish readers as a memorial of the passion of Christ. It is also presented as something Christ himself ordered his disciples to do.

As a matter of fact, there can be (in Justin's view) no anamnesis of the passion without an intention of Christ that such a memorial be celebrated. This view is all the more remarkable since Justin does not tell us where he found the expression of such an intention. In all likelihood, he regards it as contained in the account of institution (as reported in the *First Apology*). The eucharist, or memorial of the Lord, is then not an institution of the Church in the sense that the Church would be obligated to create an organism capable of accounting for it or of bringing men into contact with it.

Finally, the eucharist is an action of Christians. Jesus has commanded us to offer this bread (as Justin says again in 70, 4).

The memory which the people preserve of God's actions on their behalf and which they activate, spurs God in turn to be mindful of his people. In other words, the fidelity of the people in interpreting their own history by means of this memorial is a sacred pledge; it binds God to confirm his favorable action by repeating it.[8]

2. "For the sake of those whose souls are cleansed of all evil." These words indicate the purpose of the suffering Jesus endured: he suffered in order to purify men of all evil. The term "cleanse" or "purify" shows that Justin still has Leviticus 14.10 in mind, for while the offering of fine flour reminds us of the eucharistic bread, the leper who has been cleansed reminds us of the man who is saved. This is why Justin also specifies that it is the soul which is cleansed. He is not speaking of a salvation of the soul as distinct from a salvation of the whole man; he merely wishes to emphasize the fact that the purification is not a bodily thing. The leper was cleansed only of his leprosy; the man who is saved is cleansed of every evil.

The memorial of the passion is also a *thanksgiving* for the *creation* of the world for man's sake. This way of speaking is very interesting. What exactly is being said? The accounts of institution indicate a memorial of the passion, but we cannot see in them a thanksgiving for creation, unless we insert them into the kind of blessing-prayer that we find in the *Didache*. For Justin, then, the eucharistic prayer expresses praise of God in connection with a bread that is (as Irenaeus will say later on) the bread of creation and that exists for man's sake.

In any case, it is interesting to note that according to Justin we will not find thanksgiving for creation within the anamnesis of the passion but rather coexisting with it. The bread and wine give rise to the eucharistic prayer insofar as they are precisely bread and wine, that is to say, basic gifts of God.

The thanksgiving is also for the *definitive liberation* won for us by the suffering Savior. This liberation is first and foremost a liberation "from the evil in which we were born"; this can only be a reference to sin. Moreover, the principalities and powers (who operate through this evil) have been overcome once and for all; Christ has utterly destroyed them. This passage (41, 1) is clearly of great interest and value. In fact, it forms a complete whole, containing a solid and comprehensive eucharistic doctrine. The offering of the eucharistic bread as an anamnesis of the passion of Christ gives thanks for the orientation of the entire universe to man and for the victory Jesus has won over evil. What more is there to be said?

From all this we can see the importance of Justin's testimony.

He provides, first of all, a description of the eucharist that shows how, despite variations according to country and period of history, the eucharist of today is faithful to what it was in the second century.

He also gives us a profound and rather full interpretation of the eucharistic offering. To begin with, it forms the Christian just as baptism does, for it consecrates man to God by renewing him in Christ. Next, it commits the Christian to a life of authentic brotherhood, for the sending of the eucharist to the absent shows that no community can be closed in on itself. Finally, as a memorial of the passion, it is repeated each Sunday to celebrate the renewal of creation, which took place on the first day of the world, through the resurrection of the Lord, which took place on the first day of the week. God is thus glorified by the sacrifice of his Son.

NOTES

1. The *Apology* is a kind of open letter to the emperors; its purpose is to show that Christians are being unjustly persecuted, since they are neither atheists nor enemies of the State nor criminals.

The Greek text of the *Apologiae* and of the *Dialogus cum Tryphone* may be found in the *Textes et Documents* collection of Hemmer and Lejay. The passages on the eucharist (with the exception of *Dialogus* 70, 4, and 117, 5, are given in A. Hänggi and I. Pahl (eds.), *Prex Eucharistica: Textus e variis liturgiis antiquioribus selecti* (Spicilegium Friburgense 12; Fribourg, 1968), pp. 68-74.

2. We therefore understand the opening lines of chap. 67 as does M. Hubert in his *La Messe: Histoire du culte eucharistique en Occident* (2 vols.; Paris, 1965). Christian life is an anamnesis (remembering, memorial) of Christian initiation, in the form of fraternal charity (learned in the eucharist), Trinitarian prayer (based on baptism), and the celebration of the Lord's day (celebration of creation and the resurrection).

3. J. de Watteville, *Le sacrifice dans les textes eucharistiques des premiers siècles* (Neuchâtel–Paris, 1966), pp. 72-73.

4. This connection is very important for Irenaeus (cf. *Adv. Haer.* IV, 18, 5; V, 2, 3).

5. The *Dialogue with Trypho* is a defense of Christianity against Judaism. The work raises certain questions (including the question of whether it is rightly attributed to Justin), but it is nonetheless a significant document and sheds a great deal of light on the relation of Christianity to Judaism in the second century. In this context Justin's discussion of the eucharistic sacrifice is of primary importance.

84

6. In the *Dialogue* Ml 1.10-12 is cited three times. For a study of these citations see P. Prigent, *Justin et l'Ancien Testament* (Paris, 1964), pp. 273-77. The important thing is to determine when and why Malachi became connected with the anti-sacrificial florilegia. On the florilegia, the basic work remains J. Rendel Harris, *Testimonies* (2 vols.; London, 1916). See also J. Daniélou, *Etudes d'exégèse judéo-chrétienne* (Paris, 1965); P. Prigent, *Les testimonia dans le christianisme primitif: L'épître de Barnabé (1 à 16) et ses sources* (Paris, 1961). For St. Irenaeus cf. A. Benoit, "Adv. Haer. 4, 17 et les testimonia," *Studia Patristica* 4 (Berlin, 1961), pp. 20-27.

7. Cf. Woolcombe, "Le sens de type chez les Pères," *Vie Spirituelle Supplément* no. 16 (1951), pp. 84-100.

8. Cf. L. Bouyer, *Eucharist: Theology and Spirituality of the Eucharistic Prayer*, translated by C. U. Quinn (Notre Dame, 1968), p. 48.

IRENAEUS OF LYONS

Life led Irenaeus, Bishop of Lyons, along unexpected paths.[1] He was by temperament a missionary and a pastor of souls; his only concern was to preach the gospel in Gaul and to strengthen his community in faith and fidelity. If he wrote, it was not because he felt called to be a theologian, but because it was another way of teaching and of defending the orthodox faith against the obscure utterances of the gnostics.

One of the most dangerous of the gnostics, a man named Markos, had come to Lyons from Asia Minor. He led the people of Lyons astray with his thinking, as he played upon their emotionalism and their penchant for mysticism. Like his masters, he taught a radical dualism that set the world over against God. In various ways, the gnostics were always playing off the just God of the Old Testament against the good God revealed in Jesus Christ.

When confronted with this gnostic dualism and docetist idealism, Irenaeus sought to be only a witness to the faith that had been handed down, and to the living consciousness of the Church which was commissioned to guard the revealed deposit. Fidelity and unity are the foundation of all his teaching: unity of faith, unity of the plan of salvation that underlies the whole of history.

Far from opposing the Old Testament to the New and stripping Jewish history of its meaning, the Bishop of Lyons brought out the wonderful unity of the economy, or unfolding plan, of salvation, an economy in which mankind, shaped by the Son and the Spirit, those "two hands of God,"[2] moves forward slowly and gradually, achieves its liberation from sin, and advances toward its fulfillment.

In Christ, who is hidden at first but then revealed at the moment of his incarnation, God leads human history to the goal he has set for it. "The Father decides and commands, the Son carries out and forms, the Spirit nourishes and gives increase, and man advances little by little and ascends toward perfection, that is, he draws near to the Uncreated" (*Adv. Haer.* IV, 48, 3).

This splendid historical overview provides the framework within which we must read what Irenaeus has to say about the eucharist. He does not discuss the eucharist for its own sake but is concerned rather to situate the eucharistic mystery within his theology of history. In his eyes, the eucharist is the sacrament of the economy of salvation, and in it the Church finds its faith summed up.

THE NEW WORSHIP[3]

Irenaeus disagreed with the gnostics: for him the creation that came forth from God's hands is good and has been blessed by him. It is even in a sense his fellow worker, since it serves the plan of salvation. Christ uses it to unveil the mystery he came to reveal, and he uses it as well to bring out the generosity of his Father.

Irenaeus gives us an example of this interpretation of creation when he comments on the wedding feast at Cana, for this gives him an opportunity to explain the process of spiritual growth and progress. The miracle Jesus performed at Cana, like the multiplication of the loaves, announces and prefigures the institution of the eucharist.

"This wine was good, which the vine of God produced in accordance with the laws of creation and which the guests drank first at the wedding feast of Cana. None of those who drank it criticized it, and even the Lord himself took some of it. But better still was the wine which the Word, in a simple, momentary action, made out of water, for the use of the invited guests.

"Although the Lord could have served wine and fed the hungry without using any preexistent matter, he did not do so. On the contrary, he took the loaves produced by the earth and gave thanks over them; so too did he change water into wine. Thus he fed those who were eating, and quenched the thirst of the wedding guests. He showed us thereby that the same God who created the earth and commanded it to bear fruit and who created the waters and made the springs flow, now, in these last times, gives the human race the blessing of good food and the gift of drink through his Son" (*Adv. Haer.* III, 11, 9).

At the beginning, there is the gift given by God the creator. Everything is ultimately the fruit of his creative act and of the created order as it follows the laws he has impressed upon it. Jesus accepts and uses bread and wine because they are gifts from the divine goodness. He makes them vehicles for his missionary purpose and his revelation that he is himself the "blessing and gift" which henceforth, in the new order of things, becomes the living sacrifice of the new worship.

What the Bishop of Lyons says briefly here he develops at greater length in Book IV of his *Against the Heresies*, to which we now turn.

THE SACRIFICE OF THE NEW COVENANT

The entire history of salvation leads up to the coming of Christ, who puts an end to the period of preparation and reveals the goal of all man's searching. The sacrifice of the new covenant fulfills and replaces the institutions of the old covenant: law, circumcision, sacrifices. In this context, Irenaeus sketches a theology of the eucharist as the sacrament of the entire recapitulation (or: renewal and completion) of everything in Christ the head.

The Catholic Church alone, and not the heretics, can offer to God the sacrifice that pleases him and was foretold in prophecy, especially in the prophecy of Malachi. The latter assures men of the coming of the pure sacrifice proper to the new covenant; he foretells the eucharistic sacrifice.

Like Jesus at the wedding feast of Cana, the Church uses the bread and wine which creation produces, for, contrary to what the gnostics think, creation is good. The Church consecrates this bread and wine by means of Christ's words which have been passed on to her by the tradition. The history of the seed that is put into the ground, rises up as wheat, becomes bread, and is eventually turned into the body of Christ, expressively sums up the history and mystery of Christ.

"The Jews no longer offer sacrifice; their hands are full of blood, for they have not accepted the Word through whom men offer sacrifice to God. The same is true of all the assemblies of the heretics. . . . How could they have the certainty that the bread over which the thanksgiving is spoken is the body of the Lord and the cup his blood, when they do not acknowledge that he is the Son of the Creator, that is, the Creator's Word by which the tree bears fruit, and the springs flow, and 'the earth produces the blade, then the ear, and then the wheat in the ear'" (*Adv. Haer.* IV, 18, 4).

The supreme blessing for creation is to become eucharist, that is, the body and blood of Christ, and thereby the vehicle of grace, life, and incorruptibility. "The Church has received this sacrifice from the apostles and throughout the entire world offers it to God who gives us for our nourishment the first fruits of his gifts under the new covenant," that is, his own Son (IV, 17, 5). This sacrifice is the one that Malachi predicted the whole world would offer.

"The oblation which the Lord commanded the Church to offer throughout the entire world is a pure sacrifice in God's sight and pleasing to him. It is pleasing to him not because he needs a sacrifice from us but because the one who offers it is glorified by his gift if it is accepted. . . . The Church alone offers this pure sacrifice to the Creator, offering to him with thanksgiving what comes from his own creation" (IV, 18, 1. 4).[4]

The Church offers the sacrifice of the new covenant which completes and recapitulates all the sacrifices of the past. In her offering she gives expression to her faith, her gratitude, and her expectation. Irenaeus makes his own the theme of the interior worship by which the Christian completes the eucharistic sacrifice by the sacrifice of his life. "We ought to offer our sacrifice to God and be grateful in everything to God our Creator, by offering him the first fruits of his own creation with a pure disposition, sincere faith, firm hope, and ardent love" (IV, 18, 4).

FROM THE EUCHARIST TO THE FUTURE RESURRECTION

The gnostics made a demiurge responsible for creation, and regarded matter as hostile to man. The body was taken to be a manifestation of man's fall and therefore incapable of sharing in man's future blessedness. Thus did the dichotomy between soul and body, so dear to Platonic philosophy, lead to a denial of the resurrection of the flesh. But the doctrine of the eucharist enabled Irenaeus to refute the gnostic claims. He develops his thought at length in the final book of the *Adversus Haereses*,[5] where he spells out his ideas on the subject and shows the place of the eucharist in the plan of salvation.

As Irenaeus sees it, the entire man, body as well as soul, shares in salvation, because the entire man has been redeemed and saved by the blood of Christ and is now nourished by the eucharistic offerings, that is, the body and blood of Christ in which we participate.

"If the flesh cannot be saved, then neither did the Lord redeem us with his blood, nor is the cup of the eucharist a participation in his blood, nor the bread we break a participation in his body. For blood comes only from veins and flesh and the rest of that human substance which the Word of God assumed so as to become man and truly redeem us. As his apostle says: 'In him we have redemption and the forgiveness of sins through his blood.'

"We are his members and we are nourished by his creation. He himself gives us that creation as he makes his sun rise and his rain fall at his good pleasure. The cup which comes from his creation he declared to be his blood that mingles with ours, and the bread which comes from his creation he asserted is his body which gives growth to our bodies" (*Adv. Haer.* V, 2, 1-2).

Here we see the marvelous continuity of God's plan: creation serves our bodily life; it receives its supreme consecration in becoming the body and blood of Christ and thus the food that renders man incorruptible.

"For, as the bread that comes from the earth, when it receives the invocation of God is no longer ordinary bread but the eucharist which comprises two elements, an earthly and a heavenly, so our bodies which participate in the eucharist are no longer corruptible, since they now have the hope of resurrection" (*Adv. Haer.* IV, 18, 5).[6]

Irenaeus returns once again to the image of the wheat and the vine. What happens to these illustrates not only what happens in the eucharist, but also the hope that the body buried in the earth will rise up for eternal life.

"The vine that is planted in the earth bears fruit in its season, and the grain of wheat that falls into the soil and cracks open there rises up multiplied by the Spirit of God who holds all things together; the bread and wine are wisely put to man's use, and when they receive the word of God they become the eucharist, that is, the body and blood of Christ. So too our bodies that are nourished by the eucharist are placed in the earth and dissolve into it, but they shall rise when their time comes, for the Word of God will make them rise for the glory of God the Father, who clothes this mortal body in immortality and gives this corruptible body an unmerited incorruptibility, since the power of God is made perfect in weakness" (V, 2, 3).

Paul uses the image of the seed to explain the resurrection of the body (1 Corinthians 15.35-38). Irenaeus here applies it to the eucharistic mystery which is the bond linking Christ's resurrection to ours. Our salvation is illustrated by the history of bread from seed to loaf and is sacramentalized in the eucharist, which is the pledge and prophetic anticipation of our integral resurrection and incorruptibility. Even before St. Irenaeus, St. Ignatius of Antioch had spoken of the "bread which is a remedy bestowing immortality, an antidote preventing death and giving life in Jesus Christ forever."[7]

Such are the chief statements Irenaeus makes about the eucharist. Their context is the unfolding economy of salvation, in which God's single plan is being worked out, amid the forward movement of history, as a universal recapitulation. Now that we have seen these various texts we can sketch an outline of Irenaeus' teaching on the eucharist.

THE DIVINE DISPENSATION

The gnostic vision of man and history was essentially a vision of descent. It described a process of degradation: the fall of an angel, or the snaring of a spirit in matter. Man was thought of as a spirit which discovers that it is in a prison and has been degraded by the flesh in which it is robed. In such a vision of things, salvation requires a return to an ideal world; it requires liberation from matter and the body.

Irenaeus reverses the entire perspective and describes an ascending curve; his vision is one in which man, an indissoluble unity, is an animated body, not an embodied spirit. Irenaeus understands the story in Genesis of God breathing a "breath of life" into clay (Genesis 2.7) to be a story of humble beginnings, with man being meant to develop to his perfect state.

Men enters upon the scene of creation as part of a history that has already begun. God takes earth, a lowly but innocent material (neither evil nor sin have as yet touched it) and breathes his own life into it. This marks the beginning of man's existence, but also of his call from God and his ascent to perfection. The journey will be a slow one, for man is still a child who must learn through painful experience to use the royal gift of freedom.

God who shapes the clay uses his own Son for the model, since he is the first to achieve the perfect "image and likeness." He is the true Adam, the firstborn of creation. In him we see in fullness what we saw in an embryonic form in the first human beings. Thus he is also the new Adam, the archetype of Christian man (cf. *Adv. Haer.* III, 21, 10–22, 2. 3. 4).

RECAPITULATION

Christ is the center and focal point of history. Being linked to matter through the virginal body he received from his virginal mother, he is part of the line of human beings; he shares the history of mankind with its wretchedness and sinfulness. He has entered into the human condition in order to assume it in its entirety and save it.

"The Word, our Savior, became what lost man was, thus establishing in himself a communion with man in order to win man's salvation. What was lost possessed flesh and blood, for God had formed man out of the muddy earth, and it was for this man's sake that God determined the entire manner of the Lord's coming. The Lord, too, therefore, possessed flesh and blood, in order that he might recapitulate in himself, not some other work, but the one the Father had formed in the beginning, and that he might in this way seek out what was lost" (*Adv. Haer.* V, 14, 2).

Being at the heart of the universe, of which he was a part by reason of his body and blood, Christ brought that universe through the test of death to resurrection. The power of God or of the Spirit raised Jesus from the dead, so that his bodily resurrection is the "first fruits of our own resurrection." What the head experienced, the entire body will also experience. Our body "is sown in corruption but rises up incorrupt" (1 Corinthians 15.42, as cited in *Adv. Haer.* V, 7, 2).

THE BODY OF CHRIST

Communion between God and his creatures was established once and for all in Christ, where it is sealed by the Spirit. In Christ and through Christ the Spirit rests upon the work of the divine hands, the human race. From the head this communion is passed on to all his human brothers, with whom he forms the body that is the Church. Irenaeus cites Paul's Letter to the Ephesians. "We are the members of his body, of his flesh and blood" (*Adv. Haer.* V, 2, 2, citing Ephesians 5.30).

This solidarity between Christ and the Church makes ethical demands on the Christian and the Church. More than that, it establishes a continuity, a parallelism, and a mutual involvement between head and members. The unfolding of the divine plan in history through the old covenant into the new is itself also compared to a sowing of seed that finally yields its harvest when Christ makes our flesh his own. "What was begun in Abel and proclaimed by the prophets was accomplished in the Lord, and the same will be accomplished in us, for the body follows the head" (*Adv. Haer.* IV, 34, 4).

Irenaeus develops his thinking about the solidarity of Christ with men in the parabolic image of the lost sheep (*Adv. Haer.* III, 19, 3). Christ came to look for the lost sheep, that is, the creature he had formed with his own hands; having found it, he took it up to the heights to present and return it to the Father. Thus the whole body will share in the resurrection of Christ, for Christ is the first fruits of mankind.

A EUCHARISTIC ECONOMY

For Irenaeus, the eucharist is the sacrament of the economy, or unfolding divine plan, as revealed to us in the person and work of Christ. Faith and eucharist, eucharist and faith are inseparable and reciprocal: "Our manner of thinking is conformed to the eucharist, and the eucharist confirms our manner of thinking" (*Adv. Haer.* IV, 18, 5).[8] The eucharist is the center and content of faith, and contains the whole economy of the Son of God.

In response to the heretics, Irenaeus sums up this economy:

"The Savior redeemed us with his blood and gave his soul for our soul, his flesh for our flesh; he poured out the Spirit of the Father, in order to effect union and communion between God and man by making God descend to man through the Spirit and man ascend to God through the incarnation. By his coming he surely and truly bestowed incorruption upon us through our communion with God" (*Adv. Haer.* V, 1, 2).

The history of the bread which is the fruit of the earth but even prior to that is the fruit of the divine generosity enables us to understand the changes proper to the economy. Once the products of the created world have become through consecration the body and blood of Christ, they are vehicles of grace, salvation, and incorruptibility. In them and by means of them the Church offers God the new sacrifice throughout the world. The offerings, transformed now by the presence of Christ, convey to God the earth's most marvelous fruit, the Son of the Virgin Mary, whom God has given to men as the first-born of creation and first fruits of the new earth whereon the future kingdom will be established.

The eucharist expresses gratitude for the long roll-call of God's blessings, but it is also the anticipated ingathering of scattered mankind whom the Spirit brings together in union and communion. In the eucharist the Christian already possesses the blessings promised to him and the happiness to which he is called.

In his discussion, Irenaeus reminds us of the interior dynamism associated with the eucharist; it calls for the personal effort of each communicant and for love received and shared: "If we fail to help others in their need, we deny the love of the Lord."[9] The first fruits which we offer imply our own commitment. The love bestowed upon us must bear fruit, and by that fruit we will be judged.

The eucharist, which is bread for our journey, teaches us at each moment to welcome "the Spirit who perfects us and prepares us for incorruptibility and gradually accustoms us to receiving God." (*Adv. Haer.* V, 8, 1).[10] Mankind is advancing on a long road; as it goes, the Spirit does not destroy it but transfigures it, and the earth itself even now participates in the banquet of God. With all his being, man is caught up in this universal ascent. He offers its first fruits in the eucharist; he offers his very self by making himself wholly a part of the sacrifice which comes from the Father and returns to its Creator. Man advances slowly and steadily to his perfection, to the encounter with God that will make him incorruptible. "All who have the Spirit of God are led to the Word, that is, the Son, and the Son accepts them and offers them to his Father, and the Father bestows incorruptibility on them."[11]

Such is the truth and meaning of the eucharist of St. Irenaeus of Lyons.

NOTES

1. For a general presentation of Irenaeus the churchman, see our *Guide pratique des Pères de l'Eglise* (Paris, 1967). See also J. Quasten, *Patrology* 1. *The Beginnings of Patristic Literature* (Westminster, Md., 1950), pp. 287-313.

A critical text of parts of the *Adversus Haereses* has appeared in the *Sources chrétiennes* series: Book III, in SC 34ter; Book IV, in SC 100; Book V, in SC 152-53. The *Demonstratio apostolica* is in SC 62.

2. This is a phrase Irenaeus liked; cf. *Dem.* 11; *Adv. Haer.* IV, 34, 1; V, 6, 1; 28, 3.

3. We are making use here of thoughts developed in our book *La prière* 2 (Paris, 1963), pp. 116-20.

4. This passage alludes to the sacrifice foretold by Malachi in a prophecy that is constantly used in the early tradition.

5. This is in fact the theme of the entire book, but especially of 6, 2–8, 1.

6. An important but difficult text. For the interpretation of it cf. D. Van den Eynde in *Antonianum* (1940), pp. 13-28.

7. *Ad Ephesios* 20, 2.

8. This passage has been preserved for us in Greek by St. John Damascene.

9. A fragment, published in W. W. Harvey (ed.), *Sancti Irenaei Libri quinque adversus Haereses* (Cambridge, 1857), 2:477.

10. Irenaeus calls the Spirit "the bread of God" and of immortality (*Adv. Haer.* IV, 38, 1).

11. *Demonstratio* 7. See our book *La prière* 2:123, and "Eucharistie," DSp 5:1569-70.

André Méhat

CLEMENT OF ALEXANDRIA

When we try to discuss any aspect of the thought of Clement of Alexandria, we find ourselves straightway in an area of uncertainty. This is all the more frustrating because sure conclusions regarding what he says would be valuable both because the subjects he deals with are important (he has something to say on almost every aspect of theology) and because he lived at a significant historical juncture. He wrote around the year 200 and was one of the last heirs to traditions some of which may have originated in the very earliest Christian preaching; in addition, he is the first witness to scholarly Alexandrine theology whose writings have been preserved for us.[1] And yet, as we hinted above, the many obscurities in his writings raise problems which may not in every case be insoluble but which will certainly be debated.

This general statement applies to the eucharist.[2] According to T. Camelot[3] there are only four passages in all the works of Clement that certainly speak of the eucharist[4]; if we add all the other passages which have been taken, usually with reason, as referring to the eucharist, the number rises to about forty.[5] There is equally great hesitation when it comes to the interpretation of these passages. Until not too long ago, the great debate was on the question of whether Clement held the "real presence" or opted rather for the "symbolist" view; Catholics inclined to the former view, Protestants generally to the latter. Today there is a general tendency to think that it is misleading to put such a question to Clement,[6] but this does not mean that the relevant problems have been completely solved or that there is agreement on the solutions.

99

Our understanding of theology prior to the Council of Nicaea depends on studies that are still in the exploratory stage[7] and that have as yet paid little attention to the eucharist. In any case, Clement has little to say on the subject; he speaks of it only incidentally and in passing. What he says about it depends moreover on the particular viewpoint he is adopting in a given passage, on the authors from whom he is taking his ideas, and on the authors he is rejecting. He has little interest in the outward manifestations of the Church's life[8]; thus he does not devote much attention to the sacraments, and in this area is concerned less with the eucharist than with baptism.

The writings of Clement that have come down to us are controlled by the idea that the teacher of Christian doctrine has the important task of leading the faithful to the imitation of God and his Logos, who are mankind's real teachers. He must covert the believer from pagan ways to faith and Christian discipline; then he will lead the simple believer, through lengthy study and asceticism, to the elimination of vices and passions (to a state of *apatheia*) and, on the positive side, to charity and, above all, to *gnosis* or the knowledge of divine secrets. The believer will thus become a *gnostic*, a "knower," who is the equal of the angels; when he reaches the final step in the spiritual ascent, he will possess by anticipation the divinization, the assimilation to the Logos, and the union with the Most High God that are proper to the eschatological Church. In this whole process, the eucharist is important chiefly for its effects; we will hardly be surprised to find that Clement usually speaks of the rite only insofar as it signifies these effects.

When the sensible world is thus seen on terms of its spiritual meaning, various terms are applied to it: allegory, symbol, enigma, type, and so on. This kind of reading is made of various objects: sacred Scripture, the structure of the Church, the sacraments. We must not play down the value of such interpretation for the objects subjected to it;

we must not say, "This is only allegory,"[9] but rather "This is allegory," that is, a mystery sacralizes, or more accurately, enables us to recognize the sacrality of, both the sign and the thing signified. In most cases, the relation of allegory holds not only between words but between things as well. In order to avoid as much as possible misleading the present-day reader, and indeed in order not to mislead ourselves as well, we shall look primarily for "correspondences" in a sense close to that which Beaudelaire borrowed from Swedenborg, for poetry is the only domain in which people willingly accept symbolic thinking.

According to Clement, these correspondences give us access to things divine, to authentic reality. We shall therefore follow the procedure Clement himself generally follows, by ascending from sensible appearances to the spiritual reality which the symbol both hides and reveals. We shall look at the eucharist (1) in *Scripture*, (2) as a liturgical *rite* and celebration, (3) as a *meal*, a gathering inspired by love, and a sacrifice, and (4) finally and above all as *spiritual food*; this in turn will lead us to consider (5) the eucharistic *"mingling,"* and (6) the *eating of the Logos*.

THE EUCHARIST IN SCRIPTURE

Theology, for Clement, does not take the form of a summa that is divided into parts, questions and chapters or articles. It embraces rather a number of Scriptural passages which are linked each with the others and accompanied by glosses in the margin of the text. Thus the "treatise on the eucharist" consists, first, of the series of accounts of the institution of the eucharist: 1 Corinthians 11.24-27, Matthew 26.26-28 and parallels,[10] and then (and above all), of the discourse on the bread of life in John 6.31-58.[11] In the many passages in which Clement uses the discourse, the eucharistic meaning is not always evident, but it certainly is in some instances,[12] and this allows us to assume that it is present in almost all. The Scripture texts are often loosely quoted and mixed up with one another;

nowhere do we find the lengthy quotations which indicate that the writer has gone back to the text of Scripture and verified his quotations. On the contrary, everything suggests that Clement is quoting from memory and relying on an already long tradition.

Besides these basic texts there are some others. The manna (Exodus 16.4), which has already been picked up in John 6.59, is the basis for the frequent expression "heavenly food"[13] or (via 1 Corinthians 10.3) "spiritual food."[14] At least once, Melchisedech (Genesis 14.18; Hebrews 7.1), "who gives consecrated food—bread and wine—as a pre-figuration of the eucharist," becomes a type of Christ who gives himself as food.[15] "He ties his young ass to the vine, to its stock the foal of his she-ass. He washes his coat in wine, his cloak in blood of the grape" (Genesis 49.11). These obscure words from the blessing of Judah, whether cited in full or in the reduced form of "blood of the grape," are generally interpreted by Clement, as by Tertullian, as referring to the eucharistic wine-blood.[16] The wedding feast at Cana[17] and the water mingled with blood that came from the side of Jesus[18] are some other figures of the eucharist.

We hesitate to add to this list various citations from Scripture which the tradition regards as referring to the eucharist[19] but which Clement does not explicitly consider to be such. Some examples: Psalm 33 (34).9 (cited as early as 1 Peter 2.3): "Taste and see how good the Lord is"[20]; Malachi 1.10-11: "I shall not accept sacrifice from your hands, for my name has been glorified among the nations and in every place a sacrifice is offered to me"[21]; finally, Isaiah 58.9: "While you are still speaking, he will say, 'I am here.'"[22] In view of his practice of suggesting rather than explaining, it is likely that Clement did not explicitly mention the eucharistic meaning but had it in mind.

On the other hand, it seems that no text from pagan literature made him think in a specific way of the eucharist. The only exception is a passage attributed to Thespis in the fifth book of the *Stromata*; but the reference is fleeting and debatable.[23] This state of affairs explains why the eucharist comes into the *Stromata* so little; the eucharist is something reserved to the Christian community and has to do solely with Christ and the Bible. The work in which the eucharist comes up most frequently is the *Paedagogus*, the only one of his major writings that is meant solely for Christians.[24]

THE EUCHARIST IN THE CHURCH

There is a somewhat clear reference to the eucharistic rite in only three passages.

The first of these is *Paed.* II, 32, 2–33, 1. Amid practical advice against the drinking of wine, Clement notes that it may nonetheless be licitly drunk; he appeals to the example of Christ, especially at the Last Supper and comments: "So much for the people called 'Encratites'!"

The allusion to the Encratites is clarified in the second passage, *I Str.* 96, 1, in an exegetical note on Proverbs 9.18: "I exhort those who lack understanding, and I say to them: Delight in touching the mysterious loaves and the water of a pleasing sacrifice." In the Book of Proverbs it is Lady Folly who addresses these words to those whom she is leading astray; in the latter Clement sees the heretics. "Evidently, Scripture here mentions bread and water only as a rebuke to those who use bread and water in the sacrifice, contrary to the rule of the Church. For there are in fact some who celebrate the eucharist using plain water."

Clement is here referring to the Encratites, whom he assimilates to the Aquarians or Hydroparastatae, although later students of the phenomenon of heresy at times distinguished the two groups. This is the only controversy regarding the eucharist that Clement, like Cyprian in the West (*Letter* 63), refers to. From this we can see what a great measure of unanimity there was on the meaning of

103

the sacrament. As a general rule, Clement did not enter into discussions between heretics and churchmen.

The third passage in which there is a relatively clear reference to the eucharistic rite is *I Str.* 5, 1. Here, when Clement is on the point of revealing a secret teaching, he suddenly grows afraid lest he be revealing it to disciples who are unworthy, but then he justifies his boldness by the analogy of the eucharist. He will proceed like some who, appealing to 1 Corinthians 11.27-28, "when they distribute the eucharist according to custom, allow each believer to take his share of it," since conscience is the best judge of what the individual should do or not do. Ecclesiastical custom, supported by St. Paul's authority, is thus a norm, even if it is not followed generally but only by "some."[25] What Clement makes clear here is the importance of the Church's practice; for this reason we may well be receptive to the suggestions of the scholars who find a large number of allusions in Clement to the eucharistic liturgy.

One such allusion is to be found, we believe, at the end of the *Protrepticus* (119-120).[26] Clement here contrasts the "mysteries of the Logos" with the mysteries of Dionysos, and he reminds his readers of the former. The psalms sung by virgins, the chorus of the just, the hymn to the God of the universe: all these seem to refer to liturgical singing. The glorification of God by the angels, which is mentioned twice,[27] may be an allusion to the singing of the Sanctus (Isaiah 6.3),[28] while the word of the prophets may refer to the Old Testament readings, the exhortation of the "eternal Jesus" may refer to the reading of the gospel,[29] and the "reception of the Father" may refer to communion.[30]

The whole passage draws its inspiration from baptism rather than from the eucharist. On the other hand, we know from Justin Martyr and the *Apostolic Tradition* of St. Hippolytus that the paschal celebration of the eucharist immediately following a baptism served as a model for every eucharist,[31] just as an initiation into the pagan mysteries was the form par excellence of celebrating those mysteries.

The allusions to the eucharist are even clearer in *VI Str.* 113, 3. Here we are told that the gnostic soul studies how to "be God," while "constantly thanking God on every occasion through the hearing and reading of things divine, through authentic study, through a holy offering, through a blessed prayer, and through praising, singing hymns, and chanting psalms." The "offering" can only refer to a liturgical action, the eucharist.[32] The thanksgiving, too, therefore, may well refer to the celebration of the eucharist, the "hearing" to the homily, and the "reading" almost certainly to a liturgical reading.[33] We may note the importance given to songs of praise, which foster union with the higher choirs of angels. Admittedly, it is difficult to engage in "authentic study" during the celebration of the eucharist; other ideas, too, are intermingled in the passage.[34]

The kiss of peace is mentioned elsewhere,[35] while the attitude of the celebrant or his assistants may be described in the following lines:

"We raise our heads, we extend our hands up toward heaven, and we stand on tiptoe[36] at the final acclamation in our prayer, as we direct the thrust of our minds toward the Intelligible Substance. By attempting through words to raise our bodies above the earth and by raising up our souls to which a longing for heavenly things has given wings,[37] we force them to advance toward the Sanctuary,[38] for we scorn the bonds that still link us to the flesh" (*VII Str.* 40, 1).[39]

The prayer described in this passage may well be the prayer of prayers, the eucharist. The bodily posture adopted in the eucharist is interpreted in a very Platonic way as being the outward sign of a soul that seeks to rise up and be detached from the body so that it may go forth to God, who is the Intelligible Substance, or locus of the Ideas. In short, the prayer is interpreted as a means of knowing God, and this is indeed one aspect of the eucharist. There may be other allusions to the eucharistic celebration in these pages that describe the prayer of the "gnostic," but it is difficult to isolate them.[40]

SPIRITUAL MEAL AND SACRIFICE

The eucharist is a prayer, but for us it is also and above all a meal, the Lord's Supper.[41] Clement speaks often enough of spiritual meals or banquets,[42] but rarely does he relate these directly to the eucharist. The "sacred meal" of which he speaks is not the Last Supper but the meal Jesus took in the home of Simon the Pharisee (Luke 7.36-50).[43] The two chapters of the *Paedagogus* (III, 1 and 2) which speak of meals deal with ritual meals which do not seem to be celebrations of the eucharist.[44] We think, however, that what Clement writes here is not unrelated to his conception of the eucharist. Just as the existence of the eucharistic banquet sheds a sanctifying influence on every meal, so what is true of an ordinary meal and much more of an agape, which is a liturgical meal celebrated by brothers, will be true of the eucharistic meal.

Every meal that a Christian eats to the accompaniment of readings, prayers, and songs has something liturgical about it.[45] An agape is undoubtedly a liturgical meal: its very name indicates that it is an act of charity, for it is a sharing and pooling of at least part of what each person has.[46] Clement insists that an agape be distinguished from ordinary meals by the absence of luxury and gluttony; with all the better reason, then is he indignant that the Carpocratians should give the name of agape to their licentious banquets.[47]

Clement thinks the word agape (Greek for "love, charity") well chosen indeed as a name for the fraternal meals Christians take together, and he uses it (in what is more than a simple play on words) in order to preach charity which is the "heavenly food," "the banquet of the Logos," the reality which "does not come to an end" (1 Corinthians 13.8) and is an anticipation of the kingdom of God (Luke 14.15) and of the "heavenly banquet in heaven." "He who eats this meal will acquire the greatest good there is, namely, the kingdom of God, because he has thus prepared himself in this life for the holy assembly of love, the heavenly Church." For "earthly festivities contain within them as it were a spark of love that accustoms us to pass from ordinary food to eternal food."[48] Let us leave aside for the moment the term "heavenly food," which also brings out one aspect of the eucharist. The idea of the "gathering" of the earthly Church as a preparation for and prefiguration of the kingdom of God and of the heavenly and eternal Church is undoubtedly one of the basic reasons for the *synaxis* or eucharistic *gathering*.

In the abstruse language of philosophy, the *Protrepticus* invites the pagans to that eschatological Church:

"Let us hasten . . . to be gathered in a single love, passing from multiplicity to unity in accordance with the unifying action of the Monadic Substance.[49] In proportion to the good already bestowed on us, let us seek unity by seeking the Good Monad. The union of many voices, when their dissonance and dispersion have been submitted to a divine harmony, constitutes at last a single symphony, with the chorus obeying a single leader and instructor, the Logos, and finding its repose in truth itself."[50]

Tollinton thinks, and rightly so in our view, that this description of eschatological unity borrows the image of choral singing from the eucharistic assembly and seeks to bring out the real meaning of the liturgical singing.

Among the ancients every meal was preceded by a *sacrifice*. In Clement's view, every prayer is a sacrifice.[51] The eucharist, which is both meal and prayer, is also a sacrifice and linked to the sacrifice of Christ. This conception is suggested to us by a complicated passage from the fifth book of the *Stromata*.[52] Clement takes 1 Corinthians 3.1-2 as his starting point and distinguishes between the milk given to children, which is the initial catechesis, and the solid food that is the mystical contemplation[53] of the perfect:

"Such are the flesh and blood of the Logos, that is, the understanding[54] of the divine Power and Substance. 'Taste and see that the Lord is good' (Psalm 33 [34].9). For he gives such food to those who receive spiritually, when 'the soul nourishes itself,' as Plato, the friend of truth, says.[55] For to know the divine substance is to eat and drink the divine Logos. This is why Plato also says: 'It is only after having sacrificed not a pig but a great and undiscoverable victim'[56] that we may engage in the quest of God. And the Apostle writes: 'Christ, our Passover, has been sacrificed' (1 Corinthians 5.7), that truly undiscoverable victim, the Son of God who is handed over for us! But the sacrifice God finds acceptable (Leviticus 22.21, etc.; Philippians 4.18) is separation from the body and its passions."

At first reading, allegory seems to be in complete control in such a passage. This may, however, be simply due to the point of view Clement is adopting in Book Five of the *Stromata*, where, after distinguishing between gnosis and faith,[57] he seeks points of contact between Plato and Christian teaching. In any case, his attention here is to bring out one meaning of the eucharist, as the echoes of John 6 and Psalm 33.9 show. What we may retain from such a passage, then, are the correspondences between the eucharist and the acquisition of gnosis, but also between the eucharist and the elimination of the passions and, even more, between the eucharist and the paschal sacrifice of Christ (although it would be rash of us to try to pin down the precise nature of the correspondence).

SPIRITUAL FOOD

The idea of a "heavenly" or "spiritual" or "divine" food keeps recurring in one section of the *Paedagogus* (I, 5 and 6), where Batiffol and others have denied (mistakenly, in our view) that Clement is thinking of the eucharist. In this section of his book he is discussing the opinion of the Valentinians (a gnostic group) that the faith of simple believers is infantile and to be scorned and that only the "gnosis" of the "elect" is adult and therefore deserves respect. Especially in chapter 6 Clement deals at length with the meaning of 1 Corinthians 3.1-2: "I gave you milk to drink, as to those who are still children in Christ, and not solid food; you were not yet capable of such food."[58]

Clement's entire effort in these pages is devoted to showing that there is no difference of kind between the faith of the simple and the gnosis of the perfect. The sacraments play a role in the discussion because the Valentinians shared these with the Church at large[59]; the only thing peculiar to the Valentinians in this area was their tendency to think that the eucharist gave special access to the higher levels of the spiritual life, that is, to gnosis.[60] The discussion turns, however, chiefly on baptism. We shall not enter into the details of this discussion in which Clement tries various hypotheses in order to resolve the difficulty.[61] We shall only comment briefly on some expressions that may be of some importance for the eucharist, without trying to construct an impossible synthesis.

1. *Paed.* I, 15, 3-4. To those who disparage "spiritual infancy" Clement offers the challenge of the "ass" in Zechariah 9.9 (cf. Matthew 21.24 and parallels) and in Genesis 49.1. He adds: "'He attached his ass to the vine': he attached his people who are simple children, to the Logos, of whom the vine is an allegorical sign, for the vine produces wine as the Logos does blood; both of these are salutary drinks for man, the wine for his body, the blood for his spirit."

According to Batiffol, "the wine of which there is question here is not the eucharistic wine but . . . the wine commonly regarded as a remedy."[62] The affirmation in this sentence is quite valid, but the negation is risky. The parallelism Clement is establishing does not simply set up a comparison; it also (as in II, 19, 4) makes the wine more apt to serve as a visible symbol of the mysterious blood which brings men salvation, the blood which was shed on the cross and is present in the eucharist. As in I, 47, 2, a little further on, Genesis 49.11 is regarded as a prophecy of the eucharist.

2. *Paed.* I, 38, 1-3. One of the hypotheses used in explaining 1 Corinthians 3.1-2 is that the milk represents the preaching (the kerygma) given to the multitudes and the pagans, while the solid food stands for faith. Clement says:

"The Lord presented us with a similar nourishment under the veil of symbols when he said: 'Eat my fleshes and drink my blood,'[63] and thereby spoke allegorically of the visible nature of faith and the drinkable nature of the promise.[64] Thanks to these, the Church, like a man constituted of many members, is watered and grows[65]; she is formed and constituted on the basis of these two elements: the body of faith and the soul of hope, just as the Lord himself is composed of flesh and blood. Hope is the lifeblood of faith; like a soul, hope sustains faith. If the breath of hope vanishes, like blood draining out, the vital strength of faith also disappears."

In this passage Clement is engaging in theological speculations similar to those of Ignatius of Antioch who speaks of the Lord's flesh as faith and his blood as charity.[66] The reference to John 6.53 shows that Clement is relating all this to the eucharist, but the nature of the relation is not clear. He also refers to theories of the Stoic kind that regard both the soul and the blood as a vital principle; here, however, Clement is applying these theories to the theological realm of faith and hope and to the ecclesial body of Christ.

110

The correspondences can be outlined as follows:

38, 2: *blood of Christ = drink = hope = soul of the Church*
        flesh of Christ   food   faith   body of the Church

38, 1: *solid food = faith = catechesis*
      milk   hearing kerygma

To be noted is the factual identity between the second and third lines. We may suppose an ascending dynamism from the third to the first, analogous to that which we find in, for example, St. Irenaeus who uses the same texts— 1 Corinthians 3.1-2 and John 6.54-58—to describe the spiritual growth of mankind.[67]

3. *Paed.* I, 42, 1–43, 1. This passage, the text of which is probably corrupt,[68] refers to texts we no longer possess and to an esoteric doctrine which a clever commentator may someday rediscover.[69] The focus of the passage is on the idea of spiritual food. This food is the Logos, who is given to us by the Church in accordance with God's will as manifested in the incarnation and the dispensation built on the incarnation. The images or symbols of the passage mingle to the point of becoming incoherent. The symbol of milk is accompanied by that of the little child who is the body of Christ that is meant to grow; but the faithful are also children whom Christ has brought to birth. The blood of Christ serves these children as swaddling clothes for their crib, but they are also meant to grow up thanks to a nourishment which consists of the body and blood of Christ (John 6.53 is cited once again). Finally, baptismal symbols that are inspired by St. Paul appear. We would expect "to put off corruption" to be followed by "to put on incorruptibility," but Clement shifts from the symbol of clothing to that of food and speaks of man receiving Christ as food. The thought of the eucharist is present along with the allusion to John 6.51 ff., but we still have no full and satisfactory interpretation of the passage.

4. *Paed.* I, 43, 2-4. After the learned and "deep" considerations come others that Clement calls "more ordinary," but these two are enigmatic:

"By 'flesh' he [Christ] wishes us to understand the Holy Spirit [the Pneuma], for it was he who created the flesh.[70] By 'blood' he means the Logos, for the Logos has been poured out upon our life like an abundant blood.[71] The Lord, who is the food of little children, is a mixture of both, since he is both Pneuma and Logos. The food, then, that is the Lord Jesus, the Logos of God, is the spirit become flesh, the heavenly flesh sanctified."

The correspondence between the Logos and the Spirit, on the one hand, and flesh and blood on the other is paralleled in a passage of the *Gospel of Philip*[72] which explains John 6.53 in the same terms but inverting the relation: "What is his flesh? The Logos. His blood? The Holy Spirit." According to A. H. C. Van Eijk neither the author of the gnostic gospel nor Clement seems to have attached much importance to the order of the terms, and the idea of the Logos is hardly distinguished from that of the Pneuma. It is possible that Clement borrowed the idea of the correspondence from the author he is refuting, a Valentinian like the author of the *Gospel of Philip*. It is more probable, however, that it comes from a common source we cannot further identify. What is certain is that in this perspective the eucharist means the reception of the Pneuma and the Logos, that is, of Christ in his totality.

5. *Paed.* I, 47, 1.
"Since he said: 'And the bread I will give is my flesh,' and since on the other hand the flesh is watered by the blood and the wine is an allegory of the blood, we must realize that just as bread that is placed in a mixture of wine and water soaks up the wine and leaves the water, so the Lord's flesh, which is the bread of the heavens, absorbs the blood. Consequently it nourishes heavenly men in order to

lead them to incorruptibility, and leaves behind nothing but fleshly desires that are condemned to corruption."

This "allegory," which is borrowed from a rather naive "physics," is to be read in the light of the close relation constantly asserted by Christian antiquity between the eucharist and immortality. At the same time, the eucharist signifies the purification of the passions, a basic idea in the moral theology of Clement.

6. *Paed.* I, 47, 2.
"The Logos is represented by a number of allegories: food, flesh, nourishment, bread, blood, milk. The Lord is all this so that we who believe in him may profit by him. Let no one be astonished, then, that the Lord's blood should be allegorically represented by milk. Is it not also represented by wine?"

Clement wishes to prove that the "milk" of 1 Corinthians 3.2 is not essentially different from the "blood" of Christ. It is solely for this purpose that he jumbles together the various "allegories" of the Logos. It is notable, however, that of the two texts he cites (Genesis 49.11 and 4.10) one relates to the eucharist and the other to the sacrifice of the cross, two things which are inseparable.[73]

THE EUCHARISTIC "MINGLING"

It is generally agreed that the most important text of Clement on the eucharist is in Book II of the *Paedagogus*, nos. 19-20. In an exhortation against wine drinking, Clement praises water and gives, as one of his example, the water Moses brought forth from the rock (Exodus 17.6). Then he speaks of wine and of Joshua who is a figure of Jesus.

"Later on, the holy vine yielded the prophetic cluster of grapes.[74] This cluster was a sign for the travelers who were being guided by the Teacher to the rest that awaited them after their wanderings. The great Cluster is the Logos who was crushed for us, for the Logos[75] willed that the 'blood of the vine' be mingled with water[76] as his blood is mingled with salvation.[77] Now the Lord's blood is of two kinds: on the one hand, there is the carnal blood that freed us from corruption, and on the other the pneumatic[78] blood by which we have been anointed. To drink the blood of Jesus is to share in the Lord's incorruptibility.[79] But the Pneuma is the power of the Logos just as the blood is the power of the flesh.[80]

"There is thus an analogy between the mingling of the wine and the water and the mingling of man and the Pneuma: the first mingling, that of wine and water, is a festive meal given us for the sake of faith; in the other mingling, the Pneuma leads man to incorruptibility. The mingling of the two, that is, of the drink and the Logos, is called eucharist, a grace that is praised for its beauty.[81] Those who share in it with faith are sanctified in body and soul, when the Father's will mysteriously mingles man, this divine mixture, with the Pneuma and the Logos. In truth, the Pneuma is closely related to the soul which it draws along,[82] and the flesh is closely related to the Logos, the flesh on account of which[83] the Logos became flesh."

This digression on the eucharist stands alone in the *Paedagogus* and indeed is unique in the entire work of Clement; it is complicated, full of ellipses, and, in all probability, deliberately enigmatic. It starts from the comparison with wine and water as a drink and launches first into biblical symbolism, then into considerations based on theological metaphysics, among which there is undoubtedly question of the eucharistic drink. We may, of course, focus our attention on one or another phrase because of some particular question we wish to put to the author, but, for a proper understanding, we must look at the passage as a whole.

114

There can be no doubt that the words: "The mingling of the two, that is, of the drink and the Logos, is called eucharist," presuppose a "realist" view of the eucharist, but these same words acquire their full meaning only in the light of the idea of "mingling" which dominates the entire text, and of a theology of the Logos that makes use of the notion of "mingling." It must be noted, finally, that the whole passage draws upon a theory of the Pneuma that must be interpreted in the light of the ante-Nicene theology of the Pneuma, namely, the theology of St. Irenaeus and Tertullian, for whom the Pneuma is not a person of the Trinity but the purely divine element in the incarnation.

Clement did more than anyone else to Platonize Christian theology. Yet here, more than elsewhere, he seems very dependent if not on scholarly Stoicism, at least on a popular philosophy that was close to Stoicism. This dependence is due in part to the influence of the theologians who preceded him and whose formulations he has retained, and in part on his own eclectic formation. The key notion of "mingling" recalls the theory of a "total mingling," analogous to that of water and wine, by which the Stoics represented the compenetration of the cosmos by the divine Breath (Pneuma). The relation, whatever it be, between blood and Pneuma likewise belongs to Stoicism and at the same time to popular philosophy and the Bible; it springs from a kind of dynamic materialism, or even from animism.[84]

These are the representations Clement is still using to convey the idea of salvation and of the union of man with God, and this is the framework within which we must read this passage and situate what is said in it of the eucharist. The distinction between the two bloods of the Lord, the carnal and the pneumatic, seems to connote in this context not a disjunction but rather a conjunction of the divine and the material in the unity of the incarnate Logos. This means that here again the eucharist is not the focus of attention, but simply the point of departure for the digression. The use of wine and water and the symbolism of their mingling are the reason why the eucharist comes up at all. Clement's real concern is the divinization of the human in Christ and in every Christian. The blood of Christ and his divinity (his "Pneuma"), thanks to which this divinization takes place, are represented in the eucharist, but the eucharist is not effective independently of the blood shed on the cross and of the union of divinity and humanity through the incarnation. The eucharist is, from one point of view, the very mystery of redemption; even more, however, at least in this passage, it is the mystery of the incarnation of the Logos.

"TO EAT THE LOGOS"

In the passage we have just discussed the Pneuma was introduced because it is analogically related to blood and wine. Clement did not have to speak of the Logos in this context. The fact that he did shows the very important role the Logos plays in Clement's theology; even when the theme of the wine and drink do not require it, he launches once again into considerations of the "spiritual food," that is, of the Logos given to us as food! The image is, of course, an ancient one; it is found in Plato and in the Bible, and is frequently used by Philo Judaeus whom Clement had read extensively and profited by. It follows that such expressions as "banquet of the Logos" and "food of the Logos"[85] do not necessarily refer to the eucharist directly; in fact, they relate mainly to knowledge or "gnosis."

These expressions do, however, constitute the backdrop against which Clement sees and approaches the eucharist, and he uses one of them at least once in referring to the Lord's Supper. He is speaking of the necessary link between word (and thought), on the one hand, and action, on the other: "This is why the Lord, having taken bread, first spoke the words and gave thanks; then, after breaking the bread, he offered it to the guests so that we might eat *logikos*."[86]

We should not attempt to capture in a single English word what the final term of this sentence says and connotes. If we translate *logikos* (which is an adverb) as "with logos," we have already limited the meaning by omitting the article and the capital letter L. A minimalist reading of the sentence interprets it to mean that since he spoke vocal prayers at the Supper Jesus wanted us to share in the meal which commemorates the Supper, to the accompaniment of vocal prayers.[87] But it is perfectly clear that Clement intended to say more than that. He does not formally call for, but neither does he formally exclude, the meaning which *logikos* has in a passage like the following: "He who gave us being and life has also given us a share in the Logos, for he wants us to live both *logikos* and well. For the Logos of the Father and of the universe is not the Logos externalized [as instrument of creation] but the very evident wisdom and goodness of God, as well as his truly divine omnipotence . . . and sovereign will."[88]

The two adverbs "*logikos* and well" express the complementary duality of contemplation and action, thought and moral behavior, as in the other passage. Clement refers here to the two forms of the divine Logos, the immanent and the externalized; he refers, that is, to a Stoic interpretation of John 1.1.[89] But he emphasizes here the immanent Logos, or the Logos as interior to creation and transcendent over the world. It is clear, therefore, that in *I Str.* 46, 1, the sense is not simply: "so that we might eat *with* [to the accompaniment of] *words*," but: "so that we might eat *with the exercise of reason*" and, above all, "*with the intervention of the divine Logos*."

The whole theology of the Logos must also be supplied as background for two other texts that allude to the eucharist.

The first occurs in the discourse *Quis dives salvetur?*[90] The Savior speaks: "I give you food, I give you a bread: my very self. He who has tasted this bread no longer experiences death. Each day I offer you a drink of immortality."

These lines are part of an address in which Christ lists the benefits he gives and the hope he holds out; the eucharist is part of the list. In what Christ says of it we find the correspondence between eucharist and immortality which Clement maintains in common with the other Christians of the early centuries. The Savior is food insofar as he is the Logos, but he also presents this nourishment; he is both bread and giver of bread.

H. P. Casey and F. Sagnard have with good reason attributed to Clement himself, and not to the heretic whom he is summarizing and refuting, a passage of the *Extracta Theodoti* which exalts the Son and in which we find texts and expressions which recall those of the *Protrepticus* on the eucharist. Here is the passage from the *Extracta Theodoti*:

"He is the heavenly Bread and the spiritual food (John 6.31) that gives Life in the order both of nourishment and knowledge. He is the Light of men (John 1.4), that is, of the members of the Church.

"Those who ate the bread which fell from heaven have died, but he who eats the true Bread of the Spirit will not die (John 6, *passim*). The living Bread which the Father has given is the Son, for those who are willing to eat him. 'The bread that I will give,' he tells us, 'is my flesh' (John 6.51), whether the reference be to the bread by which the flesh is nourished in the eucharist, or whether the flesh rather be 'his body which is the Church' (Colossians 1.24), the Bread of Heaven, and the gathering that is blessed, insofar perhaps as the elect are born of the same substance as to their essential being, and destined for the same end."[91]

118

This passage, too, is a commentary on John 6.31 ff. and elaborates the idea of "spiritual food." It does not make a choice between "real presence" and "symbolism." The words "in the order both of nourishment and knowledge" may be taken as expressing an equivalence ("and" in the sense of "that is to say") as well as a disjunction ("on the one hand," "on the other hand"). The similarity to *Paed.* II, 19, 4, inclines us to see a disjunction: at the physical level, the eucharist, along with asceticism, gives immortality to the body that is destined for resurrection; at the spiritual level, the eucharist, along with teaching, gives the knowledge that likewise assures man of immortality.[92]

One thing special about this text is the naming of the Son; this, even more than the name "Logos," links the eucharist to what will later become the theology of the Trinity.[93] Even more important, however, is the introduction of the Church. "Church" here certainly means the "Church in which everyone is a 'first-born son' and a citizen of heaven" (Hebrews 12.23), the Church which exists before the creation of the world and is the model and goal of the earthly Church, and to which all the elect belong by right. In this we have the explanation of the somewhat obscure statement that ends the passage: the adoption of the elect as sons assimilates them, in substance, to the Son whose body the Church is.

Participation in the body of Christ thus is achieved through membership in the Church: in the Church as a visible evolving organism, but above all in the Church as invisible. It is probable, in our view, that the parallelism between the eucharistic bread, which nourishes the flesh, and participation in the ecclesial body of Christ signifies, in Clement's thinking, the unity of a single operation which takes on two different modalities at different levels of reality. The distinction does nonetheless exist, and it is only the bread "by which the flesh is nourished" that is linked to the eucharist.

At the end of this examination of texts, despite all the ambiguities and uncertainties, we seem to have established some of the *correspondences* we were seeking.

There is correspondence between the eucharist and certain texts from the Bible; as a result, there is also a correspondence between the visible aspects of the eucharist and what Clement calls the "economy," that is, the history of salvation. Not only is the eucharist connected to the passion of Christ, which the blood signifies; not only is it presented, at least in one text, as closely related to the paschal sacrifice of Christ; there is also a significant parallelism established between the incarnation of the Logos by the power of the Spirit (Pneuma) at his coming on earth, and the Spirit's action in the eucharist.

On the other hand, the eucharist is also connected with Christian life and the three terms in which St. Paul sums up that life: faith, hope, and love. Clement apparently is unembarrassed by the variety of the ways in which he combines these terms with those by which he defines the eucharist as well as with others that he introduces occasionally, such as the symbol of milk or the milk and honey of the promised land. Amid these variations there emerges the idea that the eucharistic mystery is related to Christian life in its entirety. This idea may not be the final word about these various terms and symbols, but it is certainly one important meaning. Similarly, the eucharistic mystery cannot be disjoined from the mystery of the Church as the body of Christ that was created before the world came to be, and as the ingathering of the elect at the end of history; the Church is responsible for the eucharist, and to it the eucharist is ordered.

If everything said of spiritual food is to be related to the eucharist (and perhaps it is), then the chief correspondence is the one between the spiritual food that is the eucharist, and the spiritual food that is the acquisition of knowledge or gnosis. The close connection between the eucharist on the one hand, and the relation of Father and Son on the other undoubtedly shows us at least the partial object of such gnosis. For, in this sense the mystery of the eucharist is the mystery of the end of time, the mystery of the salvation, immortality, and eternal life of which the eucharist gives an anticipation. On all these points, Clement is heir and witness to the orthodox tradition, to which he gives new expression.

Once we have established these various relationships, the next step would be to define their nature. We said at the beginning of this essay that the time is not ripe for attempting the solution of this and similar problems. We may, however, at least point out some of the orientations Clement seems to be adopting. First of all, in dependence on an earlier theology of a more or less Stoic cast, he thinks, or at least expresses, these relations in materialist terms of contact and mingling. Thus the physiological compenetration of man's body by the eucharistic flesh and blood has for its consequence the physical preservation and indestructibility of this body. This is a very ancient idea that had a long life in Christianity, and Clement seems to accept it.

To this kind of relations others must certainly be added. The most obvious is the one designated by the word "allegory" and related terms. It serves especially to link eucharist and gnosis.

The use Clement makes of allegory in his eucharistic theology is especially difficult to define and evaluate. In this matter it is surely a good method to interpret the more obscure by the less obscure, Clement by his successor Origen. There does not seem to be any major difference between the two writers in this area; only a detailed study, such as has not yet been made, would perhaps enable us to determine whether Origen has at times corrected, or possibly distorted, Clement's thought, but for the moment at least, the differences between the two thinkers seem to be quite minor. We are thus confronted with the difficult problem so well stated by H. Urs von Balthasar,[94] of interpreting Alexandrian theological thought. One principle which we think must be applied in seeking a solution is not to let ourselves be led astray by the philosophical, purely intellectual vocabulary these writers use. It is quite clear that gnosis leads to spiritual union as well as to intellectual knowledge, and it is in this perspective that we must consider Alexandrian eucharistic theology.

It may be, however, that like the gnostics he is refuting, Clement attempts to situate all doctrine, all of Christian life, and the eucharist in particular around two opposed poles: the level of the simple faithful and the level of the "perfect."[95] The distinction he makes between the "carnal" blood and the "pneumatic" blood of Christ may point in this direction. Origen will think that the eucharist has a different meaning for the "simple" than it does for the "intelligent"; it may be that Clement already took a similar view. At present, however, we are not really sure we have penetrated to the real foundations of his thinking; in fact, we are so sure that we have not as yet discovered the secret of his "gnosis," that any firm conclusion would be premature.

NOTES

1. The most important book of Clement is still W. Völker's *Der wahre Gnostiker nach Klemens von Alenxandrien* (TU 57; Berlin, 1952). It does not, however, entirely replace R. B. Tollinton, *Clement of Alexandria: A Study in Christian Liberalism* (London, 1914). Useful introductions in French are provided by A. de la Barre, "Clément d'Alexandrie," DTC 3 (1907), cols. 137-99, and J. Lebreton, "Clément d'Alexandrie," DSp 2/1 (1953), cols. 950-61. In English: J. Quasten, *Patrology* 2. *The Ante-Nicene Literature after Irenaeus* (Westminster, Md., 1953), pp. 5-36, and H. von Campenhausen, *The Fathers of the Greek Church*, translated by S. Godwin (New York, 1959), pp. 29-39.

E. de Faye, *Clément d'Alexandrie* (2nd ed.; Paris, 1906), is still of interest despite a "liberal" viewpoint that has now been generally abandoned. J. Daniélou's *The Theology of Jewish Christianity*, translated by J. A. Baker (Chicago, 1964), and *Gospel Message and Hellenistic Culture*, translated by J. A. Baker (Philadelphia, 1973), contain some new insights into Clement, but Daniélou has not, to our knowledge, given an overall view of this Father.

G. Bardy, *Clément d'Alexandrie* (in the collection *Moralistes chrétiens*; Paris, 1926), gives a series of extracts from Clement's writings, but in a limited perspective. There is a very succinct presentation with texts in J. Valentin, *Clément d'Alexandrie* (Paris, 1963). The *Sources chrétiennes* series contains translations (with text, introductions, and notes) for the *Protrepticus*, the *Paedagogos*, *Stromata* I and II, and the *Extracta Theodoti*.

In our dissertation *Etudes sur les Stromates* (Paris, 1966), we have attempted a comprehensive interpretation of this important work. For two particular aspects of Clement's work cf. T. Camelot, *Foi et gnose: Introduction à la connaissance mystique de Clément d'Alexandrie* (Paris, 1945) and C. Mondésert, *Clément d'Alexandrie: Introduction à sa pensée religieuse à partir de l'Ecriture* (Théologie 4; Paris 1944).

Abbreviations for the principal works: *Protr.* (*Protrepticus*), *Paed.* (*Paedagogus*), *I Str.*, *II Str.*, etc. (*Stromata* I, II, etc.), *ET* (*Extracta Theodoti*), *QDS* (*Quis dives salvetur?*). We shall use the text in the *Sources chrétiennes* series, as well as the notes there, especially those of H. Marrou for the *Paedagogus*; for the texts not yet published in SC, we shall use O. Stählin's edition in the GCS (2nd revised ed.; vol. 1, 1936; vol. 2, 1960; vol. 3, 1970). We shall follow the divisions and subdivisions of the text as established by Stählin (and used in the SC editions as well).

2. Clement is treated in general works and articles on the eucharist; among these J. Batiffol's now standard *L'Eucharistie: La présence réelle et la transsubstantiation* (Etudes de théologie positive sur l'Eucharistie, 2nd ser.; 9th ed.; Paris, 1930) will serve as point of reference and, if need be, target for criticism. The eucharist plays little part, however, in books concerned only with Clement, except in that of Tollinton which we shall generally be following. Völker's big book has only four pages on the subject (pp. 598-602); in a note (p. 598, n. 1) he briefly outlines the history of the question.

Some articles: T. Camelot, "L'Eucharistie dans l'Ecole d'Alexandrie," *Divinitas* 1 (1957), pp. 72ff. (deals especially with Origen);

C. Mondésert, "L'Eucharistie selon Clément d'Alexandrie," *Parole et pain*, no. 46 (1971), 302-8.

The publication of the Nag Hammadi papyri has turned up some interesting parallels to Clement. Cf. especially A. H. C. Van Eijk, "The Gospel of Philip and Clement of Alexandria: Gnostic and Ecclesiastical Theology on the Resurrection and the Eucharist," *Vigiliae Christianae*, 25 (1971), 94-120. We have not been able to consult H. G. Gaffron's dissertation *Studien zum koptischen Philippusevangelium unter besonderer Berücksichtigung der Sakramente* (Bonn, 1969), nor the second part of the *Tractatus Tripartitus* (fourth work in the Jung Codex), which is soon to appear and which H. C. Puech has called to our attention.

3. Camelot, *op. cit.*

4. *Paed.* II, 19-20; *I Str.* 5, 1-3; 96, 1; *IV Str.* 161, 3. Only the first of these passages is important and will be studied here.

5. We have found almost fifty references.

6. Tollinton observes that we have no right to expect answers from Clement to questions which had not yet been asked in his day (*op. cit.*, 2:156).

7. This is the case, for example, with the studies of J. Benoît, A. Orbe, J. Daniélou, and J. Moingt. But none of these, as far as I know, has dealt with the eucharist.

8. Clement has often been characterized (most recently by von Campenhausen, *op. cit.*, p. 38) as "unecclesiastical." This is evidently an exaggeration, but it is true enough that he is concerned with the Church as an eternal, invisible, eschatological reality rather than with its visible form in our present world.

9. As did A. de la Barre in his DTC article.

10. It is difficult to decide to which of these biblical texts reference is being made in *I Str.* 46, 6 (Lk 24.10, which Stählin suggests, seems to us to be excluded) and *Paed.* I, 46, 1; Matthew's text is followed in *Paed.* II, 32, 2.

11. E.g., *Paed.* I, 36, 5; 42, 3; 46, 2; 47, 1; *I Str.* 7, 1; *III Str.* 87, 1; *V Str.* 66, 2; *ET* 13, 1-4; *QDS* 23, 4.

12. E.g., *ET*, 13, 1-46.

13. *Paed.* I, 41, 2; II, 4, 2; cf. II, 6, 1-3; 9, 3; *II Str.* 50, 1. "Heavenly

food of angels" (*Paed.* I, 45, 1) is also based on Ws 16.20; Ps 77.25; Ezr 10.19.

14. *Paed.* I, 35, 3; 40, 2; 41, 3; 49, 3; 50, 3; II, 9, 1; 112, 2; III, 76, 2; *VII Str.* 104, 4.

15. *IV Str.* 161, 3.

16. *Paed.* I, 15, 3-4; 17, 2; II, 19, 3; 29, 1; 32, 3; *V Str.* 48, 8. Most of these allusions have not been noted by the editors. Cf. Tertullian, *Adversus Marcionem* IV, 40, 6 (CCL 1:657).

17. Jn 2.1-11. Cf. *Paed.* II, 29, 1, but not II, 19, 3 (despite Marrou, *op. cit.*, p. 48, n. 1).

18. Jn 19.34.

19. On these texts, cf., e.g., J. Betz, *Die Eucharistie in der Zeit der griechischen Väter*, 2/1 (2nd ed.; Freiburg, 1964).

20. *Protr.* 88, 1; *Paed.* I, 44, 1; *V Str.* 66, 3.

21. *V Str.* 136, 2-3. Cf. *Didache* 14; Justin, *Dialogus cum Tryphone* 28; Irenaeus, *Adversus Haereses* IV, 17, 5.

22. *Protr.* 116, 4.

23. *V Str.* 48, 8.

24. We leave aside the question of the possible influence of pagan cults, and especially of the Greek philosophers. The end of the *Protrepticus*, which we cite further on, mixes sure references to the Eleusinian mysteries with possible allusions to the eucharist. It would take too long to review the history of sacred meals from Homer on and of the idea of the food of the soul and the banquet of wisdom in Greek philosophy, especially after Plato. Expressions of the idea of spiritual food are common in Philo Judaeus, one of the authors whom Clement most surely used. But when Clement comes to the eucharist proper, he draws his references solely from the Bible.

25. It is not certain, therefore, that we must number Clement among the latter; it may be that he favored a stricter or, in any case, more authoritarian discrimination.

26. With Mondésert in his edition of the *Protrepticus* (and despite the reservations he expresses in his article, cited in n. 2 above), we follow A. Fortescue, *The Mass: A Study of the Roman Liturgy* (New York, 1917), pp. 28-30.

27. *Protr.* 119, 2; 120, 2.

28. The singing of the *Hagios* in the liturgy is not attested with certainty prior to the *Euchologion* of Serapion (ca. 350), but this relates to Egypt. The Apocalypse (4.8) may perhaps be evidence that it was already being sung in Asia Minor in the first century.

29. It is doubtful that the torches of 120, 1 are liturgical candles; the reference is rather to the Eleusinian mysteries.

30. Christ the Logos was also called "Father"; cf. H. Marrou's notes on *Paed.* II, 101, 1, and his edition of the *Ad Diognetum* (SC 53), p. 192, n. 3. Cf. also the Index to Stählin's edition, p. 547.

31. There may be other allusions to the eucharist in *Protr.* 88, 1; 116, 4. See text at n. 50, below.

32. Cf. *I Str.* 96, 1.

33. The word *anagnōsis* almost always refers to a reading from Scripture in an ecclesiastical if not a liturgical setting.

34. "Authentic study" is hardly an adequate description of preaching. We must keep in mind that Clement's main concern in this passage is with the gnostic, not with the liturgy.

35. *Paed.* III, 81, 1-2. Clement is afraid the practice may lead to disorder.

36. Cf. *Paed.* I, 16, 3: "Hardly touching the earth with our toes" (citation from a pagan writer?).

37. Cf. Plato, *Phaedo*, 246bc.

38. The "sanctuary" is the "holy place" of the temple, in front of the "holy of holies." Cf. Heb 9.15.

39. The interpretation of this passage is uncertain. We follow the generally accepted meaning.

40. The prayer of the gnostic here is often indistinguishable from the gnostic's continual silent prayer and the prayers at fixed times which Clement mentions, although he does not greatly favor them. Cf. A. Bekes, *De continua oratione Clementis Alexandrini doctrina* (Rome, 1942). The *eucharistia* mentioned in *V Str.* 61, 4-5, with reference to Col 8.7, may be either a private prayer of thanksgiving or the liturgical prayer accompanying the sacrifice, that is, the "canon of the Mass" (to use an anachronistic term), or both at once. Communion is envisaged in the images of food and

banquet, which we shall be discussing further on. Some of these passages (*Paed.* I, 34, 3; 51, 1) associate communion with the milk and honey of the promised land (Ex 3.8; etc.) there may be an allusion in these passages to a rite attested by the *Apostolic Tradition* (23, 1) of Hippolytus, according to which the newly baptized drank from three cups, one of wine, one of milk and honey, and one of water. According to Tollinton, Clement nowhere mentions the consecration or the epiclesis.

41. The name "Lord's Supper" is based on 1 Co 11.20. Clement does not use the expression.

42. E.g., *Paed.* II, 5, 3; *I Str.* 12, 3; *IV Str.* 92, 4; *VII Str.* 145, 5.

43. *Paed.* II, 61, 1.

44. The historians are in general agreement that the agape, which was still connected with the eucharist in the time of Ignatius of Antioch and Justin Martyr, had become a separate rite for Clement as well as for his contemporary, Tertullian, and his successor, Origen. Cf., e.g., F. J. H. Hort and J. B. Mayor, *Clement of Alexandria: Miscellanies, Book VII* (London 1902), Appendix C.

45. *Paed.* II, 77, 1; *VII Str.* 49, 4.

46. E.g., *Paed.* II, 6, 1.

47. *Paed.* II, 4, 3-4; 7, 1; *III Str.* 10, 1.

48. For the quotations in this paragraph cf. *Paed.* II, 4, 3–7, 3.

49. I.e., God.

50. *Protr.* 88, 2.

51. Cf., e.g., *Frag.* 61 (Stählin, p. 227, line 27); *VII Str.* 31, 7; 32, 5. Cf. Bekes, *op. cit.*

52. *V Str.* 66, 1-5. This passage is not usually listed among the texts that have a eucharistic meaning. Van Eijk is an exception among the authors.

53. Literally, "epoptic contemplation," a pleonasm which in the philosophers originally referred to the Eleusinian mysteries. The interpretation Clement gives here of 1 Co 3.1-2 differs from the one he gives in *Paed.* I, 6 (which we shall examine in our next section). Here his interpretation is close to that of the gnostics whom he opposes in the *Paedagogus.* It is difficult to explain this shift of view.

54. *Katalepsis* is a technical term in Stoic philosophy and means the act which gives a true and complete knowledge of an object.

55. The quoted words are from Plato, *Letter* VII, 341cd, and are to be understood in the light of the Platonic soul–body dualism.

56. Plato, *Republic* II, 378a. Such a sacrifice is the condition for revealing to a small number of initiates the secret interpretation of the myths relating to the gods. Clement again identifies the "undiscoverable victim" with Christ a little further on, in *V Str.* 70, 4 (where, with L. Früchtel and the ms, we read *aporon*).

57. In his earlier writings Clement had tended to identify gnosis and faith (cf. *Paed.* I, 6; *II Str.*). See n. 53, above.

58. *Paed.* I, 34, 3–52, 3.

59. Irenaeus relies on the same community of thought when engaging in controversy on disputed points, especially in Book III of the *Adversus Haereses*.

60. Cf. Van Eijk's remarks (based on *Paed.* I, 39, 1) in *op. cit.*, pp. 114-15. The Valentinians doubtless distinguished between the baptism of the simple and the eucharist of the gnostics.

61. *Paed.* I, 35, 1. But nothing indicates that the difference between baptism and the eucharist was connected with a difference of "kind" or "nature" between "faith" and "gnosis."

62. *Op. cit.*, p. 252.

63. Jn 6.53, modified in accordance with Mt 26.26 ff. There is no explanation for the plural "fleshes."

64. With A. Orbe we follow the mss and supply only the article: (*to*) *enarges*; there is a chiasmus.

65. A reminiscence of Plato, *Republic* VIII, 550b1, where the father "waters" (irrigates) "the young man's mind" and makes it grow. Cf. the *Phaedrus*, 243a4.

66. *Ad Trallenses* 8, 1.

67. *Adversus Haereses* IV, 38, 1-2.

68. See the critical apparatus in Stählin's edition, and Marrou's notes. None of the emendations proposed is fully satisfactory.

69. Evidence of the esoteric doctrine is (a) the two exclamations:

"Astonishing mystery!" (42, 1) and "Paradoxical mystery!" (43, 1); (b) the transition to the subsequent explanation is phrased thus: "Perhaps you do not wish to understand these words in this way, and prefer a more ordinary (*koinoteron*) explanation" (43, 2); and (c) the kinship with *VI Str.* 94-95; *VII Str.* 68, 1-2; 107, 3-6; *QDS* 37, 1-5, and other texts to which we refer in our *Etudes sur les Stromates*, pp. 483-88. Chapter 4 of St. Paul's Letter to the Ephesians seems to underlie the whole passage. We find disappointing the explanation offered by J. Quatember, *Christliche Lebenshaltung nach Klemens von Alexandrien* (Vienna, 1946), p. 192.

70. In what sense? Cf. Irenaeus, *Adversus Haereses* IV, 7, 4, and A. Orbe's commentary on it in his *Antropologia de San Ireneo* (BAC 286; Madrid, 1969), pp. 42-44 (the Logos and the Holy Spirit are the two hands of God the Creator). "Flesh" here can be taken as the flesh of Christ; cf. Mt 1.18-20; Lk 1.35.

71. A citation?

72. *Gospel of Philip*, Saying 23 (p. 57, lines 3-8, of the codex); cf. Van Eijk, *op. cit.*, p. 102.

73. We shall say nothing of the passing allusions to the eucharist in *Paed.* I, 49, 3.

74. The allegory is not completely clear. The cluster of grapes which Joshua (Jesus) brought back from the promised land (Nb 13.23-24) is a symbol of the incarnate Logos. The teacher or tutor (*paedagogus*: literally, "leader of children") is Moses or Joshua, who leads the Hebrews through the desert to rest in the promised land and, by his writings, leads them toward the Messiah; he seems to be a symbol of Logos who leads the faithful to rest in the truth and the beatific vision. The sign is perhaps the cross, perhaps also (and compatibly) the blood of the Passover lamb (Ex 12.13; 13.9). On all this see Marrou's notes.

75. Here in the sense of the revealed word, although at the beginning of the sentence the reference is to the incarnate Logos, Christ.

76. Allusion to the mingling of water with the eucharistic wine (cf., e.g. Justin, *Apologia I* 65, 3); it is a symbol of man united to Christ (cf. Cyprian, *Epist.* 63, 13, and perhaps Jn 19.34).

77. The meaning doubtless is: as his (eucharistic) blood is mingled with mankind, which is saved by its reception.

78. I avoid the term "spiritual" here because it may have misleading connotations for the reader. I know of no parallel for the distinction Clement is making, and it may be original with him, although it is based on an equivalence that goes back to St. Paul: flesh:spirit=human:divine.

79. On the connection between eucharist and immortality, cf. the discussion above on *Paed*. I, 47, 1, and cf. also Irenaeus, *Adversus Haereses* IV, 18, 5: "Our bodies which participate in the eucharist and are no longer corruptible."

80. On the relation between Pneuma and Logos cf. n. 72, above. The relation comes from a Stoicizing theology; cf. M. Spanneut, *Le Stoïcisme des Pères de l'Eglise* (Patristica Sorbonensia 1; Paris, 1957; 2nd ed., 1969), pp. 331 ff. Van Eijk, *op. cit.*, pp. 110-11, discusses Pneuma and Logos and gives references.

For the relation between the blood and the pneuma or soul cf. Fr. Rüsche, *Blut, Leben und Seele* (Paderborn, 1930); Tertullian, *De anima* 5, 2, with J. Waszink's commentary in his edition *Tertullianus: De anima* (Amsterdam, 1947), and Origen, *Discussion with Heraclites* 10, 16, with the introduction and notes of J. Schèrer in his edition, *Origène: Entretien avec Héraclite* (SC 67; Paris, 1960).

81. An obscure expression; is it a citation or allusion?

82. "Draws along" instead of "sustains" (with Mondésert in his SC translation).

83. The meaning is doubtless: "for the salvation of which."

84. On the relation between Pneuma and Logos, cf. n. 80, above.

85. E.g., *Paed*. II, 5, 3 (charity); 40, 1 (meal regulated by reason); *V Str*. 70, 1 (gnosis); etc.

86. *I Str*. 46, 1. On the difficulty of translating the word logikos̄, cf. C. Mondésert, "Vocabulaire de Clément d'Alexandrie: Le mot 'logikos,'" *Recherches de science religieuse* 42 (1954), pp. 258-65, and Marrou's introduction to the translation of the *Paedagogus* (SC 70), p. 46; Marrou speaks of "the fruitful ambiguity Clement cultivates in his use of the word *Logos*."

87. In another context, we might also understand this to be advice concerning hygiene and moderation: "Eat reasonably."

88. *V Str*. 6, 3.

89. Cf. Spanneut, *op. cit.*, pp. 310 ff.: "The Word and His Father: *Logos endiathetos* and *Logos prophorikos*," and cf. R. P. Casey, "Clement and Two Divine Logoi," *Journal of Theological Studies*, 25 (1924-25), 43-56.

90. *QDS* 23, 4.

91. *ET* 12, 3–13, 4.

92. Cf., e.g., *VI Str.* 68, 3.

93. Compare St. Catherine of Siena, "O eternal Trinity, not only have you given your Word in redemption and the Eucharist, but you have given us yourself entirely out of love for your creature"; cited in M. V. Bernadot, *De l'Eucharistie à la Trinité* (Paris, 1943), p. 35.

94. "Le Mysterion d'Origène," *Recherches de science religieuse*, 26 (1937), 513-62; 27 (1938), 38-64.

95. Cf. E. H. Pagels, "A Valentinian Interpretation of Baptism and Eucharist and Its Critique of 'Orthodox' Sacramental Theology and Practice," *Harvard Theological Review*, 67 (1972), 153-69.

TERTULLIAN

Tertullian wrote treatises on baptism and penance,[1] but none on the eucharist. What he has to say about the eucharist is fragmentary and occasional, and is scattered through his writings; it is marked more by warmth of feeling than by clarity, and provides bits of information about the eucharist at Carthage in the first twenty years of the third century. Locating these bits and pieces in the framework of the life and thought of that Church in that era is a task requiring great patience. Its successful execution is not guaranteed by the pains we take to do it well.

Those interested in pursuing the study of the eucharist in Tertullian's writings are thrown back on a secondary literature that is chiefly German and Protestant and that is evidently influenced rather heavily by the anti-sacramental and anti-eucharistic positions of the Reformation. The Catholic works written in the first decades of the twentieth century were intended as replies to the Protestant interpretation of the Fathers of the Church, Tertullian among them, and consequently were written under the aegis of the apologetics to which the writers felt constrained when it came to the dogma of the eucharist. This tendency is especially evident in the work of Pierre Batiffol. But, if we bear these facts in mind and take account of the shifts in emphasis and perspective that are often required, these Catholic works of the past continue to be indispensable tools for us today.[2]

It is in these writings that we have collected the texts of Tertullian which we shall be analyzing here. Our aim is to discover the characteristic vocabulary of Tertullian on the

eucharist and to see what he has to say about the nature
and celebration of the eucharist.

A EUCHARISTIC VOCABULARY

Tertullian introduced a certain number of Latin words and
expressions for the eucharist that were to become an integral part of the Church's traditional eucharistic vocabulary.

When Tertullian is thinking chiefly of the meal in the
course of which the eucharist was instituted, he speaks of
"the supper of God," "the banquet of God," or "the banquet of the Lord."[3] He speaks frequently of "oblation" or
"to offer"[4]; this noun and verb, though referring properly
to a specific moment of the celebration, can be used by
metonymy for the entire service. The same is true of the
word "eucharist," whether it be transliterated from the
Greek or transposed into Latin[5]: The "thanksgiving"
which is the central part of the service ends by referring not
only to the eucharistic rite in its entirety but also to the
mystery of salvation that finds expression in the rites.
Other terms indicate an aspect of the eucharistic assembly;
for example, the means used to enter into communion with
God, namely, "the prayer of sacrifice," or the solemnity
which characterizes the entire rite, as in "the solemnities of
the Lord."[6]

In other passages, Tertullian speaks of the matter of the
sacrifice. He describes it either in the usual terms of bread
and wine, or by expressions that bring out the sacral
character the material now possesses: "the sacrament of
the bread and cup," or by the expression that would become the standard one: "the sacrament of the eucharist,"
or even by the Lord's own words: "This is my body; this is
my blood."[7] When speaking of the eucharistic species, he
uses the adjective *sanctus* in its neuter form (*sanctum*) which
becomes a noun with a technical meaning and passes on to
posterity with this connotation.[8]

These various expressions and terms were quite traditional, for we find Greek equivalents of them in the authors of the first two centuries.[9] What Tertullian did was to establish the Christian meaning and usage of the corresponding Latin terms.

A EUCHARISTIC CELEBRATION

In many passages of his works Tertullian speaks of eucharistic assemblies, even if he does so incidentally. There are two passages which give us some detail.

GENERAL TEXTS

The lengthier of the two is from the *Apologeticum*, chapter 39, numbers 2-6:

"We gather into an assembly so that we may besiege God with hands full, as it were, of petitions. This kind of violence pleases God. We pray for the emperors, their ministers and men of authority, for the well-being of the world, for peace, and for the postponement of the end.

"We gather for the reading in common of the divine writings, according as present circumstances urge us to admonition for the future or acknowledgment of the past. We carefully nourish our faith with these holy words, restore our hope, strengthen our trust, and at the same time confirm ourselves in good habits by bringing the precepts home to ourselves.

"There too we hear exhortations, chastisements, and reproaches from God. For one is judged there with great severity, as is fitting for those who are sure of God's presence. It is indeed a supreme anticipation of the future judgment for a sinner to be excluded from the community of prayer, from the assembly, and from the entire holy exchange.

"Presiding over the assembly are tested elders, who have not bought the honor but possess it by reason of witness.[10] In fact, no gift of God can be bought with money. We do have a treasury, but it is not filled by initiation fees, as though we bought our religion. No, each person makes a modest contribution once a month or whenever he wishes, but he must be willing and able to do so. No one is forced to contribute; he contributes freely. The contributions are as it were the deposits love makes, and are not spent on banquets or drinking parties or fruitless visits to taverns, but on feeding and burying the poor, young men and women who are without fortune and family, aged servants who cannot work any longer, and people who have suffered shipwreck, while those who have been condemned to the mines or exile on the islands or prison (provided it be for belonging to the religion of God) are provided for as soon as they have made their confession."

This passage, in addition to telling us something of the ordinary life of the Christian community at Carthage, indicates the principal features of the Christian assemblies: prayers, readings from Scripture, exhortations, collections for the sake of the poor and the confessors of the faith. The community's life, daily and liturgical, is carried on under the authority of "tested elders."

A second passage, much shorter, again lists the features of an assembly, but with the conciseness Tertullian likes: "The Scriptures are read, psalms are sung, sermons are given, prayers are offered" (*De anima* 9, 4).

We must note, however, that in neither passage does any detail tell us that Tertullian is talking about assemblies for the eucharist. The general course of the gathering as here described applies to a non-eucharistic agape as well as to a eucharistic synaxis. If we are to turn this framework into one specifically for a eucharistic assembly, we must look for other scattered hints and indications.

In the sentence from the *De anima*, Tertullian lists the components of a Christian assembly—readings, songs, preaching, and prayers—in the order in which they already appear in Justin Martyr's *First Apology*.[11] It is the traditional order, and we shall follow it as we attempt to reconstruct the eucharistic celebration of Tertullian's day.

The Readings [12]

The readings are taken chiefly from the "sacred literature" or the "writings." Tertullian speaks expressly of readings from the prophets and the letters of the apostles. The word "prophet" should doubtless not be taken in its narrow sense but understood rather as meaning "an author of the Old Testament." As for the letters of the apostles, if we take Tertullian with complete literalness, we must conclude that in his day they were read only in the Churches to which they had been addressed. This restrictive interpretation is not certainly correct, however. We know, for example, that the Scillitan Martyrs (died 180), who were from an unidentified town in North Africa, had with them during their hearing before the proconsul "the sacred books and the letters of Paul, a just man."[13] It is likely that these sacred texts were not meant solely for the private edification of these martyrs but for public reading in the course of the liturgy.

In what order were the writings read? There can be no question of a "continuous reading" such as has become popular once again in our day, for Tertullian explicitly mentions readings chosen according to circumstances.

We know that in Africa, in the time of Tertullian and later, readings were taken not only from the Bible but from non-biblical sources as well, and especially from the Acts of the martyrs. The *Passion of Perpetua and Felicity*, which dates from a little after 203 and may have been given its form by

Tertullian himself, seems to have been composed with liturgical reading in view.[14] It was still being read during Mass in Augustine's day, as he himself tells us on several occasions.[15]

The Psalms [16]

The singing of psalms was very widespread among both Catholics and heretics, whether for private devotion or for assemblies: the agape, the synaxis, and funerals, especially those of the martyrs. The entire Christian use of the psalms was an outgrowth, of course, of earlier Jewish custom.

Tertullian is the first to give us any information on how the psalms might be sung. In *Apologeticum* 39, 18 we read: "Each person is invited to take the floor and sing to God according to his ability, whether he draws upon the divine writings or upon his own creative talent." The person thus described is the cantor or leader of song, but the congregation also takes part. In *De oratione* we learn that "those who are more fervent in prayer usually add to their prayers the alleluia and the kind of psalm to which the congregation may respond by using the final words" (no. 27). Here we have one of the earliest witnesses to Christian responsorial singing.

Preaching [17]

We know almost nothing about this. Tertullian mentions it simply in the form of "exhortations" or "sermons" that are meant to "confirm ourselves in good habits by bringing the precepts home to ourselves." It was thus concerned chiefly with morality. Tertullian tells us nothing of its themes and methods or of the point in the assembly at which it took place.

Prayers

In the long description in *Apologeticum* 39 prayers are mentioned at the beginning, while in the *De anima* 9, 4 they come at the end of the list. It is very likely that the last place is the proper one, if at least "prayers" refers to the prayer of the faithful and the eucharistic prayer. Could Tertullian be referring, in *Apologeticum* 39, to another category of prayer, comparable to our present prayer of the day, which would have come first in the liturgy of the word? It is possible that this is the correct interpretation of the text on which we drew above, when speaking of singing and the psalms,[18] but this is a point on which we really cannot gain any certainty. We can, however, shed a bit more light on the prayer of the faithful and the eucharistic prayer. We shall turn now to these two kinds of prayer.

The Prayer of the Faithful

The historians of the Christian liturgy generally distinguish two forms of the prayer of the faithful. One resembles that which has been restored in the West as a result of the recent liturgical reform. The other is a litanic prayer. It is not always easy to determine to which of the two the Fathers are referring. In the discussion of Tertullian, in particular, the scholars have tended to blur the distinction. For this reason, we think it necessary to approach the problem of the prayer of the faithful somewhat differently for Tertullian, and to distinguish the intentions of this prayer from its forms.[19]

It is easy to discern two types of prayer intentions, one relating to the Church, the other to the civil authorities. The ecclesial intentions are listed in those treatises which deal with instruction and discipline within the Church, as, for example, the *De oratione*. The intentions relating to the civil authorities are mentioned in the apologetic treatises addressed to emperors or proconsuls, as, for example, the *Apologeticum* and the *Ad Scapulam*. Ecclesial intentions are not necessarily omitted, however, in this second class of treatises; the passage from *Apologeticum* 39 which we cited earlier is good evidence of this.[20]

Tertullian is not as clear when it comes to the form of this prayer of the faithful. In particular, he tells us nothing of the way in which the faithful participated in it. He does tell us, as clearly as we could wish, how such a prayer concluded: it is "offered to God through Jesus Christ." He also refers to the posture adopted at prayer: in praying, Christians raised and opened their hands.

One further question may be asked about this prayer of the faithful: How is it related to the Lord's Prayer? Why should such a question arise? Because in one passage Tertullian seems to be saying that the Lord's Prayer was said just before the kiss of peace.[21] But, as we think we have shown elsewhere,[22] at Carthage, from the time of Tertullian to that of St. Augustine exclusive, the kiss of peace was exchanged before the offertory. This means that the Lord's Prayer, too, was said before the offertory. But, in our opinion, this amounts to saying that the Lord's Prayer was part of the prayer of the faithful.

The Offertory

We just mentioned the offertory in connection with the kiss of peace. Many texts of Tertullian show quite clearly that the faithful took an active part in the offertory.[23] He never had occasion to describe the action of the faithful, but he does tell us the material brought to the altar at the offertory, namely, bread and wine and, at a baptismal Mass, milk and honey.[24]

The Eucharistic Prayer

Tertullian speaks of offering thanksgiving to God over the bread.[25] He also mentions in passing several of the themes elaborated in this eucharistic thanksgiving. Basic, of course, is the very "thanking" which gave the Christian liturgy its very name of "eucharist." Another theme closely linking to the first is that of "anamnesis" or "remembering," since praise and thanksgiving almost necessarily in-

139

volve a recall of God's blessings and benefactions. Tertullian puts it this way: "It is right that every man in every time and place should praise God when he recalls, as he should, God's blessings."[26]

We should observe that Tertullian's words here are to be found almost unchanged in the traditional Roman prefaces. Other words and phrases which became part of the later anaphoras may have won their place in the Carthaginian form of the eucharistic prayer by the beginning of the third century. We recently studied the case of the phrase "figure of the body and blood of Christ" as applied to the eucharistic species; Tertullian attests its use, and it may go back, via the Marcionites, to the eucharistic prayers of about 150 A.D.[27] A number of words found both in Tertullian and the ancient Roman Canon[28] raise an analogous question: Is Tertullian citing them from eucharistic prayers of his day? Or is the Roman Canon deriving them from the writings of Tertullian? The answer is not as easy as the conclusion to which our just-mentioned study of *figura corporis et sanguinis Domini* led us.

The Communion
The faithful usually accepted the eucharistic bread in their hands and immediately consumed it. Usually, too, they received under both kinds.[29] After receiving the species they responded with an "Amen,"[30] which supposes that the minister distributing communion spoke some words of presentation. In certain circumstances the faithful took the eucharist home with them: to distribute it to the sick or to communicate themselves on days on which the eucharist was not celebrated.[31] Daily communion seems to have been the regular practice.[32]

A EUCHARISTIC FAITH
We must not attempt to reconstruct Tertullian's beliefs concerning the eucharist by forcing his texts into our cus-

140

tomary theological categories. Instead, we must learn of these beliefs from Tertullian himself by poring over the important texts in which he speaks of the eucharist and in the light of which we must try to understand his faith in the eucharist.

ESSENTIAL TEXTS

We shall give these texts in their chronological order and offer enough comment on each to make it immediately intelligible. The first text, then, is from the *De oratione* which was written between 200 and 206.

"This petition 'Give us today our daily bread' we understand rather in a spiritual sense, for Christ is our bread because he is life and bread of life. 'I am the bread of life,' he says, and, a little earlier, 'The bread is the word[33] of the living God that has come down from heaven.' In addition, his body is a kind of bread: 'This is my body.' Consequently, in asking for daily bread, we are asking to live forever in Christ and never to be separated from his body" (*De oratione* 6, 2).

Tertullian gives two interpretations of the words "daily bread": material bread and bread that feeds the soul. He prefers the second interpretation, and in regard to it makes a further distinction between the spiritual food contained in the word of God, and the spiritual food which is the body of Christ.

The reader may have noticed that the Latin text of John 6.33 is not the same as in the Vulgate.[34] This is not surprising, of course, since the Vulgate did not yet exist. The text of Scripture with which Tertullian was familiar is called the African text. On the other hand, the African text is attested only from Cyprian's time forward,[35] and in none of the recensions of the African text that have survived do we find the word *sermo* ("word," "discourse") in John 6.33 as Tertullian does: "The bread is the word of the living God

141

that has come down from heaven." We may think, therefore, that Tertullian had Matthew 4.4 in mind and introduced the word *sermo* into John 6.33 because he was thinking of Christ's doctrine as one form of food for our souls.

A second text is from the *Adversus Marcionem*, which was
written in 207–208:

"Jeremiah gives you an allusion to this wood [Psalm 96.10:
'The Lord has reigned from the tree'], when he tells the
Jews that they will say: 'Come, let us cast wood into his
bread' (Jeremiah 11.19 LXX), that is, into his body. For
thus has God revealed it in the very Gospel you [Mar-
cionites] accept, when he calls bread his body. He thus
enables you to understand that he who made bread the
figure of his body is the same whose body the prophet had
formerly described under the sign of bread, while the Lord
himself would later interpret this mystery" (*Adv. Marcion.*
III, 19, 3-4).

In approaching this text we must keep in mind that Tertullian's main objective in the *Adversus Marcionem* is to refute
Marcion's dualism, according to which the two Testaments
are the work of opposing gods, so that the Old Testament
cannot be an anticipation of the New. Tertullian has an
easy time showing the harmony of the two Testaments. In
our passage he emphasizes the harmony by the two adverbs "formerly" and "later" (*retro* and *postea*): Christ, by
his life and teaching, is the "interpreter" of the "mystery"
of the Old Testament. Tertullian, a born debater, does not
pass up the opportunity for an *ad hominem* argument; here
he uses a text from the gospel which the Marcionites themselves accept.[36] For our purposes, however, we should
note especially the implicit citation of the account of institution.

The next passage is from the fourth book of the *Adversus
Marcionem*; here Tertullian is attacking not only the dualism
but the docetism of Marcion:

142

"The bread which he [Christ] took and gave to his disciples he turned into his body with the words 'This is my body,' which means 'This is the figure of my body.' There would have been no figure had the body not been real, for a phantom is an empty thing and there can be no figure of it. In addition, if Christ has only pretended to make the bread his body, because in fact he had no real body, then it is also bread he must have handed over for us; in other words, he catered to Marcion's docetism [*vanitatem*] by causing bread to be crucified! But then we should go a step further and ask why Christ called bread his body and not rather a melon which Marcion put in place of the heart? No, Marcion did not understand that bread was an ancient figure of the body of Christ, who tells us through Jeremiah: 'They have plotted against me, saying, "Come, let us cast wood into his bread,"' that is, impose the cross on his body. Thus Christ, interpreter of the things of old, made it quite clear what he had intended the bread to mean [in the prophecy] by calling bread his body" (*Adv. Marcion.* IV, 40, 3-4).

In refuting Marcion's dualism Tertullian bases the harmony of the Scriptures on the unity of God's action. The same God spoke through the prophets and speaks in the New Testament; or rather it was already Christ himself who spoke through Jeremiah. The divine action was also progressive: first, through the mediation of the prophets, Christ spoke using figures; later on, speaking and acting in his own name, he interprets and fulfills what the figures meant.

To the docetists, the body of Christ was a phantom, an empty thing (*vacua res*). It is in this perspective that we can understand Tertullian's words *vanitatem Marcionis* which we have translated interpretatively as "Marcion's docetism." In proving that the historical body of Christ was real and not a pretense, Tertullian takes the eucharistic body as his starting point, and develops an argument from the absurd consequences that follow from the Marcionite

143

presupposition. If Christ's body was only a phantom, then all of his activities were fictitious; indeed, if we are to be logical, we must say that Christ should have handed bread over to be crucified. Tertullian does not make explicit the contrasting, valid argument; he leaves that to his readers. The argument is that if Christ handed his body over and not bread, then his body was real; not only was his historical body real which was nailed to the cross, but his eucharistic body, given to us in the bread, is also real.

Our final text is from this same passage of the *Adversus Marcionem* (IV, 40, 6):

"With much greater clarity, the Book of Genesis[37] . . . , had already forecast the traits of Christ in the person of Judah: 'He will wash his robe in the wine and his garment in the blood of the grape' (Genesis 49.11). His robe and garment mean his flesh, and the wine his blood. He has now also [*ita*] consecrated his blood in the wine, who long ago made the wine a figure of his blood."

Tertullian makes two comparisons in this passage. One has to do with the passion of the Lord, the second with his eucharist, but each is correlative to the other. Genesis 49.11 was one of the classical "prophecies" of the passion, according to the Fathers,[38] and this is why Tertullian speaks of Judah as prefiguring Christ. The other comparison, as we said, concerns the eucharist, and in this context we may repeat an observation made long ago, that Tertullian uses the word "consecrate" to designate a "sacramental action."[39] It is less easy to know for sure to what Tertullian is alluding when he speaks of Christ having long ago made "the wine a figure of the blood." Yet, unless we do violence to the context, must we not say that it undoubtedly refers back to the text of Genesis that was quoted only a moment before, and that the blessing given to Judah contains not only a prophecy of the passion but a prefiguration of the eucharist?

This twofold prophecy brings the cross and the Supper into close relationship. The words "now" and "long ago," in the last sentence relate simply to the "figure" and the "sacrament" of the eucharist, but the adverb *ita*, which we have translated as "also," connects the two meanings, soteriological and eucharistic, of the blessing of Judah. In another work, Tertullian seems to give the reason for this connection when he says that Christ "consecrated the wine as a memorial of his blood."[40] In these words we hear an echo of Christ's words: "Do this as a memorial of me," and of St. Paul's commentary on them: "Until the Lord comes, therefore, every time you eat this bread and drink this cup, you are proclaiming his death."[41] This means that Tertullian is tacitly attributing to Christ himself the connection between passion and eucharist: each corresponds to the other, not only because the second is the ritual memorial of the first, but because the second draws its power from the first.

ASPECTS OF THE DOCTRINE

We must be careful to avoid giving systematic form to teaching which its author never pulled into a synthesis. We shall therefore present Tertullian's teaching rather as a series of aspects which the texts bring to light.

The first aspect is that of "figure" (*figura*). The noun and the related verb *figurare* occur several times in texts in which Tertullian is speaking of the eucharist. We recently studied the liturgical origins of the term *figura* as applied to the eucharist[42]; here we shall simply try to determine the meaning Tertullian gives it.

The chief difficulty in making such a determination arises from the fact that in his debate with the Marcionites Tertullian uses any argument he can find and plays with meanings as well as words. This kind of play is especially evident when he attacks the docetism of Marcion.[43] Here, without giving his reader any warning, he shifts from the current meaning of *figura*, which depends on the verb *fingere* from which it is derived and which points to something objectively real, to its prophetic meaning.[44] We may suspect that at times Tertullian was fooled by his own playing with meaning; others certainly have been so fooled.[45] In any event, as far as *figura* is concerned, this kind of shift is the exception rather than the rule, since Tertullian habitually give it its prophetic meaning.

The prophetic meaning is clearly the one intended in *Adervsus Marcionem* IV, 40, 3-4, which we cited a few pages back. Here Tertullian speaks of Jeremiah's words (in 11.19 LXX)[46] as "an ancient figure of the body of Christ" because they foretell both the passion and the eucharist, since the eucharist is the "bread in which he renders his body present anew,"[47] that is, makes the passion present and effective. The prophetic sense also shows clearly in *Adversus Marcionem* III, 19, 3-4: "He who made bread the figure (*figura*) of his body is the same whose body the prophet had formerly described (*figuravit*) under the sign of bread."

In this last passage the parallelism, which is certainly deliberate on Tertullian's part, forbids us to give two different meanings to *figura* and *figuravit*. The meaning is rather that, just as the body of Christ was "figured," that is, foretold, in the bread of which the prophet speaks, so the eucharistic bread is a figure, that is, foretells, the body of Christ as handed over to death on the cross.

In the third passage from the *Adversus Marcionem* (IV, 40, 6) in which the word appears, the prophetic or typical sense is quite clear, as we have seen.[48]

It follows from our analysis that the historians, both Protestant and Catholic, who have dealt with Tertullian have been mistaken in their interpretation of the eucharistic use of *figura*. The Protestants have seen in "the figure of the body of Christ" a mere symbol, while the Catholics have attempted to show that the "figure" is coextensive with the reality, just as in the Scholastic analysis the species are the sign of the real presence.[49] In fact, however, Tertullian never even raised the problem the historians are dealing with. For him the eucharistic bread is a "figure" of the body of Christ because, as St. Paul tells us, the eucharist proclaims the death of the Lord until his second coming. We may deliberately turn Tertullian's formula around and say that the eucharist is the figure of the passion or that the eucharistic body of the Lord is the figure foretelling his crucified body.

The second aspect of Tertullian's eucharistic thinking to which we would like to call attention is his belief in the *real presence*. The words "real presence" do not occur, but the reality meant by these words is there. Tertullian's eucharistic realism shows in several texts. According to the *De oratione*, to communicate is to receive the body of Christ. On fast days some Christians were afraid that they would break their fast by receiving communion. Tertullian tells them that they should receive the body of Christ but not eat it until the hour comes for ending the fast; in this way they will be doubly blessed: by participating in the sacrifice that unites them to God and by fulfilling their duty of observing the fast.[50] We know, of course, from other sources that the Christians of Carthage used to take the eucharistic species home with them so that they might communicate themselves on days when there was no liturgy.[51]

Those who distribute or receive the eucharist unworthily "attack the body of Christ": "The Jews laid hands on Christ only once, these people wound his body every day."[52] In the eucharistic bread, then, the historical Christ really "renders his body present anew,"[53] not only during the time when the eucharist is being celebrated, but in a lasting way.

The reality transcends the limits of the eucharistic species, so much so that the sacrament provides a food as abundant as the banquet that greeted the prodigal son on his return home; the communicant "feeds upon the abundance of Christ's body, that is, the eucharist."[54] This realism, which a modern scholar has characterized as "dynamic,"[55] suggests that we should think of the eucharistic bread at Carthage as being not a thin wafer of unleavened bread but a piece of bread that could indeed allay hunger. Elsewhere Tertullian says in even earthier terms that our "flesh feeds on the body and blood of Christ so that the soul too may grow fat on God."[56]

Tertullian does not speculate on the precise moment of consecration nor on the manner of the real presence. We shall look in vain in his writings for a hint of the doctrine of transubstantiation.[57] He is satisfied to know that the Lord made bread into his body by saying: "This is my body."[58] In our day too (ita et nunc),[59] the word of God "consecrates" the eucharist.[60] Tertullian does not say whether this consecration takes place in virtue of the words of institution or in virtue of an epiclesis.

The last aspect of the eucharist that should be noted in Tertullian is the *sacrificial aspect*. To begin with, the eucharist is a genuine sacrifice that fits into the general framework of the sacrifices of old: it is a "prayer of sacrifice," it is celebrated at an altar, it binds (*obligat*) man to God, and communion is a "participation in the sacrifice."[61] Above all, however, it is the true sacrifice, "the new sacrifice" which was prefigured by the Old Testament sacrifices, and the priest of which is Christ.[62] But depending on whether he is addressing the faithful or refuting non-Christians, Tertullian emphasizes either the ecclesial or the spiritual character of the sacrifice.

The eucharistic sacrifice is celebrated under the presidency of elders,[63] but the whole community takes an active part in it by means of two very definite rites: the offertory and the communion. Each of these requires the ministry of a priest.[64] Thus Tertullian clearly affirms both the ecclesial and the hierarchic character of the Christian sacrifice.

At the same time, the Christian sacrifice is eminently spiritual in nature. It is rather surprising to see what difficulties of interpretation this emphasis in Tertullian has caused one of the recent historians of his thought. It is our opinion that if the texts and the words are not forced to answer questions and satisfy an exegetical outlook that are on the whole rather modern, but are instead placed in their proper historical context, terms like *censeri*, *repraesentare*, and *figura* will cause difficulty to no one who does not depend on a philosophy and vocabulary that originate with Kant. We showed earlier in this essay that *figura* does not mean symbol as opposed to reality. Similarly, the other two words, far from excluding the reality of the eucharistic sacrifice, make no sense unless they presuppose this reality.

It is, however, chiefly because modern scholars have failed to situate some other texts in their true historical context, that they have found these difficult to harmonize with Tertullian's eucharistic realism. Thus the treatise *Adversus Judaeos* and the defenses addressed to emperors and other civic authorities attack practices and mentalities that emphasize bloody sacrifices and funeral rites which are unconnected with any moral and religious conscience and instead are reduced to the level of magic. It is to these practices and this mentality that Tertullian contrasts the spiritual nature of Christian worship. He can say that as compared with such pagan practices and attitudes Christians have no altars; they do not offer sacrifice in that way.[65] By comparison with pagan sacrifices the Christian sacrifice is spiritual and pure, and supposes, on the part of the faithful who offer it, "a chaste body, an innocent soul, a holy spirit."[66] It consists in a prayer by which they offer God the Christ who is present in the bread[67] and immolated again.[68] Such statements are, of course, quite traditional. They are to be found in Justin[69] before Tertullian, and in Cyprian after him,[70] but always in a comparable anti-pagan and anti-Jewish context.

A genuine sacrifice, a sacrifice of the Church, a spiritual sacrifice: these are the main points in Tertullian's teaching on the eucharistic sacrifice. He was not concerned to integrate them, or his views on *figura* and on the real presence, into a synthesis. He is content simply to emphasize them when they are relevant to his defenses and polemics. We have tried to approach them as he did.

In conclusion, let us try to isolate the main lines of Tertullian's eucharistic practice and thinking.

As far as the eucharistic celebration is concerned, we should observe that as reflected in Tertullian's writings it is traditional and Catholic until the Montanist period of his life. In fact, if liturgical customs could acquire a hold on a mind so strong and easily roused, they must indeed have belonged to a sure and well-defined tradition. On the other hand, there is an evident disproportion between the information he gives us on the liturgy of the word and that which he gives us on the eucharistic liturgy proper. He speaks often of the former, and usually in detail; by contrast, he has little to say about the latter. The difference may be due simply to his not having had occasion or need to speak more often of the eucharistic liturgy proper. In addition, once the organized catechumenate began (and such a catechumenate is first attested at Carthage in Tertullian's day), the "discipline of the secret" (*disciplina arcani*) also came into play.[71] Whatever the cause, we must accept the fact: Tertullian tells us less than Justin did about the eucharistic rites proper.

The opposite is true of the Church's eucharistic faith; on this, Tertullian's testimony is clear, even if it is also occasional. What he bears witness to is less a theology than the faith itself, a faith whose Scriptural foundations are many and obvious. The Old Testament is for him an arsenal of eucharistic "figures," the fulfillment of which he sees in the sacrifice of Christ. In the New Testament he looks chiefly for the words, teaching, and precepts of the Master. He elaborates simultaneously a defense of the person and work of Christ and an attack on the sacrificial theories and practices of the enemies of Christianity.

It can be said, however, that in the apologetic and polemical writings we see the first outline of a positive teaching that follows a method of investigation and certain lines of thought. The method of investigation is typological exegesis, while Tertullian's eucharistic thinking has for its focus a sacramental and sacrificial realism; for Tertullian, the eucharist means real presence and true sacrifice. On the other hand, contrary to his procedure in dealing with baptism, he has little to say about the sign aspect of the eucharist. This is unfortunate, since by emphasizing it for baptism he ended up giving us not only a detailed description but a developed doctrine of the sacrament. He has given us neither for the eucharist.

NOTES

1. *De baptismo* (PL 1:1197-1224; CSEL 20:201-18; CCL 1:277-95; SC 35, ed. F. Refoulé). *De paenitentia* (PL 1:1227-48; CSEL 76:129-70; CCL 1:321-40).

2. F. X. Dieringer, "Die Abendmahlslehre Tertullians," *Der Katholik*, 44/1 (1964), 277-318. C. L. Leimbeck, *Beiträge zur Abendmahlslehre Tertullians* (Gotha, 1874). A. d'Alès, *La théologie de Tertullien* (Paris, 1905), pp. 355-70. A Struckmann, *Die Gegenwart Christi in der hl. Eucharistie nach den schriftlichen Quellen der vornizänischen Zeit* (Vienna, 1905), pp. 227-74. Ph. Scharsch, "Eine schwierige Stelle über die Eucharistie bei Tertullian (Adv. Marcion. 4, 40)," *Der Katholik*, 89/2 (1909), 21-23. B. Stakemeier, "La dottrina di Tertulliano sul sacramento dell'eucarestia," *Rivista storico-critica delle scienze teologiche* (1909), pp. 199 ff., 265 ff. P. Batiffol, *L'Eucharistie: La présence réelle et la transsubstantiation* (9th ed.; Paris, 1930), pp. 355-70. Fr. Dölger, "Sacramentum infanticidii," *Antike und Christentum*, 4 (1934), 108-228. *Idem*, "Zu

151

dominica sollemnia bei Tertullianus," *Antike und Christentum*, 6 (1940), 108-17. F. R. M. Hitchcock, "Tertullian's Views on the Sacrament of the Lord's Supper," *Church Quarterly*, 134 (1942), 21-36. E. Dekkers, *Tertullianus en de geschiedenis der liturgie* (Brussels–Amsterdam, 1947). J. Quasten, *Patrology* 2. *The Ante-Nicene Literature after Irenaeus* (Westminster, Md.), pp. 335-37. J. de Watteville, *Le sacrifice dans les textes eucharistiques des premiers siècles* (Neuchâtel–Paris, 1966), pp. 103-24.

3. *Cena domini* (*De spect.* 13); *Convivium Dei* (*Ad uxor.* II, 8); *Convivium dominicum* (*Ad uxor.* II, 4).

4. *Oblatio* (*De cor. mil.* 3; *Ad uxor.* II, 2; *De exhort. cast.* 11; *De praescr.* 40); *offerre* (*De virg. vel.* 9; *De exhort. cast.* 7; *De cult. fem.* II, 11; *Adv. Marcion.* IV, 9).

5. *Eucharistia* (*De praescr.* 36; *De pudic.* 9, 6; 17, 8; *De orat.* 19; *De cor. mil.* 3; *Adv. Marcion.* IV, 34); cf. Th. Schermann, "*Eucharistia* und *eucharistein* in ihrem Bedeutungswandel bis 200 nach Christus," *Philogogus*, 69 (1910), 375-410. *Gratiarum actio* (*Adv. Marcion.* I, 23; IV, 9).

6. *Sacrificiorum orationes* (*De orat.* 19); *dominica sollemnia* (*De fuga in presec.* 14; *De anima* 9, 4); cf. Fr. Dölger, "Zu dominica sollemnia bei Tertullianus" (n. 2, above). *Sacrificium* (*De cultu fem.* II, 82; *De orat.* 18; *De exhort. cast.* 11).

7. *Panis et calicis sacramentum* (*Adv. Marcion.* V, 8); *eucharistiae sacramentum* (*De cor. mil.* 3; *Adv. Marcion.* IV, 34). Allusions to the gospel account of the Last Supper: *De anima* 17, 13; *De orat.* 6; *Adv. Marcion.* IV, 40. *Corpus domini* (*De idol.* 7; *De orat.* 19).

8. *Sanctum* (*De spect.* 25).

9. For these authors see the other essays in this volume.

10. "Witness" can be taken actively, as the testimony these elders have given to Christ, or passively as the testimony others have given to them. Either interpretation is possible, but the second seems more probable.

11. Cf. the essay on Justin in this volume.

12. *Apol.* 22; 39; *De anima* 9, 4; *De cult. fem.* II, 11; *De praescr.* 36; 41; *De pudic.* 1, 7.

13. Cf. H. Leclercq, "Scillitains (martyrs)," DACL 15 (1950), col. 1020.

14. Cf. H. Leclercq, "Perpétue et Félicité (saintes)," DACL 14 (1939), col. 398.

15. *Ibid.*, cols. 410-11.

16. *Adv. Marcion.* V, 8; *Ad uxor.* II, 8; *Apol.* 2.39; *De anima* 9, 4; *De carne Christi* 20; *De exhort cast.* 10; *De ieiun.* 13; *De orat.* 28; *De spect.* 25; 29; *Scorp.* 7. Among these texts we must distinguish those that refer to private usage from those that refer to the liturgical use of the psalms.

17. *Apol.* 39; *De anima* 9, 4.

18. See, above, the citation from *De orat.* 27.

19. *Ad Scap.* 2; *Adv. Marcion.* IV, 9; *Apol.* 21; 28; 30; 32; 39; *De bapt.* 20; *De idol.* 7; *De orat.* 2, 29.

20. At the beginning of this section, "A Eucharistic Celebration."

21. *De orat.* 18, 1-2: Some, "when they fast, say the prayer with the brethren, but refuse to exchange the kiss of peace which is a seal set upon the prayer. But when are we to exchange peace with our brothers if not at the moment when the prayer which has been especially recommended to us (*oratio commendabilior*) is rising up? . . . What prayer can be complete when separated from the holy kiss?"

22. V. Saxer, *Vie liturgique et quotidienne á Carthage vers le milieu du IIIe siècle* (Vatican City, 1969), pp. 231-43.

23. In addition to the texts listed in n. 4, above, cf. *Ad uxor.* II, 5; *Adv. Marcion.* I, 14, 23; III, 19; IV, 26; *De resurr. mort.* 26; *De monog.* 10.

24. Cf. *Adv. Marcion.* I, 14, 3: even the "superior god" of the Marcionites has not rejected "the mixture of milk and honey with which he [the Creator] feeds his infant children." The Africans called neophytes *infantes*, whatever their biological age.

25. *Adv. Marcion.* I, 23, 9.

26. *De orat.* 3, 2.

27. V. Saxer, "Figura corporis et sanguinis Domini," *Rivista di archeologia cristiana*, 47 (1971), 65-89.

28. Dekkers, *op. cit.*, pp. 57-59, refers to *Deus vivus et verus, oblatio rationabilis, Melchisedech summi Dei sacerdos*, and others.

29. *Apol.* 39; *De resurr. mort.* 8, 3.

30. *De spect.* 25.

31. *De orat.* 19.

32. *De idol.* 7.

33. Or "discourse" (Latin: *sermo*).

34. [The Vulgate reads: *Panis enim Dei est, qui de caelo descendit.*—Tr.]

35. Cf. H. von Soden, *Das lateinische Neue Testament in Afrika zur Zeit Cyprians* (TU 33; Leipzig, 1909), p. 519. Cf. also Augustine, *Tractatus in Joannem* 25, 13 (CCL 36:255).

36. We should remember that Marcion simply cut out of the New Testament any texts contrary to his thesis.

37. In the blessing of Judah (Gn 49.8-12).

38. Cf. J. Daniélou, *The Theology of Jewish Christianity*, translated by J. A. Baker (Chicago, 1964), p. 105; P. Prigent, *Justin et l'Ancien Testament* (Paris, 1964), p. 322.

39. Batiffol, *op. cit.*, p. 224.

40. *De anima* 17, 13.

41. Lk 22.19; 1 Co 11.26.

42. See n. 27, above.

43. See, above, the translation and discussion of *Adv. Marcion.* IV, 19, 3-4, IV, 40, 3-4, and IV, 40, 6.

44. The "prophetic sense" is also and more often called the "typical sense."

45. Cf., e.g., Batiffol's exegesis of the passage, *op. cit.*, p. 221.

46. The words "Come, let us cast wood into his bread" are found in the ancient translations that were based on the Septuagint; modern translations based on the original Hebrew have an entirely different reading.

47. *Adv. Marcion.* I, 14, 3.

48. Again, see our translation and discussion of the passage, above.

49. Cf. Batiffol, *op. cit.*, p. 221.

50. Cf. *De orat.* 19.

51. Cf. *Ad uxor.* II, 5.

52. *De idol.* 7, 3.

53. *Adv. Marcion.* I, 14, 3.

54. *De pudic.* 9, 16.

55. De Watteville, *op. cit.*, p. 111.

56. *De resurr. mort.* 8, 3.

57. Cf. Batiffol, *op. cit.*, p. 225, n. 1.

58. *Adv. Marcion.* IV, 40, 3.

59. *Adv. Marcion.* IV, 40, 6.

60. *Ibid.*

61. *De orat.* 19.

62. Cf. *Adv. Jud.* 5, 4 and 7; 6, 2; 7, 1.

63. Cf. *Apol.* 39, 5 (*seniores* = the Greek *presbuteroi*).

64. Cf. *De exhort. cast.* 11, 2 (*per sacerdotem*).

65. Cf. *De spect.* 13.

66. *Apol.* 30, 5.

67. Cf. *Adv. Marcion.* I, 14, 3.

68. Cf. *De pudic.* 9, 11.

69. Cf. the essay on Justin in the volume.

70. Cf. Cyprian, *Testimonia* I, 20, 21; II, 2, and Saxer, *Vie liturgique*, pp. 197-99.

71. Cf. Batiffol, *Etudes d'histoire et de théologie positive*, first series (7th ed.; Paris, 1926), pp. 19-24, 24-29.

CYPRIAN OF CARTHAGE

Everyone is aware how important a witness Cyprian is to Christian tradition. His well known *Letter* 63 is "the only ante-Nicene writing that deals exclusively with the celebration of the eucharist."[1] It has even been called "the most notable document on the eucharist in the Christian literature of the first three centuries"[2] and is thus uniquely important for our knowledge of the life of the Church in the third century and for the history of dogma. We may look beyond this particular document, moreover, and assert that the whole movement of Cyprian's thought is eucharistic. In this essay, we shall first situate Cyprian's pastoral action, in its general lines, against the background of the third-century African Church. We shall try to define the above-mentioned movement of thought by seeing how Cyprian treats the eucharist as a memorial, in its relation to the Church, and its relation to martyrdom.

THE CONCERNS OF A PASTOR

Cyprian was first and foremost a pastor. He was an African by birth and temperament, a man whose head was "full of a tradesman's good sense and a sailor's dream."[3] Though he did not possess the genius of a Tertullian or an Origen, he was nonetheless one of those personalities who attract others and who thus exert a considerable influence on the course of events. He knew his own limitations but also his own abilities and his own dignity. He knew men and how to govern them; he was prudent but also dogged, level-headed and yet a mystic.

Cyprian was converted to Christianity around the year 245, under the influence of an elderly priest, after being a

156

rhetorician and a great pleasure-seeker.[4] He was ordained a priest in about 248 or 249 and consecrated a bishop shortly after; it is as a bishop that we see him at work. His election to the episcopal office led to disaffection on the part of five older priests, but this became secondary when in the first months of 250 the Decian persecution put the Carthaginian Church to the test. Cyprian chose flight and exile; his purpose, according to *Letter* 20, was that he might be able still to advise and help his people at this critical time. His exile did not last long, for he was reunited to his people a little after Easter, 251.

He now found himself in a difficult situation, for in the short time he was away a good deal had happened. Some blamed Cyprian for having fled, and even went so far as to try to usurp his authority. This situation had to be straightened out, and the task was not easy. He also had to try to handle the matter of the *lapsi* or "fallen," those who had not been able to hold out in the face of persecution. In general, he had to give new life to the Christian community.

Meanwhile, other events complicated things. At Rome, the attacks of Novatian on the papacy led to a schism and created a real storm (*Epist.* 55, 3) that made itself felt even in the churches of Africa. At Carthage, a violent and devastating plague swept through the city. The bishop acted with great energy, organizing the necessary help and keeping up the courage of the people. For "among us strong hope and firm faith are flourishing; amid the ruins of a collapsing world our spirit remains erect, our courage unshaken, our spirit ever joyous, and our souls sure of their God.[4a]

In his last years Cyprian had to deal with the question of the validity of baptism administered by heretics and, in so doing, he came into conflict with Pope Stephen. In the persecution of Valerian (257) martyrdom put an end to this and all the other battles. It also made it perfectly clear that here was a man who, when the Lord's time came, was willing to put the seal of his blood on a life completely dedicated to the service of the Church.

This very brief outline of Cyprian's career will enable us to appreciate his activity. This activity was crowded into a short period full of events that were sometimes brutal and always decisive for the life of the Church. Cyprian had to do his work amid persecutions and the numerous difficulties that beset the Christian community of Africa both in its internal life and in its relations to the other Churches, especially the Church of Rome. Like every great period of development and persecution, this one tested the faith of Christians; it led to defections that at times were staggering in number, but it also led to manifestations, spectacular or not, of extreme heroism.[5] Cyprian's age was an age of confessors and martyrs but also of crowds and renegades.

Cyprian has left us an unsparing picture of the period; it cannot fail to impress us, even when we have made allowance for exaggerations due to style or circumstance. A period of peace leads to laxity in almost every area of life, says Cyprian in his *De lapsis*: "There is no religious zeal left among the priests, no unalloyed faith in the ministries, no compassion in works, no moral discipline."[6] Everyone knows how virgins consecrated to the Lord have taken to sleeping with men, and that one of the latter is a deacon.[7] But should that surprise us? "At the first threats of the enemy a great number of the brethren betrayed their faith. It was not the assault of the persecutor that overthrew them; no, they threw themselves down in a voluntary fall."[8] The cowardice of Christians, their greed, their fear of torture: Cyprian puts it all down in his treatise.

At the same time, we must not forget the throng of those who remained faithful, all the "confessors who won renown by proclaiming publicly their beautiful name [of Christians] and who covered themselves with glory by their courage and faith."[9] Defection and fidelity are thus the two sides of the picture; both characterized a period in which the Church showed an astonishing vitality and range of activity. In the episcopate of St. Cyprian alone seven councils were held (from the spring of 251 to the fall of 256); some of them were extremely important, since they determined how the *lapsi* were to be handled and what position was to be taken on the rebaptism of heretics.[10]

Even these few indications will give us an idea of the trials the Church of Africa had to endure in this period of its growth. Against this background we are better able to handle and understand Cyprian's *Letter* 63, which deals with the eucharist and was long entitled "On the sacrament of the cup of the Lord."

LETTER 63 ON THE EUCHARIST

The letter was written in 253 and is a remarkable document on the sacrament of the Lord's body and blood; it provides testimony of the utmost importance on the Church's eucharistic faith and practice in the third century.[11] It will therefore be worth our while to analyze the text carefully by following the movement of Cyprian's thought, and only then to attempt a synthesis of this thought.

We know the circumstances that gave rise to the letter: some bishops, out of ingnorance or simplicity, were not doing what Jesus Christ, author and teacher of this sacrifice, had commanded should be done with regard to the consecration of the Lord's cup and its distribution to the Christian people (1, 1). In some places it had become customary to place only water in the Lord's cup (11, 1); the reason for this, it seems, was the fear that "by using wine for the morning sacrifice one might smell of Christ's blood" (16, 1) and thus be more readily found out in time of persecution. But surely this is to be ashamed of Christ. In addition it is contrary to evangelical and apostolic teaching.

159

"We must be faithful to tradition and do only what the Lord did before us, by using a mixture of wine and water in the cup we offer as a memorial of him" (2, 1). For "the blood of Christ, by which we have been redeemed and given life, cannot be in the cup unless it contains wine, since wine symbolizes the blood of Christ, as the figures and testimonies of the entire Scriptures show" (2, 2).

The problem Cyprian had to deal with was "aquarianism," the practice of using water alone, instead of wine mixed with water, for the celebration of the eucharist.[12] The practice had doctrinal roots in the Encratites and Ebionites; it persisted and even became a rather significant problem from the time of Irenaeus to that of Pope Gelasius. Are we to see in the practice which Cyprian criticizes a remnant or ramification of some kind of Judaizing Christianity? Possibly, but Cyprian's silence on the point leaves it a mere hypothesis.

Cyprian is careful not to accuse his brother bishops; he prefers to attribute their behavior to ignorance or thoughtlessness (hardly a convincing explanation) and, in the case of the faithful who receive such a eucharist, to fear (which may well be a manifestation of a doctrinal deviation). Cyprian confesses that he does not know where such a practice can have come from (11, 1); we are not in any better position to determine its origin. Such, then, are the facts as Cyprian's letter makes them known to us.

Having given the circumstances which led to his writing, Cyprian sets about showing the solid reasons for using wine in the eucharist. The basic reason is that wine is a figure of Christ's blood, as the Scriptures prove. In the Old Testament, Noah (3, 1), Melchisedech (4, 1), Abraham (4, 2), Solomon (5, 1), Judah (6), and Isaiah (7) foretell that the Lord will use wine and not water.[13] Water by itself is a figure of baptism, not of the eucharist: "whenever water is mentioned by itself in the sacred Scriptures, it is baptism

that is foretold" (8, 1). Only after being baptized with
water and receiving the Holy Spirit through this baptism
can one drink the cup of the Lord (8, 3).

But why spend time on long arguments when the example
of the Lord himself is evident? He taught us "by the authority of his example to mix wine and water in the cup"
(9, 1).

"On the eve of the day when he suffered, he took the cup
and blessed it and gave it to his disciples with the words:
'All of you, drink of this. This is the blood of the covenant,
which will be offered for many for the forgiveness of sins. I
tell you: I shall not drink again of this product of the vine,
until I drink new wine in the kingdom of my Father.' In
this passage we find that the cup the Lord offered contained a mixture and that what he called blood was wine.
We can see, then, that the blood of Christ is not offered if
the wine is missing from the cup, and that the sacrifice of
the Lord is not properly celebrated unless our gift and
sacrifice correspond to the passion. Then again, how shall
we drink new wine, product of the vine, with Christ in the
kindgom of his Father unless in the sacrifice of God the
Father and Christ we offer wine, and unless we mix the
cup according to the tradition of the Lord?" (9, 2-3).

Cyprian is here citing the account of institution as given by
St. Matthew (26.28-29). Subsequently, he relies on Paul in
his First Letter to the Corinthians (11.23-26). His point is
clear: we must do at the eucharist what the Lord did at the
Last Supper and thus fulfill the prophecies; if we do not do
what the Lord did, we do not do as he commanded: "If the
Lord prescribes, and his apostle repeats and confirm, that
whenever we drink the cup in the Lord's memory we are to
do what he himself did, then evidently we do not observe
what has been commanded us unless we do what the Lord
did and hold to the divine instruction by mixing wine with
water in the cup" (10, 2).

161

The conclusion is obvious: The disciples must not depart from the evangelical prescriptions; they must, in their turn, do what the Master did and taught.

But we must still try to grasp the symbolism of the water and wine. The water by itself cannot represent the blood of the Lord, since the cup of the Lord is a cup that intoxicates and is wholly good (Psalm 22 [23].6) and since a cup that inebriates surely has wine in it, [14] inasmuch as water never makes anyone intoxicated. On the other hand, the water does represent the people, as the Apocalypse (17.15) shows. This symbolic meaning of water is to be found in the mystery of the cup:

"Since Christ carried us all and bore our sins, we can see that the water rightly symbolizes the people, and the wine the blood of Christ. When the water is mixed with the wine in the cup, the people are being mingled with Christ, and the throng of believers are brought into union with him in whom they believe. The mingling and union of wine with water in the cup of the Lord is indissoluble, just as the Church, that is, the people who are in the Church and who faithfully and courageously persevere in the faith can never be separated from Christ but will remain bound to him by a love that makes of the two one.

"When we consecrate the cup of the Lord we cannot offer water alone, any more than we can offer wine alone. If we offer wine alone, the blood of Christ is present but without us; if the water is alone, then the people are there alone, without Christ. But when the one is mingled with the other and the two fuse to become one, then the spiritual, heavenly mystery is accomplished.

"The cup of the Lord, then, cannot contain water alone or wine alone but only a mixture of the two, just as the body of the Lord cannot be flour alone or water alone but only a mixture of the two that is required for making bread. Here we also find the unity of the Christian people represented: Just as many grains are brought together, ground, and mixed so as to form a single loaf, so in Christ, the heavenly bread, there is, as we well know, only one body, and with it our multiplicity is united and fused" (13).

This beautiful passage is very important for Cyprian's thinking. It points out not only the symbolism of the water and wine, but also and especially the ecclesial dimension of the eucharist, the very close relation between Church and eucharist. The eucharist "makes" the Church. In the eucharist the bread and the wine are inseparable, both as regards their reality and as regards the symbolism inherent in their union. In the eucharist which the Church celebrates, the people of God are united to Christ and become one in him. We shall return later on to this basic text when we come to speak of the ecclesial aspect of the eucharist.

For the moment, and given the point which Cyprian's thinking has reached at this stage of the letter, one conclusion is inescapable: We cannot follow those who offer water alone in the Lord's cup, for in so doing they do not themselves follow the Lord; we must rather obey without reserve and "do what Christ did and ordered us to do" (14, 1), for he led the way in offering himself to the Father in sacrifice. The need for such obedience is evident, since "for certain, the priest exercises the same function as Christ only if he does what Christ did; he offers to God the Father, in the Church, the true and complete sacrifice only if he offers as he sees Christ himself offering" (14, 4).

There is thus no reason for not faithfully observing what has been divinely commanded. Besides, if we are ashamed to drink the blood of Christ,[15] we run a great risk; we condemn ourselves to impotence when it comes to shedding our own blood for Christ. Martyrdom is a consequence of the eucharist; that is, men draw strength for martyrdom from the eucharist, and we may even say that martyrdom has its roots in the eucharist.

Cyprian's argument is now complete. He spends the rest of the letter refuting the objections of the Aquarians. This refutation is of less interest in itself than for the further information it can give us. Thus we learn that the eucharist was celebrated in the morning in memory of the resurrection, and not in the evening, as some wanted, in memory of what Christ did in the evening at the Supper. For, says Cyprian, "the reason why Christ offered his sacrifice toward the end of the day was to signify by the very hour itself that the world's day was declining and had reached its evening" (16, 2). What he has in mind here is surely that the paschal mystery of Christ has renewed the world.[16] The eucharist is celebrated in memory of the passion and resurrection of Christ (17, 1).

Cyprian's letter to Caecilius, Bishop of Biltha, now draws to a close. He has written this letter from a sense of piety and fear of the Lord, from a sense of duty, and from a concern to be faithful and to correct certain deviations (19, 1).

What have we learned from this letter? In addition to the information Cyprian gives us concerning the Church's life at the time, as he tells us of his pastoral concerns, the letter also gives us a broad view of the meaning of the eucharist. With the testimony of the Old and New Testaments as his basis, Cyprian develops a whole typology of the eucharist, and this in turn leads him to explain the symbolism of the water and the wine.

In so doing, Cyprian also conveys a theology of the eucharist, since image and reality are not opposed but go together. The image refers us to the reality, and the reality can be understood only by means of the image. Because of this relationship and interaction, it becomes clear that the eucharist is Christ's great gift to his Church and that it is his sacrifice. Cyprian certainly thinks of the eucharist as a true sacrifice; it contains the sacrifice of Christ, and from this sacrifice it derives its efficacy. The Church celebrates the eucharist in memory of Christ and in obedience to his will.

In addition, the Church is kept in being by the eucharist. Cyprian pushes this idea quite far: as he sees it, the eucharist "makes" the Church, it may even be said to be the Church. Logically, then, it is very important that those who offer the eucharist and those who partake of it should conform their lives ever more fully to that of Christ; they must become like him to the point of being wholly united to him by martyrdom.

We shall now discuss in greater detail these three essential aspects of the eucharist according to Cyprian: the eucharist as memorial sacrifice, the eucharist and the Church, the eucharist and martyrdom.

IN MEMORY OF CHRIST

Cyprian is undoubtedly "one of the Fathers that insisted most" on the sacrificial character of the eucharist.[17] This is clear from his vocabulary in which terms such as *sacrificium*, *commemoratio*, *passio*, and *oblatio* appear almost automatically. *Letter* 63 is especially eloquent in this respect.

We who have been redeemed and given new life by the blood of Christ offer the cup in memory of him or as a memorial of him (*in commemoratione ejus*: 63, 2, 1). In fact, the entire celebration is a memorial of the Lord (63, 10, 2), for it is *dominicae passionis et nostrae redemptionis sacramentum*: the sacrament or sacramental representation of the Lord's passion and our redemption (63, 14, 3). In this action the priest takes the place of Christ, the High Priest who first offered himself in sacrifice, and offers the sacrifice *in commemoratione*, "in memory of him," as has been

165

prescribed (63, 14, 4). The priest celebrates a memorial of the passion; he offers a sacrifice. In fact, the sacrifice consists in being a memorial or remembering of the passion (*mentio passionis*); the memorial of the passion must be understood as being, however, the very passion of Christ: *passio enim Domini sacrificium est quod offerimus*, "The Lord's passion is the sacrifice we offer" (63, 17, 1). There is an identity between Christ's sacrifice on Calvary and his sacrifice in the eucharist. For Cyprian, the eucharist is a true sacrifice; it is the sacrifice of the cross. Strong language, indeed!

But how are we to understand these various statements? On the one hand, there is the sacrifice of Christ; on the other, the *commemoratio* of this sacrifice, that is, a sacramental action which contains within itself the full reality of Christ's sacrifice or *passio*. The sacrifice, then, is alway one and the same, but its mode of existence varies. Cyprian emphasizes both the *commemoratio* and the correspondence there must be between the sacrifice of Christ on Calvary and the eucharist. For "the sacrifice of the Lord is not properly celebrated unless our gift and sacrifice correspond to the passion" (63, 9, 3).

To what, concretely, does the term *passio* refer? For Batiffol, "the word *passio* always means the Supper, and it is extremely important to remember this when we interpret the text we have cited (93, 17, 1). For it follows first of all, that in our sacrifices, that is, when we offer the sacrifice, we mention not the passion in the sense of the Savior's death on the cross, but the Supper."[18] But is it valid thus to oppose the Supper and the cross? According to de la Taille it is not: "The Supper, the Supper at which the eucharist was celebrated, is included in the passion; it is part of it." The two are aspects of a single mystery and "the two form, in Cyprian's view, a unity that is in no way artificial."[19]

What de la Taille says is true enough, but it remains a fact that in *Letter* 63 *passio* refers most of the time to the Supper.

On the other hand, Cyprian knew that Christ accomplished his sacrifce fully in the Supper and the cross taken together as two parts of a single totality. Thus there is no opposition. The eucharist is the memorial of the Lord's Supper; it is also the memorial of his passion and resurrection. It is a memorial which contains in a mysterious way the reality of the historical fact. [20] For Cyprian the eucharist is a *commemoratio*, a true sacrifice, and a *sacramentum*, a true sacrament. [21] It is the memorial of Christ.

In summary, we can say that for Cyprian there is an identity between the sacrifice of Christ and that of the Church by way of the *mentio passionis* that is made in the eucharistic prayer. [22] The Church commemorates the sacrifice of Christ, and it is in the *mentio*, the *commemoratio* of the sacrifice of Christ that the Church's sacrifice consists. At the same time, however, the sacrifice of Christ as commemorated by the Church must find expression and actualization in the Christian's life, [23] in the form of a sacrifice that may lead him to martyrdom. But, before we take up this point, we must say something about the ecclesial aspect of the eucharist.

EUCHARIST AND CHURCH

The ecclesial aspect of the eucharist is very clear in Cyprian's writings, especially in *Letter* 63, in the essay on *The Lord's Prayer*, and in the treatise on *The Unity of the Catholic Church*; it also emerges in the *De lapsis* and in the letters dealing with the problem of the apostates and with their readmission to ecclesial communion. The dates of the first three works just mentioned is of some importance. For the date of *De oratione dominica* we must, in accordance with M. Réveillaud's convincing arguments, "go back before the beginning of the Novatian schism and thus before the spring of 251." Réveillaud proposes that Cyprian composed this little work for beginners (that is, those who had just received baptism) in the first months of 250. [24] The treatise *De unitate ecclesiae catholicae* is from the Novatian period, when Novatian rose up in opposition to Cornelius who had just been elected pope in 251, and created a schism and sent delegates to Africa.[25] Finally, *Letter* 63, as we noted earlier, was written in the fall of 253. We shall begin our discussion, therefore, with the *De oratione dominica*.

In this little treatise Cyprian refers three times to the eucharist. First, he urges his readers to recall the reserve and modesty that are proper "when we come together in union with our brothers (*in unum cum fratribus convenimus*) and celebrate the divine sacrifices with God's priest" (4). In the second text, Cyprian is commenting on the fourth petition of the Our Father: "Give us this day our daily bread." He writes:

"The words can be understood both in a spiritual sense and literally. In God's providential plan, each of these two interpretations is useful for salvation.

"Christ is the bread of life; this bread does not belong to everyone, but to us. Just as we say 'our Father' because he is the Father of those who know him and believe in him, so too we say 'our bread' because Christ is the bread of those who, like us, are united to his body. We ask that this bread be given to us each day. We do so for fear lest, though we are in Christ and receive his eucharist daily as the food of salvation, we may be brought up short by some serious sin; then we would be excommunicated and proscribed, the heavenly bread would be forbidden us, and we would be separated from the body of Christ.

"Christ himself tells us this when he says: 'I, who have come down from heaven, am the bread of life; if anyone eats of my bread, he will live forever. The bread I shall give is my flesh for the life of the world.' He says here that whoever eats his bread will live eternally; he means to say that they live who are united to his body and who, having the right to communicate, do in fact receive the eucharist. We must pray with fear, then, lest any of us, being excommunicated, be separated from the body of Christ and thus be deprived of salvation. For Christ warned of this when he said: 'If you do not eat the flesh of the Son of Man and drink his blood, you will not have life in you.' This is why each day we ask that our bread, Christ, be given to us: so that we may remain in Christ, be sanctified by him and thus receive life, and not be separated from his body."[26]

Finally, in no. 23, Cyprian speaks of the people as united (*plebs adunata*) by the unity which exists in the Father, Son, and Holy Spirit. This unity of the people, however, has the eucharist for its context, as *Letter* 63 makes clear (cf. *Epist.* 63, 13).

These three texts relate to the eucharist and unity.[27] It is in unity that the brethren gather in order to celebrate with the priest the sacrifices, that is, the eucharist, which, in *The Unity of the Catholic Church*, is called the sacrament of unity (no. 7). The brethren must persevere in their unity. Now that they are in him, they are united in his body, his mystical body. To be separated from this body means that after being excommunicated or proscribed they can no longer have access to his eucharistic body.

This, then, is the sequence of ideas: To receive Christ's body is to be joined to his body; to be forbidden, through excommunication, to be in communion with Christ's body in his eucharist is to be separated from the body of Christ; and to be separated from his body is to be no longer authorized to receive his body. "Body of Christ," for Cyprian, evidently means either his eucharistic body or his ecclesial body. The two are inseparable. If we are in Christ we are in the Church and have access to the eucharist. The two bodies are united, and their unity depends in turn on the unity of the Triune God, who is Father, Son, and Spirit.

Such is Cyprian's thought at its deepest level. We find it expressed, no less vigorously, in response to the threats leveled at the ecclesial body. It is with these that the *De unitate ecclesiae catholicae* deals. Here the emphasis shifts. Dissensions are growing among the faithful and even among the heads of the Christian communities (*Epist.* 11; 14; 16; 41; 42; 43; 44). This is the period when Novatian's activity is in full swing and threatening the unity of the episcopal college. Carthage soon has direct experience of two schismatic bishops, Maximus and Fortunatus (beginning of 252). All these circumstances cause a shift in Cyprian's pastoral and theological activity; he now concentrates on developing the ideas of the *sacramentum unitatis* (*Epist.* 45) and the *Ecclesia mater*. [28] The result is a collection of fine texts (*De unit. eccl.* 5; 6; 7; 19; 23 . . .) in which Cyprian endeavors energetically, and with tender affection, to give expression to his great love for the Church.

For our purposes, three texts are especially important, since in them the relation of eucharist to Church emerges clearly.

First of all, Cyprian lifts his voice against those who dare rend the unity of God, the Lord's garment, the Church of Christ; these are the people who leave the Church and establish their dwelling elsewhere, thinking that they can also celebrate elsewhere the Passover of Christ. But the Lord's Passover must be eaten in a single house! "The flesh of Christ, which is the holy thing of the Lord, cannot be thrown outside; and for believers there is no other house than the one Church."[29] The eucharist is to be celebrated in the Church of Christ; outside that Church there can be no true eucharist.

In addition, to break peace with the brothers and withdraw from the Church is to break peace with God and separate oneself from his body. That is why the Lord tells the man who approaches the altar to offer a gift, that if he has a disagreement with his brother he should first go and make peace with that brother and only then return and offer his sacrifice (Mark 11.25).

"Christ turns away from the altar the man who comes for the sacrifice with dissension in his heart. He orders such a man to be reconciled to his brother and only then, once peace has been restored, to return and offer his gifts to God. God turned his face away from Cain's offerings, and Cain could not find God's welcome because his heart was filled with jealousy and was not at peace with his brother.

"What peace can they expect who are enemies of their brothers? What sacrifices do these rivals of the bishops think they can celebrate? Do they think that Christ is with them when they assemble outside Christ's Church?" (*De unit. eccl.* 13).

After all, how can we be united to Christ if we are separated from his body? And how can we have access to his body, the eucharist, if by our own fault we are separated from our brothers?

"There is only one God, one Savior, one Church, one faith, one people united in a solid physical unity by the cement of concord. Unity is indivisible; a body cannot lose its cohesion or be broken apart, its vitals torn and fragmented [and still remain a body]. Anything that separates itself from the life-giving center cannot live and breathe in isolation; it loses its saving substance" (*De unit. eccl.* 23).

We must not fool ourselves: the unity of a body cannot be fragmented! In a striking aphorism Cyprian writes: "You cannot have God for Father if you do not have the Church for mother" (*De unit. eccl.* 6). A person condemns himself when he separates himself from the Church outside which there is no salvation.

"Does he think he remains united to Christ when he acts against the priests of Christ and when he breaks with

Christ's clergy and people? He turns his weapons against the Church and does battle against the ordinances of God. He is an enemy of the altar, a rebel against the sacrifice of Christ, a foe of the faith instead of remaining loyal to it, sacriligious instead of devout; he is a disobedient servant, an insolent son, a brother turned enemy. He scorns God's priests and bishops and dares erect a different altar, compose illicitly a different prayer, and dishonor the true victim, our Lord, with false sacrifices. He does not realize that the man who resists God's will is punished for his reckless boldness with chastisement from on high" (*De unit. eccl.* 17).

There can be no true sacrifice, then, outside the true Church of Christ. To break away from the unity of the Church is not to have access any longer to the body of Christ, not to be able to share that body any longer, and not to be mingled any longer in the cup of Christ.

"When the Savior takes the bread that is made from the coming together of many grains, and calls it his body, he shows the unity of our people, which the bread symbolizes. And when he takes the wine that is pressed from many grapes and grains and forms a single liquid, he shows that our flock is composed of many who have been brought into unity" (*Epist.* 59, 5, 2; cf. 63, 13, 4).

This very expressive text recalls the well-known petition of the *Didache* (9, 4): "Just as the bread broken was first scattered on the hills, then was gathered and became one, so let your Church be gathered from the ends of the earth into your kingdom."[30] Whatever judgment may be passed on the similarity and dependence between the two texts, it is clear that for Cyprian the unity of the bread, the unity of the wine, the union of the water and wine in the cup (cf. *Epist.* 63, 13), the unity of the people, the unity of the Church, and the unity of the eucharist all form a whole, the elements of which cannot be separated. To attack one of the elements is, in the long run, to attack the whole. For

Cyprian, as for Ignatius of Antioch,[31] there is but a single Lord, a single eucharist, a single Church, a single faith, a single Spirit, and, beyond a doubt, a single baptism. How, then, can Novatian and the heretics claim to offer the sacrifice when they do not maintain the unity of the Church (cf. *Epist.* 69, 5, 2; 70, 2, 2)? They are cut off from the sources of grace because they have broken away from the unity of the body of Christ; they have lost everything in losing communion with Christ.

The word "communion" (*communicatio*) is one that occurs often in Cyprian's writings,[32] especially in dealing with the *lapsi*, that is, those who in time of persecution offered sacrifice to idols or become parties to such an action. They now need to be reconciled to the Church so that they may have access to the body of Christ; they have great need of this body if they are not to fail again in the new testing that may come.[33] *Communicatio* means their new unity with the Church and restored access to the eucharist; consequently it also means union with Christ through communion with his eucharistic body and his ecclesial body, under the leadership of the bishops as the visible bond of unity among the brethren.[34]

For Cyprian, then, the eucharist is sign, call for, source, and fruit of unity. The eucharist effects the one Church that is in communion with Christ. But at the same time the Church effects the eucharist in communion with the one shepherd and under his guidance. The unity of all looks always to Christ as to the source and goal of all true unity, for Christ contains us all. Consequently, the eucharist is the *sacramentum unitatis*, the sign and manifestation of the reality it contains and continuously effects, so that there is a ceaseless reciprocal action between Christ, the Church, and the eucharist: Christ is at the source, the eucharist at the term, and the Church at the center of this interaction. But this center is one that tends constantly to move toward the term while at the same time drawing ever closer to the source whence it derives its power. Consequently, the unity signified at the level of the assembly becomes a reality as a result of the access which the eucharist gives us to Christ, the matchless priest who offers the one sacrifice, his and ours, to the Father and thereby becomes the one in whom all fullness is found.

EUCHARIST AND MARTYRDOM

There is a final point to be discussed. In Cyprian's thinking, by celebrating the eucharist, partaking of the body of Christ, and sharing his cup, we learn to become ourselves a eucharist, that is, an offering or sacrifice. We become this in everyday Christian life, by acts of charity that express our unremitting concern for our brethren, but also and especially by the total gift of self in the act of martyrdom, which configures the Christian to the sacrifice of Christ. This relation between eucharist and martyrdom needs to be understood in several ways: it may be a question of celebrating the eucharist for those called upon to shed their blood or of remembering in the eucharist those who have already undergone martyrdom; it may be a question of the eucharist as a support or strength for martyrdom, or, more accurately, a source or principle leading to martyrdom; or it may also be a question of martyrdom understood as a sharing in the eucharistic sacrifice and thus in the sacrifice of Calvary, or of the eucharist as a connecting link between the Church and martyrdom. These various aspects are found separately or together (and at times intermingled), especially in the letters and in the other writings dealing with the *lapsi*. [35]

At the beginning of the Decian persecution (in 250), Cyprian writes from his exile to his very dear brothers, the priests and deacons of Carthage, and urges them to visit the confessors in prison (but to do so with discretion, in turns, and in small groups) and to offer the sacrifice in their presence (*Epist.* 5, 2). These confessors, who have been

174

"placed upon the threshing floor of the Lord . . . like win-
nowed grains of precious wheat . . . and like heavy clusters
of ripe fruit in the vineyard of the Lord," need to be supported "by prayer in common during the sacrifice" and by
"private prayer" so that they may have the strength to
confess Christ to the end by draining the cup of martyrdom
and shedding their blood "like wine pressed from the
grape" (*Epist.* 37, 1 and 2).

This last text, with its somewhat poetic character, has
eucharistic overtones. It even reminds us to some extent of
the desire of Ignatius of Antioch to become the wheat that
is ground by the teeth of wild beasts so that he may be a
pure bread of Christ (cf. his *Letter to the Romans* 4, 1). But
the parallel stops there. For Ignatius of Antioch, martyrdom, conceived as a form of eucharist, is something he
passionately desires for the sake of complete union with
Christ. Cyprian's outlook is calmer and broader (see his
Letter 81, which may be regarded as his testament). He had
evident mystical tendencies but he was also a realist.
Above all, he was concerned about his fellow men, who
were weak and yet were being called to become a pure
sacrificial offering for the sake of Christ. He had to help
them, support them, and give them the cup of Christ's
blood to drink, so that when the moment came they might
find in it the strength to shed their own blood for Christ as
generous, mature Christians.

Cyprian sees martyrdom, therefore, not as something to
wax enthusiastic about, but as something difficult, de-
manding, necessary, and requiring preparation. The sol-
diers of Christ must prepare for martyrdom each day, "re-
flecting that the blood of Christ is shed daily for them to
drink, in order that they in turn might be able to shed their
blood for Christ" (*Epist.* 58, 1). In this way, the eucharist
becomes an invitation to martyrdom and a preparation for
it. It gives the Christian the body of Christ for food and

thus gives him the power to reject the soul-killing sacrifices of the pagans and to cling to Christ alone by becoming like him (*Epist.* 58, 9).

Throught the daily celebration of the divine sacrifice, the eucharist prepares men to become victims and offerings to God (cf. *Epist.* 57, 3). By approaching the altar, celebrating the sacrifice, and sharing in the body and blood of Christ, a man becomes himself a sacrifice, since there ought to be conformity between the offerer and his offerings, between the eucharistic sacrifice and the spiritual sacrifice that is martyrdom, just as the *lapsi* established a bond of likeness between themselves and the gods to whom they offer sacrifice (cf. *De lapsis* 2, and various examples in 25–26).

The same forging of a bond of likeness is brought out in *De orat. dom.* 24 in connection with the sacrifices of Abel and Cain, but also on the basis of the symbolism in the eucharist: the bread and wine are called to become the body and blood of Christ, and we, like them, are called to become a sacrifice by sharing in the sacrifice of Christ. When we drink Christ's blood, we are learning to shed our own blood for him. If we are ashamed to drink the blood of Christ, we condemn ourselves to being unable to shed our blood for him (*Epist.* 63, 15). From this it is clear that the eucharist calls for martyrdom but is also the source of strength for martyrdom, just as martyrdom is a sharing in the eucharistic sacrifice and therefore in the sacrifice of Christ.

These various considerations determine Cyprian's attitude to the *lapsi*, as *Letter* 57 explains. It is to living men that communion should be restored, living men who need to be "protected by the body and blood of Christ":

"Since the eucharist is meant to protect those who receive it, the people whom we want to see protected against the enemy should be given the help the Lord's food brings with it. How can we instruct and urge them to shed their blood in confession of Christ's name if we refuse them the blood of Christ when they go out to battle? How can we instill in them the strength to drink the cup of martyrdom if we do not first permit them to drink the cup of the Lord in the Church, in virtue of the right to do so that comes through communion with us" (*Epist.* 57, 2, 2)?

All this shows how much importance Cyprian attaches to the eucharist and how concerned he is to prepare men so that when the time comes they will be able to bear witness to their faith with courage and without yielding. A person "cannot be ready for martyrdom if the Church does not arm him for the struggle, and the heart must fail that is not exalted and inflamed by eucharistic communion" (*Epist.* 57, 4).

It is fitting, then, to celebrate the anniversaries of the martyrs and offer oblations and sacrifices in their memory (*Epist.* 12, 2; 39, 3). This will keep alive the links between these heroes and the Christian community and will make their example a source of strength for all.

Such is Cyprian's teaching. It is a teaching he was to authenticate and seal with his own blood when the test of martyrdom came. He made a total offering to Christ in an act with profound eucharistic overtones,[36] in serenity and peace, according to the Lord's will and at the time the Lord determined. His martyrdom took place on September 14, 258, under Emperor Valerian.

By way of conclusion we can say that Cyprian's *Letter* 63 is a kind of treatise on the eucharist. Apart from this exceptional document, there are not very many passages on the eucharist in his writings, although there are plenty of allusions to it. But the eucharist is everywhere present in Cyprian's thinking. It forms as it were the backdrop for this thinking, or, to change the metaphor, the foundation for a solid edifice of ideas. The eucharist is the memorial of the Lord, that was foretold in the sacred Scriptures and made a reality by Christ, and that is made present and effective by the Church in a celebration marked by concord, peace, and unity, and lived by God's people as a gift of the Lord which lays claim upon their lives, even to the point of martyrdom. For Cyprian, the eucharist is something dynamic: in it Christ gives himself, from it men derive their strength and courage. It is the very reality of Christ who died and rose again for love of mankind.

NOTES

1. J. Quasten, *Patrology* 2. *The Ante-Nicene Literature after Irenaeus* (Westminster, Md., 1953), 381.

2. P. Batiffol, *L'Eucharistie: La présence réelle et la transsubstantiation* (9th ed.; Paris, 1930), pp. 237-38.

3. The description is from M. Jourjon, *Cyprien de Carthage* (Paris, 1957), p. 12.

4. Cf. *Ad Donatum* 3–4 (CSEL 3:5-7). We know the facts of Cyprian's life from Pontius, *Vita Caecilii Cypriani* (CSEL 3: xc-cx), but this document must be read with a critical mind.

4a. *Ad Demetrianum* 20 (CSEL 3:365).

5. On this period of persecutions, cf. M. Meslin and J. R. Palanque, *Le christianisme antique* (Paris, 1967), pp. 41-45. J. Moreau, *La persécution du christianisme dans l'empire romain* (Paris, 1956). J. Zeiller, "The Great Persecutions in the Middle of the Third Century and the Period of Religious Peace from 260 to 302," in J. Lebreton and J. Zeiller, *The History of the Primitive Church*, translated by E. C. Messenger (New York, 1949), 2:791-806. J. Daniélou and H. Marrou, *The First Six Hundred Years* (The Christian Centuries 1; New York, 1964), pp. 194-202.

6. *De lapsis* 5 (CSEL 3:240).

7. *Epist.* 4. For the letters we shall be using the text published (with a French translation) by L. Bayard: *Saint Cyprien: Correspondance* (Paris, 1962).

8. *De lapsis* 7 (CSEL 3:241-42).

9. *De lapsis* 2 (CSEL 3:237-38).

10. Attending these councils were the bishops of the African provinces, from Proconsular Africa to Numidia and Mauretania; this meant some ninety bishops. Cf. C. L. Hefele and H. Leclercq, *Histoire des conciles* 1 (Paris, 1907), pp. 154-56, 165-91. The letters of Cyprian are extremely important for our knowledge of the Church's life as reflected in these councils, cf. *Epist.* 48, 49, 52, 54, 55, 57.

On the times of Cyprian, his prestige, and his activity, cf. P. Monceaux, *Histoire littéraire de l'Afrique chrétienne des origines jusqu'à l'invasion arabe* 2. *Saint Cyprien et son temps* (Paris, 1902). P. de Labriolle, *History and Literature of Christianity from Tertullian to Boethius*, translated by H. Wilson (New York, 1925), pp. 131-68. L. Bayard, *Saint Cyprien: Correspondance* (Paris, 1962), vol. 1, Introduction, pp. viii-liii. J. Fontaine, *La littérature latine chrétienne* (Paris, 1970), pp. 25-37. G. Bardy and A. Hamman, *La vie spirituelle d'après les Pères de l'Eglise* (2nd, rev. ed.; Paris, 1968), 2:198-229. H. von Campenhausen, *Men Who Shaped the Western Church*, translated by M. Hoffman (New York, 1964), pp. 36-60. J. Lebreton, "Christian Writers of Africa, 2: St. Cyprian," in Lebreton and Zeiller, *op. cit.*, pp. 842-74. P. Batiffol, *Primitive Catholicism*, translated by H. Brianceau (New York, 1911), pp. 332-402. J. Tixeront, *History of Dogmas* 1, translated by H. L. Brianceau (St. Louis, 1910), pp. 355-76. J. Quasten, *Patrology* 2. *The Ante-Nicene Literature after Irenaeus* (Westminster, Md., 1953), pp. 340-83. M. Réveillaud, *Saint Cyprien: L'oraison dominicale* (Paris, 1964), Introduction, pp. 1-66. V. Saxer, *Vie liturgique et quotidienne à Carthage vers le milieu du IIIe siècle* (Vatican City, 1969), especially ch. 1 and 2.

11. Cyprian's correspondence is very important; it gives us a detailed knowledge of what life was like in a Christian community of the third century. Cf. R. Fluck, "La vie de la communauté chrétienne au IIIe siècle à travers la correspondance de saint Cyprien," *Jeunesse de l'Eglise*, 4 (1945), 89-124.

12. Cf. P. Batiffol, "Aquariens," DACL 1 (1924), cols. 2648-54; P. Lebeau, *Le vin nouveau de Royaume* (Museum Lessianum, section biblique 4; Paris–Bruges, 1966), pp. 142-84.

13. On the prefigurations ("figures") of the eucharist according to Cyprian, cf. A. d'Alès, *La théologie de saint Cyprien* (Paris, 1922), pp. 249-55.

14. For Cyprian, "the cup of the Lord inebriates souls so as to lead them beyond mere rational knowledge to spiritual wisdom. . . . Habitual reception of the blood of the Lord and his cup of salvation eradicates the memory of the old self, makes men forget their former worldly life, and gives them peace by infusing the joy that is an outpouring of the divine goodness" (*Epist.* 11, 3). This is the familiar theme of *sobria ebrietas*. For the sense and evaluation of the theme, cf. R. Johanny, *L'eucharistie centre de l'histoire du salut* (Paris, 1968), pp. 206-18.

15. Communion was received under both species: *Epist.* 68, 8, 3; 15, 2.

16. On the hour of celebration in the early Church cf. E. Dekkers, "L'Eglise ancienne a-t-elle connu la messe du soir?" in *Miscellanea liturgica in honorem L. Cuniberti Mohlberg* 1 (Rome, 1948), pp. 231-57.

17. Tixeront, *op. cit.*, 1:389.

18. *Leçons sur la messe* (Paris, 1927), pp. 176-77.

19. M. de la Taille, "Sens du mot 'Passio' dans la lettre 63 de saint Cyprien," *Recherches de science religieuse* 21 (1931), pp. 566-81, at pp. 580-81.

20. On the sacrificial aspect of the eucharist in Cyprian, cf. d'Alès, *op. cit.*, pp. 249-62; de Watteville, *op. cit.*, pp. 145-47; B. Renaud, *Eucharistie et culte eucharistique selon saint Cyprien* (unpublished dissertation; University of Louvain, 1967), pp. 257-58.

21. For Cyprian the *sacramentum* of the eucharist is that which manifests the reality of the eucharist; cf. A. Demoustier, "L'ontologie de l'Eglise selon saint Cyprien," *Recherches de science religieuse*, 52 (1964), 257-73.

On the eucharist as a sacrament cf. d'Alès, *op. cit.*, pp. 262-71.

22. There is a good study of the liturgical aspect of the celebration in Cyprian, in Saxer, *op. cit.*, 189-263.

23. Cf. *Epist.* 62, 2, 2; *Testimonia* III, 26 (CSEL 3:141); *De opere et eleemosynis* 15 (CSEL 3:384-85).

We know, in addition, that the sacrifice was offered for the repose of the deceased (*Epist.* 1, 2, 1) and in memory of the martyrs (*Epist.* 12, 2, 1; 39, 2).

24. *Op. cit.*, p. 38.

25. Cf. P. de Labriolle, *Saint Cyprien: De l'unité de l'Eglise catholique* (Unam sanctam 9; Paris, 1942), pp. xv-xviii. Cf. also Réveillaud, *op. cit.*, pp. 35-36, on the importance of the Novatian schism for the theological activity of Cyprian.

On the role of Novatian, cf. A. d'Alès, *Novatien: Etude sur la théologie romaine au milieu du IIIe siècle* (Paris, 1924).

26. It seems that in Cyprian's time not only was communion received daily but there was also daily celebration of the eucharist (cf. *Epist.* 57, 3, 2; 58, 1, 2).

27. In addition to these three texts, there are two allusions to the eucharist as calling for harmony and for conformity to Christ (*De orat. dom.* 24 and 32).

28. On the ecclesiology of Cyprian, see the following, among others: Batiffol, *Primitive Catholicism*, pp. 332-402. G. Bardy, *La théologie de l'Eglise* 1. *De saint Irénée au Concilede Nicée* (Unam sanctam 14; Paris, 1947), pp. 167-251. K. Delehaye, *Ecclesia mater chez les Pères des trois premiers siècles* (Unam sanctam 46; Paris, 1964), pp. 100-108. A. d'Alès, *La théologie de saint Cyprien*, pp. 91-224. A. Demoustier, "Episcopat et union à Rome selon saint Cyprien," *Recherches de science religieuse*, 52 (1964), 337-69. *Idem*, "L'ontologie de l'Eglise selon Saint Cyprien," *Recherches de science religieuse*, 52 (1964), 554-88.

The ecclesiology enables us better to understand Cyprian's position on the baptism administered by heretics (cf. *Epist.* 69; 70; 71; 72; 73; 74; 75). His attitude, which was approved by the Council of Carthage in the fall of 256, is due to the fact that he had no theology of the baptismal character (such a theology had not yet been developed).

29. *De unit. eccl.* 8.

30. On this text and its possible influence on Cyprian cf. L. Cerfaux, "La multiplication des pains dans la liturgie de la *Didachè*," in *Receuil Lucien Cerfaux* 3 (Gembloux, 1962), pp. 209-23; J. Gribomont, "*Ecclesiam adunare*: Un écho de l'eucharistie africaine et de la *Didaché*," *Recherches de théologie ancienne et médiévale*, 27 (1960), 20-28.

31. See our essay on Ignatius of Antioch in this volume.

32. *Epist.* 16, 2, 3; 17, 2; 57, 2, 3 and 4; 66, 9; 67, 3; 72, 2; *De lapsis* 15–17; 22; 25.

33. The position on the *lapsi* that was taken by Cyprian and approved in council by the bishops of Africa (*Epist.* 57 and *De lapsis*) is well known. Against those who want to admit the *lapsi* to communion without any formality, Cyprian maintains the necessity of penance for reconciliation. Against the purists who want to adopt a harsh and intransigent position, Cyprian asserts the necessity of giving peace to those who repent.

34. Cf. J. Colson, *L'évêque, lien d'unité et de charité chez saint Cyprien* (Paris, 1961), especially pp. 42-45; A. Demoustier, "L'ontologie de l'Eglise selon saint Cyprien" (n. 21, above), pp. 573-88.

35. The relation between eucharist and martyrdom in Saint Cyprian has been studied by M. Pellegrino, "Eucaristia e martirio in San Cipriano," in *Convivium Dominicum* (Catania, Sicily, 1959), pp. 135-50. Compare St. Ignatius of Antioch as described elsewhere in this volume.

36. Cf. *Acta proconsularia* (CSEL 3:cx-cxiv).

ORIGEN

"I want to base my exhortation to you on examples drawn from your religious practices. You regularly attend the various mysteries, and you know how reverently and carefully you protect the Body of the Lord when it is given to you, for you fear that a fragment of it may fall to the ground and part of the consecrated treasure be lost. If it did, you would regard yourselves as culpable, and rightly so, if through your negligence something of it were lost. Well, then, if you show such justifiable care when it comes to his Body, why should you think that neglect of God's word should deserve a lesser punishment than neglect of his Body?"[1]

One reason for beginning our essay with this passage from Origen on the eucharist is that it will seem very relevant to the reader who is aware of the debate about receiving the eucharist in the hand. As a matter of fact, much more explicit texts could be found in the tradition to show how ancient is the practice of receiving Christ's Body in the hand. This particular text of Origen has been chosen because it does more, in fact, than give us a glimpse of the practice current in the early Church. In a very simple and concrete way, it sums up the essentials of what the great Alexandrian catechist has to say about the eucharist, even though a number of technical qualifications would be required in order to deal satisfactorily with the much debated question of Origen's teaching on the eucharist.[2]

The passage we have quoted shows us, on the one hand, Origen's respect for the reality of Christ's Body, and, on the other, the importance he assigns to the word of God, for which he requires the same respect as for the eucharistic bread. These two themes seem to us characteristic of Origen's eucharistic catechesis, and we shall use them as the focus for the presentation of some passages from his writings. We hope that these will be an invitation to the reader to make his own fuller discovery of a body of writings that is extremely important for Christian theology.[3]

REALISM AND RESPECT

Doubts have been raised about Origen's adherence to the reality of the eucharistic presence. Questions about the "real presence" never entered his mind, of course, and we cannot look to early tradition for arguments in a dispute of which it knew nothing. In reading the early Fathers we should rather ask ourselves what place we should give to those aspects of the Christian mystery which the Fathers did emphasize.

Origen never challenges the reality of the eucharist. For him, "the bread which is called 'eurcharist'"[4] is indeed the Body of Christ. "If you go up with him [the Lord] to celebrate the Passover, he gives you the cup of the new covenant; he also gives you the bread of blessing. In short, he gives you the gift of his own body and his own blood."[5]

For Origen, this statement of the reality of Christ's eucharistic Body is situated within a more comprehensive theology of the eucharistic prayer that we are rediscovering in our day. "We give thanks to the Creator of the universe and eat the loaves that are presented with thanksgiving and prayer over the gifts, so that by the prayer they become a certain holy body which sanctifies those who partake of it with a pure intention."[6]

Notable here is the way in which Origen emphasizes, in the eucharist, the thanksgiving, the offering, and the prayer over the gifts by which the loaves become a "holy body." The epiclesis or invocation of the Spirit always played an important role in the early tradition, especially in the East. Even more notable, however, is the way in which the bread which has become a holy body is connected with the thought of those who partake of the bread and are sanctified by the eucharist. The very realism of the "Body of Christ" forbids isolating one aspect of the reality of this body, namely, the eucharistic bread, from the other aspect, which is the holy people that celebrate the eucharist.

In speaking of "those who partake of it with a pure intention," the text introduces a point often emphasized by Origen. In his eyes, the respect due to the eucharist is not simply a respect for the eucharistic species, such as he spoke of in the text we quote at the very beginning of this essay. Equally, if not more, important is the respect to be shown in partaking of the eucharist. Origen often returns to this subject, relating it to 1 Corinthians 11.28-30.

"You are not afraid to receive the Body of Christ and to approach the eucharist as though you were innocent and free of sin, and as though you were in no way unworthy. Have you persuaded yourself that in acting thus you will escape God's condemnation? Do you remember how Scripture says that 'among you there are many who are weak and sick and dying'? Why are there many who are weak? Because they do not pass judgment on themselves; they do not examine themselves; they do not understand what it means to be in communion with the Church and to approach a mystery so excellent and sublime."[7]

Some readers may feel uneasy at such a text if they recall, as they read, the exaggerations of recent centuries: those of the Jansenism that so greatly emphasized the unworthiness of the sinner and made access to the eucharist so difficult for him; those of the various kinds of puritanism that emphasized the guilt of Christians, especially in matters of chastity and therefore made their participation in the eucharist depend on repeated receptions of the sacrament of penance. But Origen has none of these things in mind. His concern is that the Christian's participation in

185

the eucharist should be a truly personal thing. The sanctification which the Body of Christ effects does not come automatically; it is not a bit of magic. It supposes rather that the person receiving the sacrament has an attitude in keeping with the meaning of the sacrament.

Such an attitude requires that each individual should examine himself. This self-examination, however, is not simply an examination of conscience concerning the individual's behavior. The person who participates in the eucharist must also be aware of what it means "to be in communion with the Church and to approach a mystery so excellent and sublime." Communion with the Body of Christ is communion not only with the eucharistic bread but with Christ's Church as well. The authenticity of the eucharistic assembly and of each of its members is no less important than the reality of the eucharistic bread. Need we spell out what this should mean not only for those who have always denounced the discrepancy between the profession of many Christians and their lives which give the lie to the profession, but also for those who are asking today how it is possible for people to be authentically gathered in the eucharist when they have nothing in common in other areas of their lives or when they are even utterly estranged from one another.

But rather than risk once again distorting the texts of the early tradition in the interests of our modern disputes, let us be satisfied to observe how Origen takes seriously the realism of the eucharist and the respect it requires. To bring home the quality of this respect, he emphasizes the need of realizing what the eucharist means, and the concern for authenticity that participants in the eucharist should have. He does so because eucharistic "realism" should be applied not only to the "holy body" which the bread becomes, but also to the real body that is made up of each member of the eucharistic assembly.[8]

186

WORD AND BREAD

In the text we quote at the beginning of this essay, Origen pointed out the respect the Christian should have for the reality contained in the eucharistic bread. He did so in order that he might then urge his hearers to be no less respectful to the word of God. This is one of the most important points Origen makes when he speaks of the Body of Christ. The eucharistic bread is the Body of Christ, but the word of God, Scripture, is equally the body of Christ. The same holds for the blood of Christ: "It is said that we drink the blood of Christ not only when we receive it in the celebration of the mysteries but also when we receive his words in which life dwells, as he himself tells us: 'The words I have spoken are spirit and life.'"[9]

When Origen thus insists on the word, he is not simply reminding his hearers that they must not separate the two tables of the word and the bread which are structurally united in the eucharistic celebration, as the Catholic Church has come to realize once again in recent years. Nor is he simply repeating what we have already heard him say,[10] that since the sacrament is a sacrament of faith, the word is essential to the reality of the Body of Christ: as stimulus to faith, the word gives the eucharist its full and true meaning for the believers who celebrate it; as invocation of the Holy Spirit, the word sanctifies the offering of bread as well as the assembly of those who partake of it. Origen is saying something more than all that: he is saying that the word *is* the Bread and the Body of Christ.

"The bread which God the Logos says is his body is the Logos himself as food of souls, the Logos who proceeds from God. Such is the bread that has come down from the heavenly bread and is placed on the table of which it is written: 'You have prepared a table before me, in the sight of those who afflict me.' And this drink that God the Logos says is his blood is the mighty Logos himself who fills the hearts that drink him with intoxication. Such is the drink contained in the cup of which it is written: 'And your cup that intoxicates, how splendid it is!'

"This drink is the fruit of the true Vine, who tells us: 'I am the true Vine.' And it is the blood of this grape that produced this drink when it was placed in the winepress of the passion. Thus, the bread is the word of Christ which is made from the grain that fell into the soil and produced an abundant harvest. For it was not the visible bread he held in his hands that God the Logos pronounced to be his body. He spoke rather of the word, in the mystery of which this drink was to be poured out. What else can the body or the blood of God the Logos be but the word which nourishes and the word which gives joy to the heart?"[11]

This text may dismay us as it has dismayed many down the centuries, but it can stimulate us to a better understanding of Christ's body in the eucharist by helping us understand what his body is in the Scriptures.[12] According to Origen, the same principles are to be applied to the eucharist as to the Scriptures. Both can be considered according to the "flesh" or the "letter." That is the approach of those who stop at the surface meaning, and it is the most common way of approaching the eucharist. We must, however, attune our ears to the deeper meaning of the words that bid us "Take and eat"; we must learn to see in them the promise and gift of divine nourishment.[13]

What is this divine nourishment? It is the very reality of the Logos of whom both the bread and the Scriptures are the sacrament; he is the ultimate reality of which both are the anticipatory symbols. In other words, Origen does not want us to stop short at the sacrament which is the eucharist or the Scriptures; he wants us rather to win through to the reality which these two signify. Origen's theology of symbol is very alien to our theological set of

mind, but we should not let this prevent us from grasping its depth and keenness of insight
.

Origen is well aware that "it is only in the kingdom of God that we shall eat the true food and drink the true drink, thereby obtaining and strengthening the true life in us."[14] At the same time, he wants to introduce us here and now to the table of the kingdom:

"The words we speak at this moment are the flesh of the Word of God to the extent that the food we give is not 'vegetables' for weak stomachs or 'milk' for little children. If our words are perfect and courageous, we give you the fleshes of the Word of God to eat. When we speak mystic, dogmatic words filled with Trinitarian faith; when we speak substantial words and push aside the 'veil of the letter' to manifest the mysteries of the coming age that are hidden in the spiritual law; when we carry the soul's hopes far from earth and set them on the blessings which 'eye has not seen nor ear heard nor the heart of man imagined': then we communicate the flesh of the Word of God. The person whose understanding is perfect and whose heart is purified can feed on it; he is the one who truly offers the paschal sacrifice and celebrates the feast with God and his angels."[15]

Origen undoubtedly seems to exalt the word at the expense of the eucharist, and Catholic theology is right to allow greater importance to the sacrament. Origen's emphasis can nonetheless help us today, as at the time of the Reformation, to react against a one-sided sacramentalism that leads to excesses and dead ends. This is all the more the case since he does not, by reaction, exaggerate the place of the word, for he is always conscious of the realities to which the word itself refers us. All ministers of the word and the bread should make their own the profound sense of the reality of Christ's body that made Origen say: "The

disciples prepare for Jesus' Passover; after their explanations . . . comes the divinity of the only Son, eating with
them in the house."[16]

Our hope is that the reading of these few eucharistic texts
of Origen will not once again stir up old controversies and
thus serve to hide the mystery of Christ. In the presence of
that mystery, Origen, a true theologian, knew how to
withdraw into the background so that Christ might share
his food with us.

NOTES

1. *Homiliae in Exodum* 13, 3; French translation by P. Fortier,
Homélies sur l'Exode (SC 16; Paris, 1947), p. 263.

2. The later Catholic tradition as formulated in the context of the
counter-Reformation has cast suspicion on Origen's teaching
concerning the real presence. The debate was revived at the end
of the last century; the reader will find an irenic presentation of
the question in G. Bareille, "Eucharistie," DTC 5 (1913), cols.
1137-39. It required however, the restatement of the question by
H. de Lubac in his *Histoire et esprit: L'intelligence de l'Ecriture d'après
Origène* (Théologie 4; Paris, 1950), pp. 355-73, before the whole
discussion could be shifted to its proper ground (the precise
meaning of symbol and allegory for Origen), and justice could be
done to the great Alexandrian master.

For the eucharistic doctrine of Origen cf. also T. Camelot,
"L'Eucharistie dans l'Eglise d'Alexandrie," *Divinitas*, 1 (1957),
71-92; J. Daniélou, *Origen*, translated by W. Mitchell (New York,
1955), pp. 61-68. For a presentation of Origen's work as a whole,
the major work is still M. Harl, *Origène et la fonction révélatrice du
Verbe incarné* (Patristica Sorbonensia 2; Paris, 1958), but it does
not deal directly with our subject.

3. We have deliberately chosen simply to present some texts of
Origen rather than attempt an impossible and illusory synthesis.
We have given priority to catechetical texts (especially homilies),
since for early tradition catechesis, whether biblical or directly
mystagogical, was the authentic theological locus for the sacraments. When possible, we use the translations of Origen that

190

have appeared in the *Sources chrétiennes* series; this will make it easier for the reader to pursue and deepen his knowledge. For texts not edited with a translation we borrow the translation given in the works of J. Daniélou and H. de Lubac where these texts are cited.

4. *Contra Celsum* VIII, 57: "We have a symbol of our thanksgiving to God in the bread which is called 'eucharist'" (translated by H. Chadwick, *Origen: Contra Celsum* [Cambridge, 1953], p. 495).

5. *Homiliae in Jeremiam* 19, 13 (GCS 3:169).

6. *Contra Celsum* VIII, 33, translated by Chadwick, *op. cit.*, p. 476.

7. *Homiliae in Ps. 37* 2, 6 (PG 12:1386CD), cited and translated in Lubac, *op. cit.*, p. 368.

Cf. *Commentarium in Matthaeum* X, 25, translated by R. Garod, *Commentaire sur Matthieu* (SC 162; Paris, 1970), pp. 263-65: "If anyone does not hear the words 'let each one examine himself,' and does not 'eat this bread' only after having thus prepared himself, and if instead he neglects the warning and partakes of the Lord's bread and cup in his present state, he will become weak or sick; he will even be stunned as it were by the power of this bread and will die."

Origen seems to be taking Paul's words literally. Would we betray Origen if we offered an Origenian exegesis of his own exegesis and suggested that the "dead" of whom he speaks are the "dead members" of the holy people?

8. After these remarks it will perhaps be easier for the reader to supply the proper background for a text which has thrown suspicion on Origen's eucharistic teaching. The text is the *Commentarium in Matthaeum* XI, 4, translated in Girod, *op. cit.*, pp. 343-47: "Just as it is not the food but the conscience of the person who eats it despite his doubts, that defiles him when he eats ('he who eats despite his doubts is condemned because he lacks good faith'), and just as for a man who is defiled and without faith no food is pure because of his defilement and refusal to believe, so also the food which sanctifies 'thanks to the word of God and the prayer' does not sanctify by the word alone the person who partakes of it. For, if it could sanctify in this way, it would sanctify even the person who eats 'in a manner unworthy of the Lord,' and no one would be weak or sick or dead because he had eaten.

Yet this last is just what Paul is telling us when he says: 'This is why many among you are weak and sick, and a good number have died.'

"When it comes to the bread of the Lord, then, the participant profits by it when he takes his share of the bread with an undefiled spirit and a pure conscience. Consequently, it is not because we have abstained from the bread which has been 'sanctified by the word of God and the prayer,' that we are deprived of some advantage, nor is it because we have eaten that we receive some profit. What causes the privation is the evil in us and our sins, and what produces the profit is justice and an upright life. In saying this we are almost using Paul's own words: 'If we eat, we gain nothing, and if we do not eat, we lose nothing.' Moreover, if 'everything that enters the mouth passes into the stomach and is discharged in the privy,' then the food that has been 'sanctified by the word of God and the prayer' also, insofar as it is material, 'passes into the stomach and is discharged in the privy.' But, because of the prayer said over it 'in conformity with our faith,' it becomes useful and produces the clear vision of the spirit which discerns what is useful. It is not the material bread but the words spoken over it that are the source of profit for the person who eats it in a way not unworthy of the Lord."

We may disagree with the way in which Origen speaks of matter and word with regard to the sacrament; we can no longer speak in just the same way today. But it seems that we can indeed regard the following points of this passage as valid: (a) the refusal to think of the eucharistic bread in isolation from the person receiving it; (b) the importance attibuted to the action of the word and to the prayer over the bread and the recipients; (c) the emphasis on authenticity in the attitude of the person receiving the body of Christ.

9. *Homiliae in Numeros* 16, 9, translated by A. Méhat, *Homélies sur les Nombres* (SC 29; Paris, 1951), pp. 334-35.

10. See the text quoted in n. 8.

11. *Mat. ser.* 85, cited and translated in Lubac, *op. cit.*, p. 359.

12. For the ensuing remarks we follow closely the indispensable commentary of Lubac, *op. cit.*, pp. 355-73.

13. We are paraphrasing here a text from Origen's *Commentarium in Joannem* XXXII, 24, given in Lubac, *op. cit.*, p. 358.

14. *Mat. ser.* 86, cited and translated in Lubac, *op. cit.*, p. 370.

15. *Homiliae in Numeros* 23, 6, translated by Méhat, *op. cit.*, pp. 448-49.

16. *Mat. ser.* 79, cited and translated in Lubac, *op. cit.*, p. 372.

THE DIDASCALIA AND THE CONSTITUTIONES APOSTOLORUM

An anonymous letter is alway perplexing to its recipient, for it raises a number of often unanswerable questions: Who wrote the letter? When did he write it? Why? Is what he says true or false? How much credence can be given to his remarks?

Anonymous or pseudepigraphical Christian writings of the early centuries often raise the same questions. This is especially the case with the entire liturgical and canonical literature, of which the works most important for their extent and contents are the *Catholic Teaching of the Twelve Apostles and Holy Disciples of Our Savior* (the *Didascalia*; henceforth *Did.*) and the *Apostolic Constitutions* (*Constitutiones Apostolorum*; henceforth *C.A.*).[1] As the titles indicate, the two writings are presented as composed by the apostles, and they were long accepted as such.

As a matter of fact, we do not know who the real authors were. Internal criticism, however, yields a few facts about them. The author of the *Did.* was certainly a bishop, for in a couple of passages he speaks as a member of the episcopal college and addresses his colleagues as "brothers."[2] He wrote in the first half of the third century, and very probably in the first decades of it.[3] His homeland was Syria.

The author of the *C.A.* was in fact a compiler who transcribed various earlier documents, chief among them the *Did.*, but also adapted and expanded them. The *Did.* provides the substance of the first six books of the *C.A.* The first thirty-two chapters of Book VII are an adaptation of

194

the *Didache*, while Book VIII follows the outline of the *Apostolic Tradition* of St. Hippolytus and uses some of its components, but in a very free way. Chapters 33 and 38 of Book VII contain a collection of blessings, Book VIII has a treatise on the charisms, and both books have numerous liturgical texts; but scholars have not yet succeeded in tracking down the sources of these various chapters. Do they perhaps represent compositions of the author-compiler? There is no proof of this; on the contrary, here too the compiler seems to have taken over earlier writings and adapted them.

The C.A. in its entirety shows a certain unity and seems to have been the work of a single compiler who has left his personal mark in expressions peculiar to him that may be found throughout the work.[4] Some of these expressions are also to be found in the long recension of the letters of Ignatius of Antioch, a fact that has long made scholars conclude that the compiler of the C.A. was also the interpolator of Ignatius' letters.[5] There is agreement that the compilation was made toward the end of the fourth century, around the year 380; the C.A. certainly does not antedate this period because it mentions the feast of Christmas which was introduced into the East only around this time. Where was the compilation made? It assigns a great deal of importance to James, bishop of Jerusalem, and describes the life of Christian communities that had a significant number of faithful and clerics; in addition, the names of the months are those of the Syro-Macedonian calendar. All this points to a Syro-Palestinian origin.

In the present state of our knowledge and research it is impossible to get a further glimpse of the authors of the *Did.* and the C.A. But still further questions arise since the writings are not only anonymous but pseudepigraphical. Why did the authors or compilers hide behind the names of apostles? What were their motives in writing at all? Do their descriptions correspond to the real practices of their time, or are they descriptions of an ideal state of affairs?

More concretely: Is what the two writings tell us of the eucharist to be taken as true or as simply imaginary?

The question of theological tendency also arises, especially for the *C.A.* The *Did.* was widely read, according to Saint Epiphanius,[6] in the sect founded by Audo, a deacon of Edessa, but the work is nonetheless regarded as orthodox.[7] As a matter of fact, the author even attacks heresies on occasion and is in reaction especially against Judaizing practices. His purpose is a pastoral one: to exhort the Christian people and give advice to pastors. Is it in order to lend greater authority to his advice that he claims apostolic authorship for his book?

Did the compiler of the *C.A.* have the same purpose in view as the author of the *Did.*? Or was he rather a dissident Christian who sought to justify the positions and practices of his community by presenting them as coming from the apostles? His compilation was long regarded as in fact an apostolic writing, but its orthodoxy also became suspect at an early date. The initial reaction to these suspicions was to try to explain how an apostolic writing could contain heterodox statements. For example, the Fathers of the Trullan Synod (691–692) imagined that heretics had thus falsified the *C.A.*[8]

Photius, the patriarch of Constantinople (d. 891), was more critical and censured the compilation for its Arianism.[9] From that time forward, opinion was divided. Some scholars emphasized all the heterodox passages in the compilation, while others played down the importance of these passages, explaining them as due to the state of theology in the early centuries. The discussion revived after the publication of F. X. Funk's edition of the text. Funk played down the importance of the heterodox formulas either by preferring orthodox variant readings or by showing that the heterodox formulas came from the compiler's sources and thus from earlier documents. C. H. Turner criticized Funk's edition and pointed out the

196

Arianisms in a manuscript whose antiquity was guaranteed by its close relation to the eastern translations of Book VIII.[10] B. Capelle was later to show that the text of the *Gloria* was not the original form of this hymn, as used to be thought, but that the compiler had adapted the original and turned the prayer to Christ into a prayer addressed to the Father.[11] It may be objected that the compiler did not proceed uniformly in this matter and left a prayer addressed to Christ, namely, the prayer which the bishop says over the possessed before their return to the eucharistic assembly. But such a prayer does not contradict Arian practice, for in ancient Christology Christ is deputized for exorcisms and the struggle against demons, and therefore it is to him that the liturgies turn for the purification of the possessed.[12]

Was the compiler of the *C.A.*, like the author of the *Did.*, a pastor concerned for the good behavior of the members both lay and clerical of the Christian communities? Or was he seeking to justify the practices of the Arian communities by presenting them as originating with the apostles? Or was he an antiquarian and canonist who wanted to spread knowledge of liturgical and canonical customs of various provenances and even to revive them? There is one fact that supports this third hypothesis: the traditions compiled in the *C.A.* do come from various communities and locales. Thus the lists of hierarchical offices differ from chapter to chapter; subdeacon, psalmist, and cantor are in one list but omitted from another.[13] In one passage there is question of but a single deacon; in another, there are several. These variations can be explained by the diversity of sources on which the compiler drew, with one tradition coming from a quite large community, another from a small one.

The same sort of variation can be seen in the prayers offered for the civil authorities: sometimes the reference is to one king, sometimes it is to kings.[14] Do we perhaps have here documents from different periods, with those mentioning more than one king being from periods when two emperors shared the power? Another type of variation is to be found in the citation of the greeting and blessing from 2 Corinthians 13.13, which appears twice in the eucharistic liturgy of the C.A. The first time it is used, it follows the same order as in Paul's text: Christ, the Father, the Holy Spirit. The second time, the succession of persons is that of classical Trinitarian theology: Father, Son, Holy Spirit.[15] The second form of the greeting may come from a more recent tradition that was influenced by the advances in Trinitarian theology.

We are left with many uncertainties; the *Did.* and the *C.A.* have not yet yielded all their secrets. As we study the eucharist in the two documents, therefore, we will be unable to give a definitive answer to this question: Does what the documents say of the eucharist represent an ideal proposed to the Christian communities, but never realized, or is it the reflection of the actual liturgical practices of one or other period? Many critics have regarded the liturgy of the *C.A.* as a fantasy.[16] But that is surely an exaggeration. Even if there is no proof that this liturgy as a whole was ever used, it is nonetheless certain that this or that component of it was in use or is still in use in some of the Eastern Churches.[17] In addition, documents contemporary with the *C.A.* allude to or describe liturgical usages identical with those presented in the compilation.[18] The two documents we shall be studying cannot, therefore, be regarded as fantasy pure and simple.

The information on the eucharist does not come in equal measure from each of the two works. The two have in common a number of brief allusions to the eucharist, as well as recommendations regarding good order and the welcome to be given to strangers. On the other hand, Books VII and VIII of the *C.A.* which draw upon sources other than the *Did.*, give a lengthy description of the eucharistic rite and the text of two eucharistic prayers. We shall first examine the information common to the two documents and then go on to what is peculiar to the *C.A.*

THE EUCHARIST IN THE DIDASCALIA AND THE FIRST SIX BOOKS OF THE CONSTITUTIONES APOSTOLORUM

The *Did.* and the first six books of the *C.A.* deal with the eucharist only incidentally, in the form of brief allusions in the course of moral or disciplinary exhortations. Some of the allusions are theological and reflect the thinking of the author concerning the eucharist; others are to the eucharistic rite.

THEOLOGICAL REMARKS

The author of the *Did.* reacts against certain customs that contradict the Christian faith. At the end of Book VI he takes up questions of sexual behavior and is sharply critical of certain beliefs. One of these beliefs was that of some women who thought that the Holy Spirit abandoned them during their menstrual periods. The author admonishes these women and reminds them of the presence of the Holy Spirit in prayer, the eucharist, and the Scriptures. The compiler of the *C.A.* has not repeated this passage in its entirety; in particular, he has omitted mention of the eucharist. There is thus no point in giving his text here; it will be enought to quote the *Did.*:

"For if thou think, O woman, that in the seven days of thy flux thou are void of the Holy Spirit; if thou die in those days, thou wilt depart empty and without hope. But if the Holy Spirit is always in thee, without (just) impediment dost thou keep thyself from prayer and from the Scriptures and from the eucharist. For consider and see, that prayer also is heard through the Holy Spirit, and the eucharist through the Holy Spirit is accepted and sanctified, and the Scriptures are the words of the Holy Spirit, and are holy."[19]

The interest of this passage lies especially in the words "the eucharist through the Holy Spirit is accepted and sanctified." Here the consecration of the offerings is being attributed to the action of the Holy Spirit. Should we see in the words an allusion to the epiclesis? Another passage, a few pages further on, suggests that we should, for it mentions, among other things, "invocations" by which the bread is sanctified. In the *C.A.* the passage has been revised somewhat; here are the two texts:

Didascalia

. . . come together even in the cemeteries, and read the holy Scripture, and without demur perform your ministry and your supplication to God; and offer an acceptable eucharist, the likeness of the royal body of Christ, both in your congregations and in your cemeteries and on the departures of them that sleep—pure bread that is made with fire and sanctified with invocations.[20]

Constitutiones Apostolorum

. . . come together even in the cemeteries, reading from the sacred books and singing psalms for the martyrs who rest there, for all the saints who have been since the beginning, and for your brothers who rest in the Lord, and offer an acceptable eucharist, the likeness of the royal body of Christ, in your churches and in your cemeteries, and at the processions of the deceased, accompany the latter with psalms, if they were believers in the Lord.[21]

The *C.A.* has omitted the words about the sanctification of the bread through invocations, but it has kept the other important eucharistic reference, namely, the term "likeness" (*antitupos*) as applied to the eucharist. The term occurs frequently in the Fathers,[22] and brings out the sacramental dimension of the offerings: these are now the body and blood of Christ, but in a mysterious way. The emphasis is not so much on the real presence as on the difference between the signs and the reality signified, between what the senses perceive and what the offerings proclaim.

These extracts thus furnish us with two interesting pieces of information. First, the author of the *Did.* refers to the action of the Holy Spirit in the consecration of the offerings, a consecration petitioned through invocations; there is an obvious allusion to the epiclesis as found in the eastern anaphoras. The compiler of the *C.A.* has not kept this reference, but in Book VIII, in the anaphora which we shall be studying later on, he does give the text of the epiclesis. Second, like the author of the *Did.*, the compiler of the *C.A.* uses the term *antitupos* in relation to the eucharist; in fact, he uses it not only here but in two other passages as well.[23] Elsewhere he also uses a related term: "symbol" (*sumbolon*), with the intention once again of bringing out the sacramental aspect of the eucharist.[24]

LITURGICAL REMARKS

The author of the *Did.* is concerned about proper order in the Christian communities and several times discussed the way in which the members of the liturgical assembly should act. He makes recommendations to bishops about assigning places to clerics and faithful in the assembly hall.[25] Thus he locates the bishop's chair and the chairs of the presbyters on the eastern side of the building; deacons are to supervise and welcome the members; different categories of the faithful—children, young men, young women, men, married women, widows—are each assigned their place. The author speaks in detail of how to welcome strangers, whether clerical or lay, and even urges the bishop to sit on the ground, if need be, so as to give a poor man a place.

The compiler of the *C.A.* has taken over this set of recommendations and exhortations, but as usual he has also introduced changes. In particular, he includes a quick description of the eucharistic liturgy, mentioning the readings, the psalmody, fraternal reconciliation through the kiss of peace, the prayer of the faithful, and the communion.[26] When he comes to the recommendations about receiving a bishop of another congregation, he introduces a significant change into the text of the *Did.*:

And do thou, O bishop, invite him to discourse to thy people; for the exhortation and admonition of strangers is very profitable, especially as it is written: *There is no prophet that is acceptable in his own place.*[27] And when you offer the oblation, let him speak. But if he is wise and gives the honor to thee, and is unwilling to offer, at least let him speak over the cup.[28]	And do thou, O bishop, ask him to address some words of instruction to the people; for the exhortation and admonition of strangers is very useful. For it has been said: *There is no prophet that is acceptable in his own place.* Ask him also to offer the eucharist, but if he is wise and respectfully leaves the honor to you and is unwilling to offer, urge him at least to give the blessing to the people.[29]

The *Did.* refers to a eucharistic prayer which can be divided between two celebrants, with the visiting bishop being asked to "speak over the cup." A century and a half later, the compiler of the *C.A.* omits this part and changes the text by leaving to the visiting bishop only the blessing of the people. Comparison with Jewish ceremonial at meals can shed some light on the practice referred to in the *Did.*: It seems that for the author of the *Did.* the eucharistic prayer comprised a series of blessings comparable to the series of Jewish blessings.[30] The compiler of the *C.A.* was no longer familiar with that kind of situation; he did not understand the allusion and therefore omitted it.

From time to time, both author and compiler make other allusions to the eucharistic liturgy, but they are not very important and simply confirm what we already know about the rite. For example, both of them emphasize reconciliation between Christians and remind their readers of what the kiss of peace requires if it is to be authentic.[31]

The information we have gleaned from the *Did.* and the first six books of the *C.A.* is not extensive. For the most part, there are only allusions, since a broader exposition of the eucharistic liturgy and its theology is not called for. The situation completely changes in the final two books of the *C.A.*; here the rite is described and eucharistic texts are given twice.

THE EUCHARIST IN BOOKS VII AND VIII OF THE CONSTITUTIONES APOSTOLORUM

While the first six books of the *C.A.* contain chiefly exhortations of a pastoral and disciplinary kind, the final two books are substantially made up of liturgical texts: rituals and prayers for Christian initiation, for the eucharist, for ordinations, for the divine Office, and so on. There is a detailed description of the ceremonies for the eucharist. We shall present this description briefly and then go on to the two eucharistic prayers.

THE CEREMONIES OF THE EUCHARISTIC LITURGY

In Book VIII the compiler follows the plan of the *Apostolic Tradition* of St. Hippolytus. After two chapters on the charisms, he describes the election and ordination of a bishop, then the lengthy eucharistic liturgy that follows upon the ordination. He says almost nothing of the liturgy of the word, but simply mentions the readings and homily.[32] In contrast, he describes in detail the entire ceremony for the dismissal of those who were excluded from the liturgy of sacrifice: the catechumens, the possessed, the "qualified" (*competentes*),[33] and the penitents. In dismissing each category, the deacon first issues a lengthy admonition and urges the congregation to pray for these brethren, while the latter prostrate themselves. Then, after the invocation *Kyrie, eleison*, the bishop offers a long prayer. This ceremony is repeated four times.[34]

Next comes the prayer of the faithful or general intercessions.[35] The deacon calls upon the congregation to pray for various intentions relating to the Church, the authorities, the destitute, the brothers and sisters who need some particular form of help, and so on. The bishop concludes this part of the service with a prayer over the people, and the congregation then prepares for the sacrifice. The kiss of peace is exchanged,[36] and the deacons prepare the offerings. The anaphora now begins and is followed by a further litanic prayer and the rite of communion.[37] The entire celebration ends with the post-communion prayers, which comprise an invocation by the deacon and prayers by the bishop.[38]

Part of this rite is the lengthy "Clementine" anaphora, so called because the compiler presents it as having been composed by Pope Clement of Rome. This anaphora, and the one in Book VII merit detailed examination.

THE TWO ANAPHORAS OF THE CONSTITUTIONES APOSTOLORUM

Each of the two anaphoras is the end result of a very extensive process of adaptation, so extensive in the case of the Clementine anaphora that the prayer no longer seems to bear any relation to its source. But let us turn first to the anaphora in Book VII, a prayer to which the manuscripts give the title: "Mystical thanksgiving."[39]

The Anaphora of Book VII

The anaphora of Book VII is an adaptation of the blessings recorded in chapter 9 of the *Didache*.[40] The reviser has taken great liberties with the text, omitting several things contained in his source and adding others. His anaphora has three parts:

First blessing (v. 2):
introduction: "We give you thanks";
anamnesis: the life revealed by Jesus, the creation of providential care exercised by the Father through the Son, the redemptive work of Christ from his incarnation to his glorification.

Petition (v. 3): prayer for the universal spread of the Church

Second blessing (v. 4):
introduction: "We give you thanks";
anamnesis: the body and blood of Christ;
mention of the sacrifice of the "likenesses" (*antitupa*) of Christ;
recall of Christ's command to proclaim his death;
final doxology.

The prayer of *Didache* 9 comprises three blessings and an invocation, each of the three blessings being concluded by a doxology. This scheme has been altered in the "mystical thanksgiving," with the petition being placed between two blessings. Each of these two blessings has an introduction and an anamnesis. In addition, specifically eucharistic references have been added to the anamnesis of the second blessing.

The anaphora of the *C.A.* also shows thematic modifications as compared with the prayer in the *Didache*. In the "mystical thanksgiving" the mention of the vine of David has been omitted, and the Christological anamnesis has been filled out. In the *Didache* thanks are offered separately for the cup and the bread; in the later text, a single prayer of thanksgiving is offered for the body and blood of Christ. We may note that in both documents the cup or the blood is named before the bread or the body.

The "mystical thanksgiving" raises certain questions. Is this a real anaphora? That is: Was it actually used for the celebration of the eucharist? The same question arises, of course, with regard to the source of this prayer; no certain answer can as yet be given concerning the real function of the prayer in *Didache* 9. In any case, at least the eucharistic purpose of the later prayer is quite clear.

In the anaphora there is mention of the sacrifice and of Christ's command to proclaim his death; this last is thus an allusion to the account of institution (1 Corinthians 11.26). The main components of an anaphora are represented in the "mystical thanksgiving,"[41] although most of them are reduced to their simplest form. Similarly, the prayer that follows the anaphora is in the form of a post-communion prayer,[42] whereas the function of its source (the prayer in *Didache* 10) is still uncertain.[43]

A further question arises: Why did the compiler retain in his collection this revised prayer from the *Didache* when he has in Book VIII a far more fully developed anaphora? Is the "mystical thanksgiving" so undeveloped because it was meant simply as an outline to guide others in composing liturgies? Or was it meant for ordinary celebrations, while the anaphora of Book VIII was meant for special occasions? These are questions we cannot answer since in VII, 25–26 the compiler has only given us blessings and prayers, without telling us of their purpose or context.

The Anaphora of Book VIII
The situation is entirely different in Book VIII where along with the anaphora we have its whole liturgical context. The Clementine anaphora represents a revision of the anaphora in the *Apostolic Tradition* of St. Hippolytus,[44] but this time the revision is so extensive that the new text is almost ten times longer than its source, even though by and large the plan of the original is kept. Here are the parts of the scheme: (1) opening dialogue (VIII, 12, vv. 4-5); (2) formula of introduction (v. 6); (3) lengthy anamnesis of the history of salvation, interrupted by the singing of the bibli-

cal trisagion (vv. 6-34); (4) account of institution (vv. 35-37); (5) prayer of offering (v. 38); (6) epiclesis (v. 39); (7) intercessions (vv. 40-49); (8) final doxology (vv. 50-51).

The anamnesis. The opening dialogue and the formula of introduction are the same as in most anaphoras and eucharistic prayers, whether ancient or modern. It is only after this beginning that the Clementine anaphora shows its originality, for it moves into a lengthy survey of the history of salvation; no other known anaphora has anything comparable for sheer length. Following L. Ligier,[45] I call this historical survey an "anamnesis." This name is better than "preface," because it represents a recalling, a remembering, far more extensive than that which follows the account of institution and for which the name "anamnesis" has traditionally been reserved. The prayer after the account of institution is in fact a prayer of offering, a sacrificial prayer, and the anamnetic element at that point simply justifies the prayer.

The lengthy anamnesis of the Clementine anaphora has itself four parts: (1) praise of the divine being and listing of God's perfections: vv. 6-7; (2) recall of creation, and praise of God's providence: vv. 8-20; (3) recall of God's marvelous deeds under the old covenant: vv. 21-26; and singing of the trisagion: v. 27; (4) recall of God's marvelous deeds under the new covenant; recall that is, of the work of Christ: vv. 30-34.

The anamnesis in the *Apostolic Tradition* is much shorter and mentions only the great deeds God has accomplished through Christ.

The praise of the divine being is directed, first of all, to God the Father; mentioned are his eternity, his utterly unique fatherhood, his absolute superiority, his changelessness, and his perfection of understanding and knowledge which is infinitely beyond the capacities of man. To praise of the Father is added praise of the Son. In particular, his primacy over all creation and his universal lordship are mentioned. The passage contains many echoes of Scripture, chiefly from the New Testament and chiefly in the part devoted to praise of Christ.

In the second part of this long anamnesis, thanks are given to God for having created everything and for continuing to watch over everything with his "attentive providence" (v. 8). In the recall of creation and the praise of providence, the Son is associated with the Father in terms partly taken from the Letter to the Colossians.[46] The section on creation lists the works of God: the angels, the universe, the light, the water and the air, the fire, the sea and the land, the rivers, the vegetation and the animals, and finally man.

Among creatures first place is thus given to the angels whom God "made before all things else" (v. 8). The various degrees in the angelic hierarchy are also named: thrones, dominations, principalities and powers, seraphim and cherubim, archangels and angels. A number of biblical texts have been gathered for this listing.[47] After the heavenly court attention shifts to the visible world and all it contains; the underlying scheme is that of the first account of creation,[48] combined with the list of the four elements. The plan is not strictly adhered to, however, and there are a number of repetitions; thus the creation of the land and of the sea, of the vegetation and of the animals is mentioned twice. The whole gives the impression of having been composed on the basis of varying partial descriptions of a given creature. The inspiration behind the description is both biblical and hellenistic; the description of the universe is based on biblical cosmology, but some parts of it draw on Stoic physics and physiology. For example, here is how the human composite is described: man is formed of an immaterial soul and a body composed of the four elements (earth, air, fire, and water); the soul is endowed with reason and discernment, the body with five senses and mobility.[49]

The account of the first sin serves as a transition to the anamnesis of the wonderful deeds God accomplished under the old covenant. The section begins with man's original happiness in paradise, the gift of the natural law to man, the fall and its consequences, and finally the oath by which God promised resurrection to Adam.[50] The rest of this section has for its guiding thread a list of the just men of the Old Testament: Abel, Noah, Abraham, Melchisedech, Moses and Aaron, and finally Joshua. The name of this last turns the composer's thoughts to Christ, the new leader who brings the people into the true promised land, the kingdom of God.[51]

This list of God's great deeds under the old covenant reminds us by its style of the historical surveys we find in the Bible.[52] But a number of scholars have looked to the literature of the synagogue for even closer parallels or even models. W. Bousset first studied C.A. VII 33–38, which contains blessings very like the anamnesis of Book VIII; in these blessings God is praised for his creation and providence, for the wonderful deeds he accomplished down the centuries, and for the protection he bestows upon the just. In these blessings Bousset detected Jewish antecedents, and he concluded that there must also have been a Jewish model for the Clementine anaphora.[53] Other scholars have likewise sought parallels; the most convincing are those proposed by L. Ligier who has shown the kinship of the lengthy Clementine anaphora with a blessing from the synagogal liturgy for Yom Kippur, which was composed during the period when the compiler was gathering his materials.[54]

The anamnesis of God's great deeds under the old covenant ends with the singing of the biblical trisagion, the formula of which combines several texts of Scripture.[55] A transitional formula, which speaks of God's holiness, then leads over to the anamnesis of Christ's work. The mystery of the incarnation is presented in a series of Christological paradoxes: the creator has become a creature, the priest a victim, the shepherd a sheep, etc.[56] The life of Christ among men is then described in a few lines and is followed by the account of the passion and glorification. A new formula of blessing ends the whole long anamnesis: "We thank you, almighty God, not as we should but as we can."[57]

The account of institution. The account of institution, which follows upon the anamnesis, could have been part of it, since it amounts to a recall of Christ's actions and words at the Supper. But, implicitly by the traditional place which it assigns to the account, and explicitly by a brief word of explanation, the *C.A.* shows that the account has a more than anamnetic function; it is precisely an account of institution, a "disposition" (*diataxis*) issuing from Christ himself. The long anamnesis is finished, and now "we carry out his [Christ's] disposition."[58] There immediately follows a detailed account of the Supper, a composite account combining elements from the different Scriptural descriptions of the scene.[59] If this account of the institution were simply an anamnesis, it should logically have taken its proper place in the series of events from Christ's life, before the mention of the passion and what followed upon it. Precisely because it plays an institutional role and embodies a disposition, it must be put in relief at the center of the entire anaphora.[60]

The prayer of offering. Since the account of institution follows upon the anamnesis of Christ's work, this last has to be summed up as an introduction to and justification of the next prayer, the prayer of offering. As I mentioned above, in treatises on the liturgy it is this prayer that usually bears the name of "anamnesis," not on its own account but because of the recall that introduces it. I prefer the title "prayer of offering" because in fact the prayer is basically a sacrificial formula: "In accordance with Christ's disposition, we offer you, king and God, this bread and this

210

cup."[61] We should note that the anamnetic introduction to the prayer mentions the return of Christ.

Epiclesis. The account of institution and the prayer of offering are found in all the major anaphoras. The same is true of the next prayer, the epiclesis, which includes several petitions: that God would look with favor on the gifts being offered; and that he would send the Holy Spirit on the sacrifice, so that the Spirit might transform the offerings into the body and blood of Christ and, through communion, give the participants the help they need and forgiveness of their sins.

The epiclesis of the *C.A.* contains a word that has been much discussed: *apophainein*. Some interpreters give the word its primary meaning, "to manifest," and infer that the epiclesis was simply a manifestation of the consecration that had already taken place. Reacting to such interpretations, S. Salaville has shown that in this context the verb means "make to become," "render," "transform," and that the epicletic formula in the *C.A.* is similar to those in the anaphoras of St. Basil and St. John Chrysostom.[62]

As with the opening dialogue, the introduction, and the Christological anamnesis, so with the account of institution, the prayer of offering, and the epiclesis, the anaphora of the *C.A.* has expanded the rather brief text of the *Apostolic Tradition*. In the latter, the account of institution contains hardly more than the words of Christ at the Supper, while the anamnetic introduction to the prayer of offering mentions only the death and resurrection of Christ.

The intercessions. In the *Apostolic Tradition* there is no trace of the intercessions which follow the epiclesis in the Clementine anaphora as they do in all the great anaphoras. In content, the prayers of intercession here are akin to the great deaconal liturgy in the prayer of the faithful.[63] In form, however, they differ: there are no invitations to pray issued by the deacon but only invocations which the celebrant addresses to God, without any intervention from the congregation. The long litany of prayers mentions in succession the universal Church and the hierarchy with its various degrees, the civil authorities, the dead, the states of Christian life, the brethren in need, non-Christians, those who are hostile or have gone astray, catechumens, the possessed and the penitents, the weather and the harvest, and finally the brethren who are absent.

The final doxology. The anaphora ends with a spacious doxology addressed to the three divine persons. In one manuscript, which has preserved some Arianisms, the doxology is in the archaic form which the Arians prized: *through* Christ, *in* the Spirit. The other manuscripts have made the text "orthodox," replacing *through* and *in* with *and*. This final doxology expands the text as found in the source by multiplying doxological words: glory, veneration, thanksgiving, honor, and adoration. The entire congregation responds and acquiesces in the celebrant's prayer by means of its "Amen."

Among all known anaphoras, that of the *C.A.* is evidently distinguished by its length, but a further distinguishing mark is its stylistic elegance, for the text shows balance and careful finish. It is its very length that has made it suspect, as we noted earlier. Was it ever used? Or was it a purely literary composition? We also noted earlier that there is no decisive proof, one way or the other. There is, however, one point that suggests the composition was actually used: the emphasis given to the priesthood throughout the anamnesis and at the end of the prayer of offering.[64] The eucharist in question seems to be one celebrated at the ordination of a bishop. Was the Clementine anaphora the anaphora for episcopal ordinations?

Did the author of the *Did.* and the compiler of the *C.A.* claim apostolic authorship in order to lend apostolic authority to new practices contrary to those then current? And did the writings achieve their purpose with the help of this usurped authority? We lack the evidence that would help us answer these questions, and the anonymity of the writings will always make them difficult to interpret. This does not mean we should treat them as exercises in fantasy. Now that our description is complete the reader can see the kinship between these documents and others of the early centuries.

Our attitude to these documents should not be mistrust but a willingness to profit. This is especially true of the lengthy anaphora in C.A. In this anaphora we can see how the Christian mind gradually worked out a complete eucharistic synthesis according to which the sacrifice of Christ recapitulates the history of salvation and brings it to its goal, and acts as both the source and the leaven of the Church. As the centuries passed, Christians succeeded in giving ever more explicit expression, in blessings and invocations, to what in the beginning was perhaps grasped only implicitly.

This is especially true of the epiclesis. In the eucharistic liturgy, bread and wine become the body and blood of Christ, so that a communion may be established between God and his people. How does this transformation of the elements take place? The author of the *Did.* already has the explanation of the mystery. The celebrant does not perform an act of magic; rather, the agent is God and his creative power, which is the Holy Spirit, as the entire Syrian tradition soon came to profess and persevered in professing. Even if we object that the epiclesis is not an absolutely necessary part of the rites and that some eucharistic prayers do not have an epiclesis, or have epicleses that are vague, or even have epiclesis of the Logos, we must admit that it is God who makes the offerings become the body and blood of Christ and that he does so in order to set a seal upon his covenanted communion with his people, even if the celebrant's words at this moment give only imperfect expression to the mystery being celebrated. The epiclesis is not simply an invocation; it is also a profession of faith, an acknowledgment of the power of God.

NOTES

1. The *Did.* was written in Greek but the original text is lost, and the document is known only through Latin fragments and a Syriac version. Modern translations of the text have been published: in English, R. H. Connolly, *Didascalia Apostolorum* (Oxford, 1929; reprinted, 1971); in German, H. Achelis and J. Flemming, *Die syrische Didascalia übersetzt und erklärt* (TU 25/2, NF 10/2; Leipzig, 1904); in French, F. Nau, *La Didascalie des douze apôtres* (2nd ed.; Paris, 1912).

A Latin translation, which includes the fragments of the ancient Latin version (these are called the Verona fragments and were first edited by E. Hauler) has been published by F. X. Funk in his *Didascalia et Constitutiones Apostolorum* 1 (Paderborn, 1905; reprinted: Turin, 1950). Funk's is the current edition of the Greek text of the *C.A.* For the first six books of the *C.A.*, the Latin of the *Did.* is given on the left-hand page, the Greek of the *C.A.* on the right-hand page. In this edition the same division into books, chapters, and verses has been adopted for both documents. We shall refer to Funk henceforth as *DCA*. We ourselves are preparing a new edition of the *C.A.* for the *Sources chrétiennes* series (with a French translation).

2. E.g., in II, 6, 16, and II, 7; Funk, *DCA*, p. 42. There is a description of the author in Achelis and Flemming, *op. cit.*, p. 378.

3. This is the conclusion reached by P. Galtier, "La date de la Didascalie," *Revue d'histoire ecclésiastique*, 42 (1947), 315-51.

4. See the arguments of F. X. Funk, *Die apostolischen Konstitutionen* (Rottenburg, 1891), pp. 123-32, 168-69, 192-206.

5. Cf. *ibid.*, pp. 281-353. Some examples of this relationship have also been given by B. Capelle, "Le texte du 'gloria in excelsis,'" *Revue d'histoire ecclésiastique*, 44 (1949), 442-43, and by F. E. Brightman and C. E. Hammond, *Liturgies Eastern and Western* (Oxford, 1896), pp. XXVII-XXVIII.

6. *Haer.* 70, 10 (PG 42:356-57). Cf. also Nau, *op. cit.*, pp. XX-XXI.

7. Funk concluded that the *Did.* is Catholic and comes from a Catholic milieu; cf. his *Die apostolischen Konstitutionen*, p. 62.

8. Funk gives the text of the conciliar decision in DCA 2:18-19.

9. Funk also prints this text in DCA 2:28.

10. Cf. *Journal of Theological Studies*, 15 (1913), 53-65; 16 (1914), 54-61, 523-28; 21 (1930), 128-41.

11. Capelle, *op. cit.*, pp. 439-57.

12. *C.A.* VIII, 7, 5-8; cf. Funk, *DCA*, p. 482. The liturgical practice of addressing prayers to Christ was a contradiction of Arian Christology, as St. Athanasius shows in his anti-Arian treatises; cf. *Contra Arianos* I, 17-18; I, 20; III, 15-16. On the prayers to Christ in the *C.A.*, cf. J. A. Jungmann, *The Place of Christ in Liturgical Prayer*, translated by A. Peeler (London, 1965), pp. 11 and 214.

13. E.g., *C.A.* II, 26, 3; VI, 17; VIII, 10, 6-10; 12, 43; 31, 2. We have made a synoptic table of these various lists of clerics in our dissertation, *La liturgie eucharistique selon les Constitutions apostoliques* (Faculty of Catholic Theology, Strasbourg, 1968).

14. "King" in *C.A.* II, 57, 18, and VIII, 12, 42; "kings" in VIII, 13, 5, and 15, 4. Cf. Funk, *DCA*, pp. 167, 512, 514, 518.

15. *C.A.* VIII, 5, 11, and 12, 4, in *DCA*, pp. 476 and 496.

16. Cf. H. Leclercq, "Constitutions apostoliques," DACL 3 (1914), cols. 2749-50. For a contrary view cf. L. Ligier, "Célébration divine et anamnèse . . . ," in the collection of essays, *Eucharisties d'Orient et d'Occident* (Paris, 1970), 2:169, and L. Bouyer, *Eucharist: Theology and Spirituality of the Eucharistic Prayer*, translated by C. U. Quinn (Notre Dame, 1968), pp. 251-52.

17. Cf., e.g., E. Lanne, "Les ordinations dans le rite copte: Leurs relations avec les Constitutions apostoliques," *L'Orient syrien*, no. 17 (1960), 81-106.

18. Cf., e.g., Cyril of Jerusalem, *Catéchèses mystagogiques*, ed. by A. Piédagnel (SC 126; Paris, 1966); Theodore of Mopsuestia, *Homélies catéchétiques*, ed. by L. Tonneau (Vatican City, 1949). See also the comparative tables drawn up by H. Engberding for the intercessory prayers in the various anaphoras, among them the anaphora in *C.A.* VIII, in *Oriens Christianus*, 45 (1961), 20-29; 46

(1962), 36-61; 47 (1963), 16-52, and in *Orientalia Christiana Periodica*, 30 (1964), 398-446.

19. Connolly, *op. cit.*, p. 244; Funk, *DCA*, p. 370.

20. Connolly, *op. cit.*, p. 252; Funk, *DCA*, p. 376.

21. *C.A.* VI, 30, 2, in Funk, *DCA*, p. 381.

22. Some examples can be found in B. Bobrinskoy, "Liturgie et ecclésiologie trinitaire de saint Basile," in *Eucharisties d'Orient et d'Occident*, 2, 217-18, and in J. N. D. Kelly, *Early Christian Doctrines* (2nd ed.; New York, 1960), pp. 440-41.

23. *C.A.* V, 14, 7: "After having handed over to us the mysteries which are likenesses of his body and his precious blood . . . [Jesus] went out to the Mount of Olives." Later, VII, 25, 4 speaks of the likenesses of Christ that are offered in sacrifice. Cf. Funk, *DCA*, pp. 273 and 412.

24. *C.A.* VI, 23, 5, in Funk, *DCA*, p. 361.

25. *Did.* II, 57-58, in Connolly, *op. cit.*, pp. 119-24.

26. *C.A.* II, 57-58. The text is also in J. Quasten, *Monumenta eucharistica et liturgica vetustissima* (Florilegium Patristicum 7/4; Bonn, 1936), pp. 180-84, and in Brightman and Hammond, *op. cit.*, 1:28.

27. Lk 4.24.

28. *Did.* II, 58, 3, in Connolly, *op. cit.*, p. 122.

29. *C.A.* II, 58, 3, in Funk, *DCA*, p. 168.

30. On the relations between the Jewish blessings at table and the Christian liturgy, see the writings of L. Ligier, especially "The Origins of Eucharistic Prayer: From the Last Supper to the Eucharist," *Studia Liturgica* 9 (1973), 161-85, in which he reviews the various studies on the question.

31. *Did.* II, 54, 1-2, and *C.A.* II, 54, 1-2, in Connolly, *op. cit.*, pp. 117-19, and Funk, *DCA*, pp. 152-55.

32. *C.A.* VIII, 5, 11, in Funk, *DCA*, p. 476.

33. The *competentes* were catechumens who had reached the end of their remote preparation and were to receive baptism during the next Easter vigil.

34. *C.A.* VIII, 6-9, in Funk *DCA*, pp. 478-88.

35. *C.A.* VIII, 10-11, in Funk, *DCA*, pp. 488-94.

36. *C.A.* VIII, 11, 7-12, in Funk, *DCA*, p. 494.

37. *C.A.* VIII, 13, 1-17, in Funk, *DCA*, pp. 514-18.

38. *C.A.* VIII, 14-15, in Funk, *DCA*, pp. 518-20.

39. *C.A.* VII, 25, in Funk, *DCA*, pp. 410-12.

40. The text of the *Didache* is in J.-P. Audet, *La Didachè: Instructions des apôtres* (Paris, 1958), and in Funk, *DCA*, pp. 410-12.

41. This can be brought out by a comparative table; we have provided one in "Les deux prières eucharistiques des Constitutions apostoliques," *Revue des sciences religieuses*, 45 (1971), 67.

42. *C.A.* VII, 26, in Funk, *DCA*, pp. 412-14.

43. Cf., e.g. Audet, *op. cit.*, or W. Rordorf in his essay on the *Didache* in this volume.

44. The text of the *Apostolic Tradition* can be consulted in the two editions of B. Botte: *La Tradition apostolique de saint Hippolyte: Essai de reconstitution* (Liturgiewissenschaftliche Quellen und Forschungen 39; Münster, 1963), and *La Tradition apostolique* (SC 11bis; Paris, 1968). The text of the Clementine anaphora has been published in Greek, Latin, French, and English (among other languages): J. Quasten, *op. cit.*, pp. 198-233 (Greek and Latin); Brightman and Hammond, *op. cit.*, pp. 3-17 (Greek); L. Ligier, *Péché d'Adam et péché du monde: Bible, Kippur, Eucharistie* 2 (Paris, 1968), pp. 403-6 (Latin); *idem*, "Anaphores orientales et prières juives," *Proche-Orient chrétien*, 13 (1963), 10-13 (French); A. Hänggi and I. Pahl, *Prex Eucharistica: Textus e liturgiis antiquioribus selecti* (Spicilegium Friburgense 12; Fribourg, 1968), pp. 82-95 (Greek and Latin); L. Bouyer, *op. cit.*, pp. 253-57, 261-65 (English); L. Deiss, *Early Sources of the Liturgy*, translated by B. Weatherhead (Collegeville, 1967), pp. 161-83 (English); A. Hamman, *Prières eucharistiques* (Paris, 1969), pp. 63-74 (French); *idem*, *The Mass: Ancient Liturgies and Patristic Texts*, ed. by T. Halton (Staten Island, N.Y., 1967), pp. 53-77 (English); *idem*, *Early Christian Prayers*, translated by W. Mitchell (Chicago, 1961), pp. 104-13 (English).

45. Cf., e.g., L. Ligier, "Autour du sacrifice eucharistique:

Anaphores orientales et anamnèse juive de Kippur," *Nouvelle revue théologique*, 82 (1960), 41; *Péché d'Adam et péché du monde*, 2:295-97; "Célébration divine et anamnèse . . . ," in *Eucharisties d'Orient et d'Occident*, p. 140.

46. Col 1.16.

47. Col 1.16; Ep 1.21; Is 6.2; Ex 25.18, 22.

48. Gn 1; cf. Dn 3.57-88 and Ps 104.

49. *C.A.* VIII, 12, 17, in Funk, *DCA*, p. 500.

50. *C.A.* VIII, 12, 20, in Funk, *DCA*, p. 502.

51. Irenaeus, in the *Démonstration de la prédication apostolique* (SC 62; Paris, 1959), pp. 78-79, proceeds in the same manner: he ends the historical exposition of the Old Testament with Joshua and passes immediately to Jesus, his namesake. The Jewish anamnesis, on the other hand, continues the historical sequence, especially by recalling Aaron, whom Christians replace with Christ, the new and eternal high priest. On this point, cf. Ligier, "Autour du sacrifice eucharistique," p. 46.

52. Ps 78, 105, 106, 135, 136; Ezk 20; Si 44–50; Ws 1; 1 M 2.51-68; Ne 9.5-31; Ac 7; Heb 11.

53. "Eine jüdische Gebetssammlung im siebenten Buch der Apostolischen Konstitutionen," *Nachrichten von der Königl. Gesellshaft der Wissenschaften zu Göttingen* (Berlin, 1916), pp. 435-89.

54. See the various studies of Ligier mentioned in earlier notes. Ligier sums up his studies in "Les origines de la prière eucharistique" pp. 186-200 (n.b., due to a technical error, p. 192 of this article must be read immediately after p. 188). The texts of the Jewish anamnesis have been published by Ligier in his *Péché d'Adam et péché du monde*, pp. 399-401 (Latin), in his "Anaphores orientales et prières juives," pp. 14-16 (French), and in Hänggi and Pahl, *op. cit.*, pp. 56-57 (Latin).

55. Is 6, 3 and Rm 1.25; 9.5.

56. *C.A.* VIII, 12, 30-33, in Funk, *DCA*, pp. 506-8.

57. *C.A.* VIII, 12, 35, in Funk, *DCA*, p. 508.

58. *Ibid.* The expression "disposition of Christ," as applied to the account of institution, occurs again a little further on in the

218

anaphora, in v. 38 (Funk, *DCA*, p. 510). It is possible to see allusions to it in two other passages: V, 19, 7, and VII, 25, 4 (Funk, *DCA*, pp. 293 and 412), where there is question of what Christ ordained with regard to the sacrifice and his death.

59. Mt 26.26-28; 14.19; 1 Co 11.23-25.

60. Cf. Ligier, "Célébration divine et anamnèse . . . ," p. 174; H. Manders, "Sens et fonction du récit de l'institution," *Questions liturgiques et paroissiales*, 53 (1972), 203-18.

61. *C.A.* VIII, 12, 38, in Funk, *DCA*, pp. 508-10.

62. *"Anadeiknunai–apophanein*: Notes de lexicographie à propos de textes eucharistiques," in *Mémorial Louis Petit* (Paris–Bucharest, 1948), pp. 413-22.

63. *C.A.* VIII, 10 (deaconal litany) and 12, 40-49 (intercessions), in Funk, *DCA*, pp. 488-92 and 510-14.

64. Cf. Ligier, "Célébration divine et anamnèse . . . ," p. 169. The prayer of offering likewise contains an allusion to episcopal ordination, since it repeats the formula already found in the *Apostolic Tradition*: "You judged us worthy to serve you through the priesthood *(hierateuein)*" (*C.A.* VIII, 12, 38, in Funk, *DCA*, p. 510).

BIBLIOGRAPHY

GENERAL

Altaner, B. *Patrology*. Translated by H. Graef. New York, 1960.

Aubin, P. *Le problème de la conversion: Etude sur un thème commun à l'hellénisme et au christianisme des trois premiers siècles*. Théologie historique 1. Paris, 1963.

Bardy, G. *La conversion au christianisme durant les premiers siècles*. Paris, 1949.

Bardy, G. *La vie spirituelle d'après les Pères des trois premiers siècles*. Revised and updated by A. Hamman. 2 vols. Paris, 1968.

Batiffol, P. *Primitive Catholicism*. Translated by H. L. Brianceau. New York, 1911.

Bouyer, L. *The Spirituality of the New Testament and the Fathers*. Translated by M. P. Ryan. New York, 1963.

Cerfaux, L. *La puissance de la foi; La communauté apostolique*. Foi vivante 93. Paris, 1968.

Daniélou, J., and Marrou, H. *The First Six Hundred Years*. Translated by V. Cronin. The Christian Centuries 1. New York, 1964.

Dauvillier, J. *Les temps apostoliques*. Paris, 1970.

Davies, J. G. *Daily Life in the Early Church: Studies in the Church Social History of the First Five Centuries*. London, 1952.

Giet, S. *L'énigme de la Didachè*. Paris, 1970.

Griffe, E. *Les persécutions contre les chrétiens aux Ier et IIe siècles*. Paris, 1967.

Hamman, A. *La vie quotidienne des premiers chrétiens*. Paris, 1972.

Jaubert, A. *Les premiers chrétiens*. Paris, 1967.

Kelly, J. N. D. *Early Christian Doctrines*. 2nd ed. New York, 1960.

Labriolle, P. de. *La réaction païenne*. Paris, 1942.

Lebreton, J., and Zeiller, J. *The History of the Primitive Church*. Translated by E. C. Messenger. 2 vols. New York, 1949.

Liébaert, J. *Les enseignements moraux des Pères apostoliques*. Recherches et synthèses, Section morale 4. Gembloux, 1970.

Lietzmann, H. *A History of the Early Church*. Translated by B. L. Woolf. 4 vols. 2nd ed.; London, 1950-1958.

Menoud, Ph. H. *La vie de l'Eglise naissante*. Foi vivante 114. Paris, 1969.

Meslin, M. *Le christianisme dans l'Empire romain*. Paris, 1970.

Meslin, M., and Palanque, J. R. *Le christianisme antique*. Paris, 1967.

Minnerath, R. *Les chrétiens et le monde*. Paris, 1973.

Moreau, J. *La persécution du christianisme dans l'Empire romain*. Paris, 1956.

Pierrard, P. *Histoire de l'Eglise catholique*. Paris, 1972.

Quasten, J. *Patrology*. 3 vols. Westminster, Md., 1950-60.

Simon, M. *Les premiers chrétiens*. Que sais-je? 551. 3rd ed.; Paris, 1967.

Simon, M. *La civilisation de l'antiquité et le christianisme*. Paris, 1972.

Simon, M., and Benoit, A. *Le judaïsme et le christianisme antique*. Paris, 1968.

Tixeront, J. *History of Dogmas*. Translated by H. L. Brianceau. 3 vols. St. Louis, 1910-16.

Turck, A. *Evangélisation et catéchèse aux deux premiers siècles*. Paris, 1962.

Viller, M. *La spiritualité des premiers siècles chrétiens*. Paris, 1930.

EUCHARIST

Alès, A. d'. *La théologie de Tertullien*. Paris, 1905, pp. 355-70.

Alès, A. d'. *La théologie de saint Cyprien*. 2nd ed. Paris, 1922, pp. 249-72.

Bardy, G. *En lisant les Pères*. Tourcoing, 1921, p. 239-77.

Bareille, G. "Eucharistie d'après les Pères," DTC 5 (1912), cols. 1121-83.

Batiffol, P. *L'eucharistie: La présence réelle et le transsubstantiation*. 9th ed. Paris, 1930.

Bouyer, L. *Eucharist: Theology and Spirituality of the Eucharistic Prayer*. Translated by C. U. Quinn. Notre Dame, 1968.

Brightman, F. E., and Hammond, C. E. *Liturgies Eastern and Western*. Oxford, 1896.

Camelot, T. "L'eucharistie dans l'Ecole d'Alexandrie," *Divinitas*, 1 (1957), 71-92.

Casel, O. *Faites ceci en mémoire de moi*. Translated from the German by J. C. Didier. Lex orandi 34. Paris, 1962.

Cerfaux, L. "La multiplication des pains dans la liturgie de la *Didachè (Did*. IX, 4)," in *Recueil Lucien Cerfaux* 3 (Gembloux, 1962), pp. 209-23.

Chirat, H. *L'assemblée chrétienne à l'âge apostolique*. Lex orandi 10. Paris, 1949.

Cullmann, O. *La foi et le culte de l'Eglise primitive*. Neuchâtel, 1963.

Daniélou, J. *The Bible and the Liturgy*. Notre Dame, 1956.

Daniélou, J. "La catéchèse eucharistique chez les Pères de l'Eglise," in *La messe et sa catéchèse*. Lex orandi 7. Paris, 1947, pp. 7-33.

Daniélou, J., and Du Charlat. *La catéchèse aux premiers siècles*. Paris, 1967.

Dekkers, E. "Liturgie et vie spirituelle aux premiers siècles," *Maison-Dieu*, no. 69 (1962), 29-38.

Dix, G. *The Shape of the Liturgy*. London, 1945.

Duchesne, L. *Christian Worship: Its Origin and Evolution*. Translated by M. L. McClure. London, 1903.

Dufort, J. M. *Le symbolisme eucharistique aux origines de l'Eglise*. Studia 23. Montreal, 1969.

Eucharisties d'Orient et d'Occident. Lex orandi 46–47. 2 vols. Paris, 1970.

Fluck, R. "La vie de la communauté chrétienne au IIIe siècle à travers la correspondance de saint Cyprien," *Jeunesse de l'Eglise*, 4 (1945), 89-124.

Goguel, M. *L'Eucharistie, des origines à Justin Martyr*. Paris, 1910.

Goossens, W. *Les origines de l'eucharistie, sacrement et sacrifice.* Paris, 1931.

Gribomont, J. *"Ecclesiam adunare*: Un echo de l'eucharistie africaine et de la *Didachè," Recherches de théologie ancienne et médiévale,* 27 (1960), 20-28.

Hamman, A. *Early Christian Prayers.* Translated by W. Mitchell. Chicago, 1961.

Hamman, A. *La prière* 2. *Les trois permiers siècles.* Paris 1963.

Hamman, A. *The Mass: Ancient Liturgies and Patristic Texts.* Edited by T. Halton. Staten Island, N.Y., 1967.

Hamman, A. *Vie liturgique et vie sociale.* Paris, 1968.

Hamman, A. *Prières eucharistiques, des premiers siècles à nos jours.* Foi vivante 113. Paris, 1969.

Hubert, M. *La messe: Histoire du culte eucharistique en Occident.* 2 vols. Paris, 1965.

Jugie, M. *"*La forme du sacrement de l'eucharistie d'après saint Irénée," in *Mémorial J. Chaine.* Lyons, 1950, pp. 223-33.

Jungmann, J. A. *The Mass of the Roman Rite: Its Origins and Development (Missarum Sollemnia).* Translated by F. A. Brunner. 2 vols. New York, 1951-55.

Jungmann, J. A. *The Early Liturgy to the Time of Gregory the Great.* Translated by F. A. Brunner. Notre Dame, 1959.

Ladeuze, P. *"*L'eucharistie et les repas communs des fidèles dans la Didachè," *Revue de l'Orient chrétien,* 7 (1902), 339-59.

Ligier, L. *"*The Origins of the Eucharistic Prayer: From the Last Supper to the Eucharist," *Studia Liturgica,* 9 (1973) 161-85.

Martimort, A. G. *The Eucharist.* Edited by A. Flannery and V. Ryan. The Church at Prayer 2. New York 1973. This is a translation of one section of *L'Eglise en prière.* Paris, 1961.

Maurice-Denis, N., and Boulet, R. *Euchariste ou la messe dans ses variétés, son histoire et ses origines.* Paris, 1953.

Metzger, M. *"*Les deux prières eucharistiques des Constitutions apostoliques," *Revue des sciences religieuses,* 45 (1971), 57-77.

Palashkovsky, V. "La théologie eucharistique de saint Irénée évêque de Lyon," *Studia Patristica* 2 (Berlin, 1957), pp. 277-81.

Pellegrino, M. "Eucaristia e martirio in San Cipriano," in *Convivium Dominicum* (Catania, Sicily, 1959), pp. 135-50.

Perler, O. "Eucharistie et unité de l'Eglise d'après saint Ignace d'Antioche," in *XXXV Congreso Eucarístico Internacional*. Barcelona, 1952, pp. 244-49.

Piolanti, A. *Eucaristia*. Rome, 1957.

Pons, A. "La communion d'après les deux grands docteurs Cyprien et Augustin et d'après la pratique de l'ancienne Eglise d'Afrique," in *XXXe Congrès Eucharistique International* (Carthage, 1930). Tunis 1931, pp. 149-70.

Renaud, B. *Eucharistie et culte eucharistique selon saint Cyprien*. Unpublished dissertation. Louvain, 1967.

Renaud, B. "L'Eglise comme assemblée liturgique selon saint Cyprien," *Recherches de théologie ancienne et médiévale*, 38 (1971), 5-68.

Rordorf, W. "La célébration dominicale de la sainte Cène dans l'Eglise ancienne," *Revue de théologie et de philosophie*, 99 (1966), 25-37.

Sauget, J. M. *Bibliographie des liturgies orientales*. Rome, 1962.

Saxer, V. *Vie liturgique et quotidienne à Carthage vers le milieu du IIIe siècle*. Vatican City, 1969.

Vloberg, M. *L'eucharistie dans l'art*. 2 vols. Paris, 1949.

Watteville, J. de. *Le sacrifice dans les textes eucharistiques des premiers siècles*. Neuchâtel–Paris, 1966.

Wilpert, J. *Fractio panis: Les plus anciennes représentations du sacrifice eucharistique à la Capella greca*. Paris, 1896.